Hardy Bamboos
TAMING THE DRAGON

Here there be Dragons

Hardy Bamboos

TAMING THE DRAGON
PAUL WHITTAKER

Timber Press

Portland · Cambridge

Published in 2005 by

Timber Press, Inc.
The Haseltine Building
133 S.W. Second Avenue, Suite 450
Portland, Oregon 97204-3527, U.S.A.

Timber Press
2 Station Road
Swavesey
Cambridge CB4 5QJ, U.K.

www.timberpress.com

Designed by Les Dominey
Printed in China

Catalogue records for this book are available from the Library of Congress
and the British Library.

Page 2: Phyllostachys leaf in the frost.

Page 3: Chu, the modern Chinese symbol for bamboo.

Dedication

This book is dedicated to three important people. My dad, Brian, who sadly is not here to read it; I learned from him, one way or another, about all the important things in life. My mum, Sylvia, who has always believed in me, but still lets me beat her at Scrabble. Most of all, this book is for Diana my wife, who is always there through thick and thin, for better or worse. She is so tolerant of the world around her whether good or bad, and always looks on the bright side of life. She deserves far more than she is given.

Thank you.

Contents

Introduction   13

The Need to Know   41

Nothing but the Plants   87

Feeling at Home   253

Vital Statistics

Foreword

As a long time admirer of bamboos both in cultivation and in the wild, I was thrilled as well as flattered to be asked to write a foreword for this book. To all who know him, especially those fellow members of the Royal Horticultural Society's Woody Plant Committee, or Committee B as it has long been known, Paul is one of life's enthusiasts and as we all know, those who are passionate about their subject share their knowledge and experience with all they meet.

Paul's passion as well as his knowledge is clearly evident in this his first book, and in describing his experiences in growing and getting to know bamboos I am reminded of my own interest in these plants which dates back to my childhood in Lancashire. A typical boy with a questioning mind, a colourful imagination and a taste for adventure, I needed no persuading when asked one day to join some pals in exploring a large, long neglected garden. It lay to the north of my home town Bolton, on a spur of the Pennine Hills and was known as The Bungalow Grounds. Planted during the early part of the twentieth century it had for many years remained in a wild state yet it contained a wealth of trees and shrubs that had grown and spread to form mixed thickets in which lay the remnants of ornamental pools, waterfalls and bridges. There was even a Japanese Garden and a grotto made from slabs of the local millstone grit. Occupying a vast area in the centre of the garden was a virtually impenetrable bamboo thicket which to our impressionable minds was the closest we had found to the jungle through which our hero Tarzan ran and swung in the movies at our local cinema.

It was a tall bamboo, probably the Japanese medake *Pseudosasa japonica*. We played for hours in this thicket acting out our own adventures looking for tigers, gorillas, snakes and long-forgotten tribes. Before leaving for home we would cut some of the canes to use as "Zulu spears" and I couldn't help smiling when on reading Paul's entry for this bamboo I find that he too has his own childhood memories. He also notes this bamboo's tolerance of wind and salt spray which makes it a useful coastal shelterbelt.

It is the thoroughness of Paul's cultivation notes and the certainty that he is writing from personal experience that help make his book so useful to the gardener be he beginner or professional. His comments on growing bamboos in pots and the use of barriers to impede their spread are just two of many examples. So often one sees bamboo clumps stuck in a lawn or lost in a border with no attempt to make the most of their individual qualities. Reading this book reveals the rich variety of bamboos currently available to gardeners as well as some of the stories associated with their introduction and cultivation.

Some of the bamboos described here I have seen in the wild in the Himalaya, China, Japan and South America and one of them, *Fargesia denudata*, I was the first to introduce to cultivation from China's Sichuan Province in 1986. This is the giant panda's preferred food plant and for many years I grew two of its seedlings in my Hampshire garden before they became too large for their position and I reluctantly decided to give them away, one to the Cotswold Wildlife Park in Gloucestershire and the other to the author's nursery PW Plants.

Seeing plants in the wild for me is more exciting and satisfying than seeing them in a garden and bamboos are no exception. Whether wading waist deep in *Sasa* on a Japanese hillside or picking my way through stands of *Chusquea* in an Andean woodland, I am happy in their company and would not be without at least one reminder of their incredible beauty in my garden. My current favourite is a magnificent golden-culmed *Phyllostachys vivax* f. *aureocaulis* given to me by a German nurseryman friend and whenever I stop to admire it I am reminded of his generosity. It is in my opinion, the most magnificent of its kind and is planted where its culms glow in the late afternoon sun when seen through the windows of our sitting room.

I have several other bamboos in my relatively small garden and have given away others that threatened to take over their allotted space. The most notable of these being the bamboo now named *Chimonobambusa tumidissinoda* but previously and still by some *Qiongzhuea tumidinoda*. This is a very fast moving colonizer, famous for the saucer-like nodes of its strong green culms. My plant was given me by my old friend Peter Addington whose bamboo collection at his home, Stream Cottage in Sussex, was the best I have seen in private hands. I was delighted, by the way, to note Paul's acknowledgement of Peter's role in encouraging him to explore the world of bamboo and his subsequent conversion.

Paul's frequent references to those who have helped him in his quest for new bamboos and bamboo news confirms his belief in giving credit where credit is due as well as bringing to the reader's attention some of those dedicated gardeners or skilled growers who hide their light under a bushel, which reminds me that even this author does not exactly trumpet his varied talents one of which, exhibiting, is given no mention here. Over the years I have had the pleasure of judging some of Paul's exhibits at the Royal Horticultural Society's Flower Shows and I have long admired his skill with the positioning of his plants so as to show them to perfection. Naturally, bamboos are a major ingredient of the award-winning exhibits and the way he uses them shows not only an artist's eye but a love of and a feel for their essential characteristics. Given the limited space his exhibits commonly occupy, I can only marvel at his ability to make the most of his bamboos and their ornamental merits, which brings me finally to the range of species covered by this book.

As explained in one of the opening chapters, the bamboo "family" is a very large one. Even omitting the tropical bamboos, which are unsuited to cultivation out of doors in the temperate regions, there are a huge number of bamboo species described here suitable for growing in British and North American gardens. Their numbers are being constantly added to and those with the necessary space, dedication and wealth could easily spend their lives collecting and enjoying them. But this book is not for the specialist alone. Its aim, as the author clearly states, is to reach out to all those to whom bamboos are either a mystery or a growing interest. Bamboo enthusiasts will find plenty to chew over here, argue about too perhaps for this is no copycat account. It records the revelations of a man who discovered bamboos, or maybe bamboos discovered him. Whatever happened, the chemistry generated by that chance meeting provided the making of this plantsman, focusing his considerable talent and potential in a way that he would never have dreamed of in those far off days as a child making bamboo spears in the woodland.

Roy Lancaster O.B.E., V.M.H., F.I.Hort.

Preface

"Bamboos for a Cold Climate" was an early choice of title for this book, which adequately conveys a vision of plants suffering the extremes of winter in temperate zones. However, as a title standing alone I soon realised it was far too limiting, as cold is only one extreme among the vagaries a bamboo can suffer in temperate regions. Wind, heat, drought, flooding, coastal exposure and altitude, together with cold, and a combination of these at any time will cause a plant to suffer stress. To these you can add a few of your own local problems: pollution, pests or pets, as the case may be, and physical damage (by children, or neighbours with brushcutters come to mind) to name but a few. So I moved on to "Hardy Bamboos" after considering the dictionary definition of "hardy", which uses words and phrases such as "robust", "capable of enduring difficult conditions" and, with reference to plants in particular, "the ability to grow outside for all of the year". The old Germanic word *hardir* translates as "become bold"; this is indeed very apt, and I could not find a better description of a bamboo.

But there are subtleties to growing bamboos beyond coping with conditions and these are encapsulated in the subtitle: "Taming the Dragon". A strange interpretation of the subject you might think, but the word taming with reference to an animal would usually mean to domesticate or make less wild; and with plants, to cultivate them. A dragon is a mythical uncontrollable beast, which also conjures up images of the East. To tame the dragon, you have to bring it into your fold and treat it with respect and favour, very much as you would care for new plants in your garden – and this is what I wish to convey.

As far as myths are concerned, we can discount many of the false notions that are attributed to bamboos. This book deals with temperate bamboos; and yes, they are hardy; no, they do not all invade the garden like triffids; yes, most are evergreen; and, no, they do not all die when they flower. Temperate bamboos make some of the finest ornamental plants. They only require that you treat them like all other plants by learning a little about them to help them succeed, thinking about their needs and giving them their own space. In effect you will be cultivating, or taming, the bamboo to survive in your garden.

The bamboos described in this book are not the beasts of the equatorial jungle, although some do need ample room to display their charms. Many from the mountains of the East are naturally compact and refined. So you have choices depending on the size of your garden.

The choice you make when selecting any plant for your garden is usually limited by its ability to cope with your set of environmental conditions. I am here to tell you simply how good bamboos are at handling a very wide range of situations and to help you make the right choices, thereby increasing your understanding and success at growing these magnificent plants.

1. *Phyllostachys violascens*
2. *Phyllostachys bambusoides*
3. *Phyllostachys bambusoides 'Castillonis'*
4. *Phyllostachys aureosulcata* f. *pekinensis*
5. *Phyllostachys vivax* f. *aureocaulis*
6. *Phyllostachys nigra 'Boryana'*
7. *Phyllostachys bambusoides 'Castillonis Inversa'*
8. *Phyllostachys aureosulcata* f. *spectabilis*
9. *Chusquea culeou* (without sheaths)
10. *Chusquea culeou* (with sheaths)
11. *Phyllostachys bambusoides 'Allgold'*
12. *Phyllostachys iridescens*

Acknowledgements

During my time spent with bamboos I have met many people from whom I have learned a great deal, and their experiences of bamboo is as important in this book as my own. Much reading has also been done, but most literature fails to enthuse when it comes to the plants, their descriptions lost with only brief detail. It is the individual plants I am asked about when meeting customers; all other information follows, usually through experience and the desire to learn further. The feedback I have received from all who have tried bamboos is enormous and I realized some time ago that there are many reasons why people grow them, and they are excited by their success.

All acknowledged here are thanked and respected for their help along the way, from when I first became self-employed and a compulsive lover of bamboos to the present day, and also for their assistance, sometimes unknowingly, with this book.

I would like to thank the following (in no particular order) for being there during my life with bamboos: Richard Childs for his excellent photography, time, patience and enthusiasm, I hope you succeed in all you do. Peter Addington, for being my original mentor and without whom this book would have been impossible. Anna Mumford for approaching me, giving me the extra time and the opportunity. Les Dominey for a fine design, Sue Viccars for her thoroughness and Barbara Haynes for the edit and her enthusiasm. Roy Lancaster for his sound advice, encouragement, thoughtful Foreword, outstanding plant knowledge and the *Fargesia denudata*. Ian Hodgson and Jon Ardle at the Royal Horticultural Society's journal *The Garden*, for their long-time support. Tim Sandall for being a true professional, and good company during some great lunchtimes. Tony Churly for being a good mate, letting me raid his garden, and Jane, his wife, for allowing him to. Mike Bell, who on the few occasions I have met him has been a valuable source of inspiration. Tony Pike for some great stock and useful advice. Michael Brisbane for those early days long ago, very late nights, good beer and banter. (Nice wok, thanks.)

The Royal Horticultural Society is a large organization and there are far too many people to thank individually, but my appreciation to the Shows and Regional Development Departments for allowing me to show my wares, and the members of the Woody Plant Committee for their support and taking me under their wing; I hope to contribute as much as I have already learned.

The Curator and staff at the Royal Horticultural Society's Garden Rosemoor, Devon, and in particular Leslie Kane, for their support. We were fortunate that we had a good day on 11 September, 2001, may those who did not, rest in peace.

The gardeners of the late Mr. Maurice Mason, Derek and Roger, have been a valuable source of plant knowledge. Sadly Derek is no longer with us but Roger continues his skills in pastures new. David and Suz for some great times and trying bamboos (under pressure). Tim Newbury for many years of friendship and learning and Kath Newbury for being you, the twenty vegetables and actually liking bamboos. The team at the Kings Head, for giving me a break and a laugh. The late John Bond, I hope he knew what a great inspiration he was to me. Chris Bond, his son, and my own son Ian are the "workers" who have (I think) tolerated my long absence while writing this book, but also for their hard work through all weathers. Derren Nugent, for being "a bit of a lad" and designing the coolest of websites. Peter Wilson for being pushy, keeping me in order and producing the best of catalogues. Noël Kingsbury for allowing me to help him with his book *Grasses and Bamboos*, it was indeed good practice.

I must not forget my two dogs, Sasa and Simba for their devotion and entertainment when I need to smile; my twin teenage daughters, Shani and Fay for making sure I never have too much money to spend; my sister, Boo, for coming back into the fold and being brave; and my trusty Powerbook, for taking the punches and never letting me down.

Last but not least, those closest to me, the dedicatees of this book, my parents for giving me life, and Diana my wife for her support, patience and positive energy.

From left to right, starting top left
Phyllostachys aureosulcata
Phyllostachys aureosulcata f. *aureocaulis*
Chimonobambusa quadrangularis
Phyllostachys nigra 'Boryana'
Chusquea gigantea
×*Hibanobambusa tranquillans* 'Shiroshima'
Phyllostachys bambusoides 'Castillonis Inversa'
Fargesia robusta
Phyllostachys vivax f. *aureocaulis*
Chusquea culeou
Fargesia robusta 'Red Sheath'
Phyllostachys aureosulcata 'Argus'

Introduction

Chapter 1
First Contact and Beyond

"Why bamboos?" I am often asked. "By chance" is the usual reply. As with most things in life such occasions are never planned, and so it was on a day many years ago in my previous employment. A visit to a private garden in the depths of leafy Sussex, in the south of England, with a fellow nurseryman to acquire propagation material of some rare woody plants was the order of the day. Astonished by the mouth-watering display of *Mahonia*, *Osmanthus*, *Viburnum* and many others, the secateurs and plastic bags appeared with the dexterity of a practised magician; all this being legal I might add, we had, of course, been invited. During the necessary chitchat with the owner he pointed almost skyward and asked my opinion of an example of his favoured collection of bamboos. My reply was polite and I quickly thought of an intelligent question to ask, not really paying much attention to his answer as I was trying snip the last viable piece of a very rare *Rubus*. It was obvious at this point that I might outstay my welcome unless I showed further interest in the bamboos, so was given a tour by the owner of his prized collection.

Initially, I was not inspired by the green, leafy, tall and dominant bamboos. I went through the motions of showing slight interest but did recognize a few key words: evergreen, quick, hardy. Then I spotted a sizeable and noteworthy form of

1. *Phyllostachys heteroclada*
2. *Phyllostachys iridescens*
3. *Chusquea gigantea*
4. *Phyllostachys aureosulcata* f. *spectabilis*
5. *Phyllostachys nigra* 'Boryana'
6. *Phyllostachys sulphurea*
7. *Phyllostachys* (dried culm)
8. *Semiarundinaria fastuosa* (old culm)
9. *Phyllostachys bambusoides* 'Castillonis Inversa'
10. *Phyllostachys violascens*
11. *Phyllostachys bambusoides* 'Allgold'

Hydrangea aspera, the sunlight darting through the overhead canopy of bamboo and dancing across the plate-like flowerheads; not quite strobe lighting but effective nonetheless. The hydrangea shone in the flickering light and was certainly well placed – out of the full sun disliked by this species but with enough light to show off. I was left alone at this point and allowed to take a few non-flowering shoots of the hydrangea, the owner in a slight huff at my digression had gone to put the kettle on.

The plant behind and arching above the hydrangea was a *Phyllostachys bambusoides* 'Marliacea'. The pale green, very thick canes and fresh leaf almost impressed at this point. I wrapped my fingers around the thickest cane and, as you do, gave it a shake; I suppose I felt compelled to test its strength and woodiness and, as I have found to this day, this is an automatic reaction by people when first presented with a tall, thick cane. I felt the longitudinal grooves and wrinkles and saw the ridges highlighted by the sunshine and shadow, and how the bamboo leaves formed shadowgraph images against the pale green, sunlit canes. Almost impressed had now moved on to my being enamoured with the bamboo as an individual plant, and also with the simple combination of its tall vertical canes and the horizontally held flowers and grey-blue felted leaves of the hydrangea. Plant association is all too often missed in favour of the beauty or interest of an individual specimen. To quote my well-used phrase: "I don't like bamboo gardens, I like gardens with bamboos in them."

The garden owner returned with mugs of tea in hand to find me fondling a massively imposing cane of a bright golden bamboo. I am sure he smiled at this point, taking delight in informing me that they were culms, not canes, and *Phyllostachys bambusoides* 'Castillonis' was the name of the bamboo. I quickly made a note and

Phyllostachys bambusoides 'Marliacea'
leaf shadow on a wrinkled culm.

much to his dismay wrote down something that looked like "filostax"; the smile dropped and he realized he had a job on his hands. At this point, my colleague who had brought me to the garden in the first place was vigorously pruning a good-looking, golden-leaved jasmine, the material falling into an expertly positioned bag. Flinching at the sight of this, the owner paused thoughtfully for what seemed like an age and then turned smiling towards me, muttering about how "it needed pruning anyway... I suppose..."; he avoided the use of expletives in his grumblings, which was remarkable as the jasmine now resembled a bonsai in the making. The owner and I then spent at least an hour looking at his bamboos. He was happier than I was, and told me all he could in

the simplest of language. The names of the genera and species were, however, meaningless and almost a foreign tongue. There was no science in his words; they were all about the plants, what you could see, his experiences of them, his successes, his losses and, most of all, his enthusiasm.

I am most grateful to the owner, Peter Addington, for that hour spent rummaging through his garden at Stream Cottage, weaving, ducking and diving through his bamboos. Peter could so easily have been angry about what I later found out was a rare *Jasminum nudiflorum* 'Aureum', which had been mutilated beyond recognition, and cut short the visit. Instead he ignored the damage and gave his time and explained his passion freely. On our departure Peter gave me a plant of *Fargesia nitida* he had propagated and potted, which I realized later was quite common, but it was my first bamboo.

Twenty Years On

Almost twenty years after that visit to Stream Cottage I sit in my small office looking through the window at my own *Phyllostachys bambusoides* 'Marliacea', only 1 m (3 ft.) away from the glass. My office faces southwest, so the bamboo gives shade from the noonday sun and shelter from the prevailing wind. Most of all it creates the tunnels and slashes of sunlight that filter through the leaves and culms just as a similar plant did when I visited Peter's garden. I did not know twenty years ago that 'Marliacea' was the rarest of bamboos and when I learned as such, I never thought I would own one (having said that, it probably owns me). Mine is a half of Peter Addington's original plant, which I received in awe when he left his garden some years later. It is still a very rare bamboo and a far cry from the *Fargesia nitida* he first gave me.

That First Bamboo

Perhaps Peter knew what he was doing when he presented me with the *Fargesia nitida*. It is a common bamboo and, compared to some, easy to grow and forms a fine specimen quickly. Do not shirk from the word common. This plant is not ordinary but used widely because of its beauty and reliability. I planted the *Fargesia* in a mixed island border in my garden, paying it no particular favour. The garden at the time was exposed on all sides and in winter it felt like Siberia was just over the horizon. The flatlands of eastern England have no barriers against the east or the west wind. In summer, with little or nothing mature enough to cast welcome shade, the sun baked the garden. Plants developed slowly, none more so than the *Fargesia nitida*. It grew a little, but sparsely. It was scorched in the first winter, it flopped in the wind and after two years it did not inspire. One more season and then out, was my principle; there were many plants to take its place.

At this time my appetite for plants was such that I was interested in most things. I visited gardens with eucalyptus, fell in love with pines, had an affair with hamamelis, worked with conifers and played with hydrangeas. Rhododendrons, azaleas and many magnolias were never considered, as the soil is too alkaline; Japanese maples burned in the arid air, as East Anglia does not have the humidity of the west of England and the locality suffers occasional continental extremes. My day with bamboos at Peter Addington's garden was just another expedition for me, although a memorable one and not forgotten. The difference between his sheltered plot and my wind-beaten dustbowl was even more noticeable because I was certainly not impressed with the bamboo.

How things change. A late spring morning the following year I did my usual circuit of the garden and spotted a ring of spiky shoots just appearing from the soil around the *Fargesia*; I had seen one or two the previous year, very spindly and weak. The quantity of shoots now was at least treble the number of the existing ones. They looked fresh, colourful, much thicker than the previous crops and the dew on each and every tip was a delightful sight to behold. Those shoots grew quickly in the next few weeks and the plant doubled in height and girth, a feast for the eyes and a transformation I had never seen before. Was this plant perennial or woody? There were no branches or leaves on the new culms, and I even questioned whether it was the same plant.

After some quick research I discovered that the branches and the bulk of the leaves were produced in the second year after shooting; not too disappointing then. While the books were open I read with a little more interest the sections on bamboos, all very terse and uninspiring, but I made a mental note to keep an eye open for a better book and a few more plants on my frequent treks to favoured gardening haunts. I never found the book, but I did come across another three or four bamboos on my travels, all short and looking like they had been rescued from a skip. So where were all the giants? My memories of Peter Addington's garden came flooding back.

The Next Step Forward

I had a passion for plants but I was losing touch because my job involved people, politics and production on a grand and very inhibiting scale, so I left my employment to start a business of my own. First I dabbled with consultancy, gardened for others, designed and maintained. My sights were set on a small nursery, but with nothing to start with except my small plot and young plant collection, I started landscaping in earnest as a means of financing my plant collection and supporting my family. I still reckon to this day I could be building brick walls, nailing cedar shingles to gazebos, digging out ponds or something equally creative. In particular I loved using recycled materials, making something new from something old, and then softening and enhancing the creations with plants. Bamboos would look good but I could not source what I needed, so I rang Peter.

My second visit to Peter Addington's garden was like Christmas to a six-year-old child. The garden was at least a 160-mile journey and I was there far too early, but Peter was more than welcoming. A whole morning was spent with a notebook, mugs of coffee and an intense survey of his garden; it was almost mind numbing. As an avid science-fiction fan I have found that the human brain is very limiting when accruing new data, or so I have read, but I did my best, and at least learned how to spell *Phyllostachys* correctly. Pronouncing *Qiongzhuea tumidissinoda*, however, was beyond me. Lunch was welcome and a

Part of the author's garden. A small, secluded wooded area has been made by surrounding a small clearing with different bamboos.

chance to calm down, review notes and talk plants. Peter was an admirable plantsman and almost finicky with his selections of rare shrubs, ground-cover plants, ferns and other exotica, but he seemed to have all the bamboos. Shortly after lunch, out came the spades and, to my horror, axes and chisels.

All afternoon we sectioned and quartered, chopped and chiselled, dug and divided, pruned, tied, labelled and bagged the pieces of bamboo Peter felt were "best removed". I worried about leaving the mess in our wake, of holes in the ground, deep scars in the leafmould and lengths of cut culms strewn haphazardly around the garden. "It will give me something to do tomorrow," Peter assured me. As darkness fell I was mentally compromised and physically shattered. (I must tell you at this point, for no reason other than I want to; the sun was shining on that day, both literally and metaphorically. All the times I visited Peter – and they were many – the sun always shone. In fact, I

have dug bamboos far and wide and the sun has always smiled on me, apart from once.)

I believe I hold the world record for the most plants in a small estate car. So, probably illegally overladen, I trundled home with bamboos overhead and on all sides, creating the most extreme tunnel vision I have ever experienced. Headlights glaring upward, exhaust scraping on uneven country lanes, I approached the house with the company of a multitude of insects vying with each other to bite the best places on my body. I finally went to bed the following day after spending hours looking at my notes, trying to remember the snippets of interest and knowledge from that visit, and deciding what to do with my new arrivals.

And Now

My new-found interest in bamboos dominated my plant time, hunting and research. One who understands human beings better than me may call it an obsession; whatever it is, it is infinitely better than stamp collecting (in my opinion). Along the way, my affection for bamboos has been noted by journalists, photographers, customers and friends. Most have been inquisitive, helpful, friendly and enthusiastic, and all in their own way have contributed to the promotion and now certain popularity of these plants. They, like me, have written or photographed, planted or praised the fruits of my labour and, as a result, brought a new dimension to gardening.

Vicky Kimm, a local, very qualified journalist, wrote an article once and made good effort in explaining the relationship between person and plant by saying I was "on an obsessive journey of discovery". I have since studied the dictionary to define clearly the keywords and unearthed such gems as: preoccupy, haunt, searching and chance. I now realize these words have meaning when I look back over eighteen years, and Vicky was right with her quote. It has been a journey, but one with no end as nearly every day I learn something new about bamboos.

Looking at my garden now, but thinking back to its infancy, I am humbled at the ability of bamboos to transform a place; to adapt to inhospitable surroundings; to survive with little care (or knowledge on my part, initially); and, most of all, to surprise and delight the visitors. I had no vision of the tunnels of vertical culms, or the foliage held high in the stately groves and billowing in the wind. Dense screens, high-rise specimens, and shady sanctuaries – all have formed naturally from living bamboos.

There is not enough information about bamboos, particularly those suitable for cool, temperate gardens. Much that is written is fact, seemingly set in stone, but little is understood. I cannot confess to knowing more than is already written, but I can tell the story differently. I will tell you all I have learnt and experienced, but you must understand that I grow plants because I like them; botanical detail is not my way. I will delve only slightly into taxonomy and using the complicated wordage of science, as I believe you do not need to know much of this to grow bamboos successfully. More important are those little idiosyncrasies of each and every plant that make it useful, special, interesting or even challenging; so if you wish to try it for yourself, at least you will know what to expect. The bulk of this book is about the plants and no brief descriptions here; all too often we are blinded by science and not told about the individual quirks and charms that a particular bamboo can offer.

Often we unknowingly form rules from facts and observations and then become blinkered into their belief and acceptance. This happens in all walks of life. Rules are rarely golden, in fact bamboos break them all the time. Rules can change, new boundaries set, facts challenged; and then much becomes possible.

Such is the beauty and character of bamboos.

Sasa palmata f. *nebulosa*.

Chapter 2
A New Acquaintance

What are Bamboos?

Bamboos can be simply defined as tall or shrubby grasses with woody stems (culms) for structure. Compared to grasses they are indeed woody. Many of the bamboos described in this book form an all-year-round, small tree-like structure, which survives the cold season as well as any evergreen shrub or small tree. Many grasses in their natural habitat are razed to the ground by the hardness of winter or the grazing of livestock, and in some cases burned or cropped annually to help their regeneration in the following year. Although some of the very short bamboos can benefit from a yearly shearing, and very occa-

sionally a plant in the wild may be naturally deciduous because of an extreme winter beating, they do not require the severe pruning that is essential for grasses. In keeping with other woody plants the temperate bamboos only require the occasional thinning of old or weak wood. This is done by removal of the older culms, or canes.

The other obvious feature of bamboos is the strange lack of flowers, these often not appearing for centuries, in comparison to the annual flowering of grasses. It would seem that temperate bamboos will flower when they feel like it, and

The tall, woody structure of
Phyllostachys bambusoides 'Castillonis'.

although flowering cycles have been predicted, these predictions are backed by little scientific knowledge and based only on assumptions drawn from the brief modern history of these plants. The flowering cycle of bamboos is a lengthy botanical subject and not the reason for this book, but it will be discussed briefly later on in chapter 6, "From Root to Roof".

Bamboos were forest plants of old and fossils have been found dating back six-and-a-half million years. DNA evidence of fossilized plant material suggests that earlier forms go back twenty-six million years. Bamboos can be considered as superior in evolutionary terms as, in general, they do not rely only on flowering for reproduction. Reproduction is mostly by vegetative propagation through the formation of rhizomes and new culms, whereas young plants from seed are always more vulnerable.

History and Uses

The symbolism of nature features strongly in the religion of China, Japan, Korea and Indonesia, and bamboos are commonplace in the gardens and temples in association with other revered objects – stones and water as well as other plants. In many of these countries bamboo is considered a friend and a travelling companion in line with the widespread belief that humanity cannot exist without nature. In many rural communities today, particularly continental China, there will always be a strong bamboo by each homestead, together with other useful plants and the livestock. The bamboo not only represents a religious symbol but is also put to practical use for building materials and creating everyday objects for the home and daily life.

In Chinese symbolism the bamboo is very important and represents virtues such as laughter, modesty or age. In fact much of the Asian community today believe it is impossible to live without bamboo. Apart from the symbolism, people also identify with the bamboo in a broader sense. In Chinese history, bamboo represents life's path; it reflects the elasticity,

Bamboo flowers, which fortunately do not appear very often.

endurance and tenacity that should prevail in a human being. Bamboo bends in the breeze and does not break, its leaves blow in the wind but do not fall; it survives and therefore it conquers. In Japan, certain species of bamboos are used for making the utensils used in the Japanese tea ceremony. Other religious, symbolic or seasonal festivals involve this revered plant in both China and Japan, usually in association with the other noble plants of plum and pine in Japan, and with the addition of chrysanthemum in China. Together these plants either represent friendship, or good luck and well being.

The past four thousand years

Bamboos have been used in Chinese gardens since 2000 BC in association with other native plants and their cultivation was unique to this vast country for almost three millennia. In the later centuries leading up to AD 1000 the Japanese started trading with China and many of the architectural or curious forms were naturalized in Japan to enhance the gardens of temples or those of wealthy traders. The bamboos were chosen for much the same symbolic purpose as in Chinese gardens, to reflect the human relationship with nature or, in some cases, as status symbols in a socially divided society.

Trade between the East and West was always limited up to the eighteenth century due to the hostile reception of foreigners by the Chinese, who had superior technology and believed themselves to be self-sufficient. Any trade that did occur was usually illegal, involving the exchange of opium for Chinese goods at the main ports. The first bamboo introduction to the West was *Phyllostachys nigra* from Japan in 1827, after the American navy had negotiated a trade agreement with the *imperium* of the time, with a few other species appearing during the following two decades of intense commerce.

The interior of China was out of bounds and exploration was impossible until the middle of the nineteenth century when the aggression of the Western powers forced movement towards free trade and exploration. The influx of voracious plant hunters from the West invaded the mountains of China, collecting mainly seeds from many of the woody plants that now provide the back-bone to many of our gardens. Unfortunately bamboos were mostly missed, not being the most reliable of seed-bearing plants, and it was the lesser-known French collectors, M. Latour-Marliac and Eugene Mazel that were responsible for many of the early bamboo acquisitions. During the last four decades of the nineteenth century the interest in gardening surged as a result of the wealth created by industry in the West. The new and intriguing plant group of bamboos was exported between countries and continents as the fascination with exotica prevailed.

In Europe, the rich and noble planted bamboos in their rapidly developing gardens and estates, botanists were kept busy, and many important reference works were written as a result: Messrs A. and C. Rivière, W. J. Bean, and A. B. Freeman-Mitford contributing much-needed data regarding this little known group.

In America bamboos were valued more for the commercial production of timber, paper and edible shoots, than for general gardening purposes. Substantial work and research were undertaken by early pioneers such as Henry Nehrling, on both tropical and temperate bamboos, and early collectors David Fairchild and Frank Meyer continued the learning process well into the early part of the twentieth century.

During the first few decades of the twentieth century the popularity of bamboos in Europe waned. The new fashion for gardening was very much the Gertrude Jekyll influence of all things flowery and the English cottage-garden style. Bamboo collecting all but ceased and existing stands were often poorly managed, giving the plants a bad reputation. However, the interest in America was at its peak at this time thanks to the studies of some influential scientists. F. A. McClure sent many species over to the United States from China and some of these are only now, in the twenty-first century, being cultivated in Europe. Further work by Robert Young continued until the Second World War stopped his research, as funding was directed into the war effort, and other science and manufacturing projects.

The war with Japan and the Communist rule in China effectively closed all the doors to these two countries, and the desire to grow anything Oriental was lost. The feuds and blemishes of the twentieth century have now passed, the scars and wounds have been healed and once again there is free trade between the East and West. However, it was during the period of isolation and insular economies that two most influential works on bamboos were written, which once again created an interest in these forgotten plants. In America Floyd McClure issued his great work *The Bamboos* in 1966 and in 1968 A. H. Lawson's *Bamboos: A Gardener's Guide to their Cultivation in Temperate Climates* was printed, an account of his experiences of bamboos in England.

In this new Millennium, the whole of the grass family is now regularly used for large scale land-scaping, whether in naturalized or mixed plantings. The bamboos, especially, have provided a new architectural dimension for contemporary design and, with their instant appeal portrayed by the media, have regained the popularity they enjoyed in the Victorian era. There is now a strong network of bamboo enthusiasts world-wide, and their imagination and perseverance has helped to provide gardeners with a far greater choice of species and forms than ever before.

Culture and craft

There is one outstanding work solely devoted to the uses of bamboos as materials rather than living plants. It is *The Book of Bamboo. A Comprehensive Guide to this Remarkable Plant, its Uses, and its History* by David Farrelly and published in 1996. In this book there is a chapter devoted to "One Thousand Things", as reference to a collection of artefacts used in everyday life in early twentieth-century Japan. Many of these objects are still fashioned widely alongside other more modern uses of bamboo. With the development of metalwork, plastics and moulding, the art of bamboo craftsmanship has become specialized, often influenced by tourism rather than need; however the use of bamboo for scaffolding and some construction work is still common-place in Asian countries.

Before the onset of the Cultural Revolution in

A section of a thick bamboo pole planted with a miniature ivy.

1966, Chinese rural life was dominated by the growing and use of all things bamboo. It could be said that a whole culture or even a civilization was developed in association with bamboos; for these plants have qualities above and beyond all others. The high tensile strength of the timber poles with their nodal cross-sections; the smoothness of the grain; the ease of splitting for weaving and matting; the ability to be heated then shaped; the hardness and durability; the belief that the silica contained in the timber gave them medicinal properties, not to mention the edible qualities, give bamboos their own niche in human evolution, as important as any animal or other plant. And so the relationship between people and bamboos exists; bamboos can be built with, lived in, slept on, eaten and eaten with, floated on and hunted with – all major necessities in civilizations of old and for human survival. Today we use bamboos in gardens, where they screen, reduce the wind and are so very inspiring with their versatile qualities; a different relationship perhaps, but one of value and, if you are fortunate, one that may even touch your soul.

Harvesting and curing

In China and other Asian countries bamboos have long been harvested over a three-year cycle and this method of production continues. The older, more woody culms are cut leaving the one- and two-year-old ones to grow on. In this way a dense grove will be selectively thinned of older culms, channelling the energy of the clump into ripening the younger culms for future cropping. After harvesting the culms are cured using different processes according to the final use. Curved or bent culms can be straightened using steam or heat from a direct flame, or the same end can be achieved by using weight or pressure from binding the culms to flat surfaces. Bamboo poles that warp when dried can also be soaked and reshaped. These methods are mostly used on thick culms used for structural work. The slender bamboo poles, or canes, used in gardens have their branches removed and are then stored in open-sided curing sheds, which protect the drying culms from the rain but are open to the breeze. The canes can take up to a year to cure before they are ready for use.

Chapter 3
Going Native

Distribution and Origin

Bamboos, including tropical bamboos, cover large areas north and south of the Equator, and occur in all continents except Europe. Temperate bamboos are limited in their distribution to areas shown on the world map. Like most woody plants, bamboos have failed to colonize the harshest environments, such as arid desert or Arctic tundra. The effect of the ice age meant that Europe and most of North America were excluded from the potential areas where bamboos could establish. (Ironically this book, which mostly relates to growing bamboos in these two continents, proves that had climatic history been different, these plants may well have been native.)

There are well over a hundred genera and fifteen times as many species worldwide, with more still to be named and discovered. The majority come from the hot tropical and equatorial regions and a select few, approximately one-fifth of the total, originate in the widely variable temperate zones. There are a few differences between the two groups, for example many equatorial bamboos can be grown from culm cuttings, which is almost impossible with temperate bamboos. However, by far the most important is that temperate bamboos effect a winter dormancy by which they can survive a prolonged period of much colder weather that occurs during at least one season of the year. In contrast tropical bamboos may experience daily or short-term temperature fluctuations but the daily average is similar throughout the year. The significance of this difference is that the "hot" bamboos cannot be cultivated

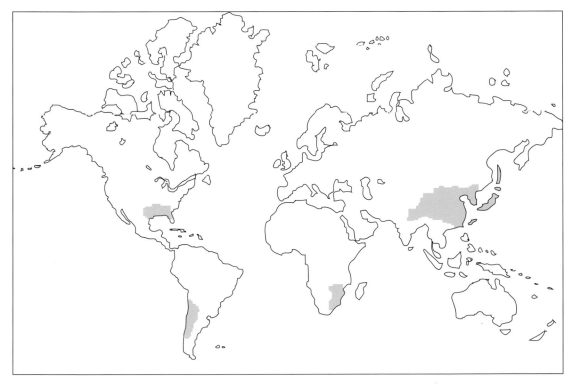

Distribution of temperate bamboos.

outside of their comfort zone, at least not without help and nurturing, whereas the "cold" bamboos, as I will continue impress on you, can adapt to environments well beyond their natural habitat – one of the most important attributes of a good garden plant.

Some bamboos have become widely dispersed from their native habitats, mainly due to their commercial value and usefulness, and this has meant the origin of certain species has been lost in time. In China and Japan some of the most useful bamboos are, in fact, introductions that have been grown for centuries and are now considered naturalized plants. Such instances are listed below under both the native and naturalized areas of distribution. In large genera, the bulk of the species may originate from one region, with a few isolated individuals occurring elsewhere, even in a different continent, for example in *Pseudosasa* and *Thamnocalamus*.

Bamboos native to China and Taiwan

Bambusa
Bashania
Brachystachyum
Chimonobambusa
Fargesia
Indocalamus
Oligostachyum
Phyllostachys
Pleioblastus
Pseudosasa
Sasamorpha
Schizostachyum
Semiarundinaria
Shibataea
Sinobambusa
Yushania

Thamnocalamus crassinodus 'Gosainkund' is one of a selection of new cultivars from the Himalayas, noted for their unique pale silvery blue culm colouring.

Bamboos native to Korea and Japan, including the surrounding islands

Chimonobambusa
×Hibanobambusa
Indocalamus
Phyllostachys
Pleioblastus
Pseudosasa
Sasa
Sasaella
Sasamorpha
Semiarundinaria
Shibataea
Sinobambusa

Bamboos native to North India, Himalayas, Nepal and Tibet

Borinda
Drepanostachyum
Fargesia
Himalayacalamus
Thamnocalamus
Yushania

Bamboos native to North America

Arundinaria gigantea
Arundinaria gigantea subsp. *tecta*

Bamboos native to South America, mainly Chile

Chusquea

Bamboos native to South Africa

Thamnocalamus tessellatus

Habitat and Diversity

The native habitats of garden bamboos fall mainly into three categories. Simply put, the divisions are due to altitude – highland and lowland – and isolation, as the third category is island.

Highland

Geologically, the high mountains of the world are very young and so is the flora that inhabits them. Compared to lowland relatives, it would appear that high-altitude plants are less set in their ways and keen to show affinity with new areas. The

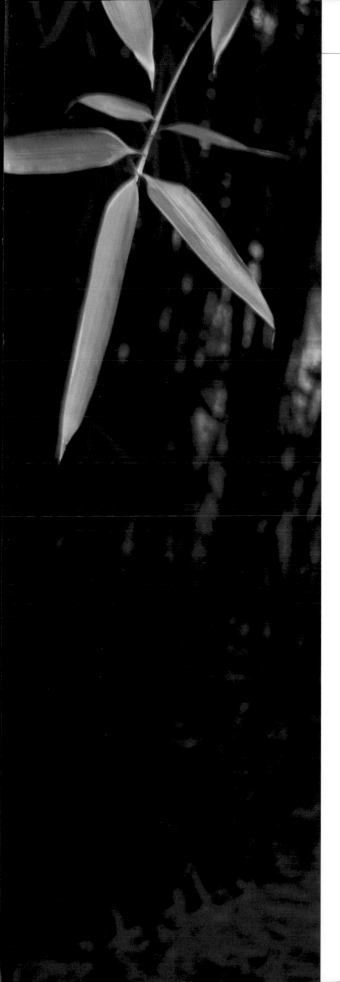

Himalayas and Andes are known for their rich tapestries of plant material, which includes many bamboos. Some of the hardiest bamboos in existence are from this montane group, surviving temperatures as low as -29°C (-20°F), as well as others that are only just frost hardy.

Most montane plants can also survive at lower altitudes and often retain their natural character, or even exhibit a superior appearance. Two of the most important genera described in this book, and by their appearance and adaptability worthy of cultivation, are *Fargesia* and *Thamnocalamus*. In their natural home at high altitude, they may suffer damage during long winters or a short, sharp, shock of a blizzard. In such circumstances they can defoliate, or at worst be cut to the ground, but always they regrow unless conditions are exceptional. Any move to an area with less of these vicious extremes would seem luxuriant, even though some of us might consider our gardens harsh and inhospitable. The reward for providing bamboos with softer conditions is some of the most attractive, tidy and easily manageable garden plants.

Broadly speaking, many highland bamboos tolerate cool coastal conditions or inland continental areas. Occasionally a species may require some protection from hot baking sun, particularly in dry soil, or possibly benefit from a sheltered location out of the wind, mimicking its natural forested habitat in the wild. Many of these plants also have great tolerance to extremes of temperature although some may require high light levels, or cool and moist summers. Some may have a low daily average temperature requirement but rarely experience a hard winter, while others have a long period of winter dormancy. Occasionally a species may need high humidity rather than dry alpine conditions, or possibly a constant supply of moisture at the roots rather than a dry summer baking.

Do not be put off by all th'
because the specific requi
plants are given under (

Phyllostachys iridescens, from China, is
and thick culms in cool, temperate gat

"Nothing but the Plants". In their favour, the highland bamboos are truly versatile, usually tidy and clump forming and regardless of their minor quirks, keen to adapt and tolerate a new home in our gardens.

Lowland

The lowland bamboos are more or less confined to the plains of eastern China and the very important genus *Phyllostachys*. In their native habitat these bamboos are generally vigorous and spreading but in cool temperate gardens are mostly the opposite, and in some cases can remain as tight clumps. The genus *Phyllostachys* is very variable and has many species, offering a great variety of form. Although they do not develop the noble proportions of the plants in the wild, there are a few that will become giants in the coolest of gardens.

This lowland group is used to seasonal extremes of temperature and precipitation, from the hot and humid to the dry and cold, sometimes surprised by summer flooding from monsoon rainfall or heavy winter snowfall. It is for this versatility in all weathers that make them most useful as garden plants. In my experience the lowland bamboos have proved tolerant of drought and waterlogged conditions, as well as cold winds from the north. In the wild many of the species withstand -26°C (-15°F) before they suffer physical damage to their woody parts.

It would appear that with the speedy industrialization of China, many of the vast lowland stands, some of single species, could be in danger of extinction. By growing these bamboos in our gardens we are going some way to help the conservation of these plants.

Island

This group is specific to the islands of Japan, Taiwan and the Kuril Isles and contains examples from the most northerly boundary of bamboos. Some are equal in hardiness to the toughest of the montane species, but usually they grow in areas of high summer humidity. Many in this group have large leaves that remain turgid and fresh in summer due to the influence of the maritime climate. In the long and vicious winters the leaves can desiccate and the plants may be covered with snow, but emerge full of life with new foliage and culms in the heat of the summer.

In cool temperate regions we are fortunate not to suffer these extremes, so in our gardens this group of bamboos remain attractive throughout the year. However, the natural character of some, such as *Sasa*, is to wander freely through surrounding vegetation, and many in this group are truly invasive, even in gardens. They do, however, provide that often desired Oriental imagery, and careful selection, planting and culture will create a tropical appearance that no other hardy plant is capable of.

Above: Large leaves on tropical-looking *Sinobambusa tranquillans*.

Right: A bright young plant of the Japanese *Pleioblastus shibuyanus* 'Tsuboi'.

Chapter 4

In at the Deep End

Botanical Classification

It is now widely accepted that bamboos are a sub-family of the grass family Poaceae and are classified as Bambusoideae, which is further divided into two tribes: Bambuseae, woody bamboos, and Olyreae, herbaceous bamboos. This book is concerned only with woody bamboos, as herbaceous bamboos are not suitable for temperate gardens. Bamboos are monocotyledons (monocots) and, like grasses and many bulbs, they emerge from a seed with one cotyledon, or seed leaf, as opposed to a dicotyledon, which has two.

In the eighteenth century Carl Linnaeus introduced a system of classification by which living organisms were assigned two names to denote genus and species. For instance, *Phyllostachys nigra*, the black bamboo, is a member of the genus *Phyllostachys*, which can be likened to a surname. The members of an individual genus share many characteristics but also display some differences. The second part of the name, *nigra*, denotes the species, but is more like the first name of a family member. The species name is often descriptive as in the case of *nigra*, which means black. There are other species of *Phyllostachys* each of which has a different epithet.

There may also be variations within a species, and these are taken into account by further divisions into subspecies, variety, forma and cultivar, and occasionally those that have a close affinity to the species (aff.). All occur in the wild except for cultivars which as "cultivated varieties" have occurred or been bred in

The woody structure of bamboos is clearly shown by the tall culms of *Phyllostachys* ranged either side of a winding lawn.

1. *Thamnocalamus crassinodus* 'Kew Beauty'
2. *Pleioblastus fortunei*
3. *Bashania faberi*

4. *Indocalamus tessellatus*
5. *Sasa veitchii*
6. *Indocalamus hamadae*

cultivation. Often there are differences in opinion as to whether a particular plant occurred in the wild or in cultivation, but the way the plant name is written varies only slightly and should not prove too confusing. For example: *Phyllostachys aureosulcata* 'Aureocaulis' is now considered to be a naturally occurring form rather than a cultivar, and is written *Phyllostachys aureosulcata* f. *aureocaulis*. To confuse matters further there is also *Phyllostachys vivax* f. *aureocaulis*, which is a completely different plant in habit and place of origin, with thicker culms than the species *P. aureosulcata*. The specific (second) name identifies the plant and is usually the most important.

The further divisions of the species are explained in the following examples.

Subspecies: *Thamnocalamus spathiflorus* subsp. *nepalensis*

Subspecies (subsp.) defines the plant geographically. A subspecies comes from a different location in the wild to the true species and any variation will be defined by the location, whether higher altitude, lower latitude or other factor, perhaps providing a different habitat or temperature tolerance.

Variety: *Semiarundinaria fastuosa* var. *viridis*

Variety, or varietas (var.), can refer to provenance in the wild that may affect certain qualities of the plant, such as its tolerance of wind or drought.

Thick and woody culms of *Phyllostachys vivax* f. *aureocaulis* from lowland China.

The plant will have adapted to cope with the specific conditions of its habitat. Alternatively, as with this example, the variety is distinct from the species because it produces taller culms of persistent green colouring that does not pale in sunlight.

Forma: *Phyllostachys bambusoides f. lacrima-deae*

Form, or forma (f.), refers to a unique characteristic of a plant that has developed in the wild. In this example the bamboo has mottled culms. In other cases the forma could differ in colour or habit from the species, such as erect or dwarf forms.

Cultivar: *Fargesia murielae* 'Simba'

A cultivar (cv.) name is always expressed in single quotes with a capital letter, and not lower case and in italics like subspecies, varieties and forma. Cultivar refers to a plant formed or produced in cultivation and *Fargesia murielae* 'Simba' for example, was produced from seed on a nursery. Problems do occur in naming cultivars where a plant has been grown in cultivation for centuries; bamboos have become widely distributed throughout China and the East for cropping purposes. Records of origin are often lost in time and a plant brought into a particular region for cultivation may have established itself in the wild and is now considered native. New forms from cultivated stands are technically cultivars but mostly listed in China as variety (var.) or forma (f.); in the Western world many of these plants are given cultivar names.

Although older cultivar names (pre-1959) are in Latin and usually describe the plant ('Variegata' for example), modern cultivars named after 1959 are more like common names and use everyday language, like 'Simba' to differentiate them from the names of subspecies, variety and forma.

Common parlance

It is worth noting at this point that most gardening books, even those that discuss a specialist plant group, will often use the words form and variety with complete disregard to the subdivisions of a species. The word form, particularly, is used widely to describe a variation from the species in its English meaning and not botanically. Your forgiveness throughout this book will be appreciated when plants such as *Phyllostachys bambusoides* 'Kawadana' and 'Marliacea' are described as magnificent forms, when botanically they are cultivars. Even the most ardent botanist will lapse in concentration when discussing plants, and when presented with something spectacular, will generalize by describing it as a very fine form.

Nomenclature

There is much confusion over bamboo nomenclature and common names are often invented to ease this bewilderment, and then used improperly. Occasionally books, magazine articles, web pages and plant labels in gardens use names that cannot be found in modern literature because they have often changed in history; plant naming is, of course, the playground of botanists and taxonomists, with name changes continuing to be commonplace. Chinese and Japanese names now appear frequently, and when translated usually provide a good individual description of the bamboo. Common English or North American names are often vague and may refer to more than one species, as they are sometimes very generalized in their description. However, misnomers are most apparent on the older generation of bamboos that were introduced late in the nineteenth and the first half of the twentieth centuries. Most of the more recent introductions have not been around long enough for name changes and there is much more botanical information available to enable accurate checks to be made before a name is published.

The main area of disorder in the use of old botanical names is among the genera but occasionally it affects the species. The information given overleaf and the list of synonyms in Appendix 2 will help you to understand the major changes and to identify an old plant with a strange name labelled many years ago.

What's in a name when you can combine a background fountain of *Fargesia murielae* 'Simba' with the willowy leaves of *Yushania maculata* to create a tranquil secluded corner for peaceful contemplation.

Simple rules

If you are confronted with an unfamiliar name, check the genus. If it is *Arundinaria* it is now likely to be listed under a new genus but with the same species name. For example *Arundinaria murielae* is now *Fargesia murielae*; *Arundinaria linearis* is now *Pleioblastus linearis*.

Bashania, *Chimonobambusa*, *Fargesia*, *Himalayacalamus*, *Pleioblastus*, *Pseudosasa*, *Semiarundinaria*, *Thamnocalamus* and *Yushania* were mostly included in the previously much larger genus of *Arundinaria*. However, when confronted with *Thamnocalmaus spathaceus*, which is also *Fargesia murielae*, the specific name has also changed, and you can be forgiven for raising eyebrows and abandoning all hope.

Chusquea and *Phyllostachys* have mostly remained unchanged within their genera, although there are some alternative species names for many *Phyllostachys*: *Phyllostachys congesta* is now *Phyllostachys atrovaginata*, and *Phyllostachys pubescens* is *Phyllostachys edulis*.

Occasionally an old species name has been used when it should be attributed as subspecies, variety, forma or cultivar of another species. For example: *Phyllostachys boryana* is now *Phyllostachys nigra* 'Boryana'; *Phyllostachys henonis* is *Phyllostachys nigra* f. *henonis*.

There is more. *Indocalamus* and *Sasaella* are now separate genera divided from *Sasa*. *Sasa masamuneana* is now *Sasaella masamuneana*; and *Sasa tessellata* is now *Indocalamus tessellatus*.

For total perplexity: *Sasa auricoma* is now *Pleioblastus viridistriatus*, and *Sasa japonica* is *Pseudosasa japonica*.

Chinese and Japanese names

These are very descriptive when translated, sometimes relating to the form of the plant and occasionally to the image it portrays. These names are frequently used in magazines, and customers regularly enquire about *Medake*, *Shima-dake* or *Yadake*, and the only method of identification is to use a table of synonyms or have many works of reference to hand.

As examples: *Phyllostachys aurea* is *hotei-chiku* (bamboo of fairyland); *Phyllostachys mannii* 'Decora' is *mei-chu* (beautiful bamboo); *Phyllostachys bambusoides* 'Castillonis' is *kimmei-chiku* or *ginmei-chiku* (golden brilliant bamboo); *Semiarundinaria kagamiana* is *rikuchu-dake* (referring to the province in Japan where it is found). Sometimes the native name is used as a modern cultivar name as in *Phyllostachys nigra* 'Megurochiku'.

Common names

These are usually created to make life simple, and sometimes they are descriptive of the most notable characteristics of the plant. For example golden crookstem bamboo is *Phyllostachys aureosulcata* f. *aureocaulis*, which has golden and sometimes crooked culms. The leopard-skin bamboo is *Phyllostachys nigra* 'Boryana', with culms mottled like a leopard (apparently).

Common names can refer to people. For example David Bisset bamboo, *Phyllostachys bissetii*, is named after him for his dedication to work in the cultivation and use of bamboos. They can also be a translation of the Latin species or cultivar name. The dragon's head bamboo is *Fargesia dracocephala* and a direct translation of the species.

In the directory of bamboos, "Nothing but the Plants", only the widely used common names and most recent botanical synonyms have been referred to unless there is a particular need to further describe a plant.

The correct and now accepted botanical names used in this book are as listed in the Royal Horticultural Society's Plant Finder 2003–2004 unless I strongly disagree with their naming. I hope most of the synonyms are listed in Appendix 2.

From left to right, starting top left
Phyllostachys bambusoides 'Allgold'
Yushania maculata
Phyllostachys violascens
Thamnocalamus crassinodus 'Kew Beauty'
Phyllostachys bambusoides f. *lacrima-deae*
Chimonobambusa tumidissinoda
Chusquea gigantea
Phyllostachys nigra 'Hale'
Semiarundinaria yashadake f. *kimmei*
Sasa kurilensis 'Shimofuri'
Phyllostachys aureosulcata 'Harbin'
Borinda albocera

The Need to Know

A note about Plant Structure

History, origins, botanical classification and nomenclature are possible unnecessaries for the average gardener and I have seen many shy away from such information with boredom and distaste. Many gardeners are vehemently opposed to anything botanical or scientific, and react like a vampire presented with a crucifix. However, to grow bamboos successfully you really do need to know about their form and structure. In fact, I insist. Bamboos are unlike any other plant group you will have grown, and understanding a little about their different parts, especially their composition and function, will go a long way in helping you select the right plant for your garden and then succeed in its cultivation.

A temperate bamboo is usually very hardy, vigorous (as in grows strongly) and evergreen. As with most plants, bamboos consist of the visible and the invisible, or the above-ground and underground parts. The roots support and feed the top growth, which in turn uses energy from the sun to manufacture carbohydrates from carbon dioxide in the air and water – a process known as photosynthesis. Surplus carbohydrate is stored in the underground rhizomes for times when the bamboo is unable to photosynthesize in balance with the plant's needs. Very occasionally, if the rhizome is unable to support the needs of the bamboo, a portion of the culms will die to balance the supply and demand for food. This balance of growth above and below ground is

particularly important when purchasing or establishing a young plant (as you will read later in "Feeling at Home").

The main structural parts of a bamboo are the underground rhizome system, which has buds and roots, and the aerial culms (canes or stems), which support the branches and leaves. All the parts, with the exception of the fine roots at one extreme and the leaves at the other, are comprised of a series of alternating nodes and internodes, producing a segmented structure. This alternating pattern of usually hollow internodes and solid nodes gives the culm great strength, light weight and flexibility, and the rhizomes with unbreakable yet elastic qualities to support the huge mass of billowing foliage in a storm.

The other noticeable feature of a bamboo, in comparison to a tree or shrub, is its development pattern. The diameter of a young bamboo shoot emerging from the ground will remain the same throughout its life; an individual culm will never thicken in girth like the trunk of a tree. The height a culm reaches in its first year will also be its final height; unlike a tree it never continues growing slowly upwards. In subsequent years, as the bamboo develops a stronger and thicker rhizome system, the culms that emerge can be thicker and taller than the previous ones. Branches and leaves form at the solid nodes on the culms and these do increase in number each year. Although bamboos are evergreen, young leaves are produced regularly as the older ones drop. The leaves and sheaths shed by a bamboo also provide a natural mulch and long-term nourishment so always leave them in situ.

The underground rhizomes form roots at the nodal rings, and buds to develop the shoots and culms above the ground. In general, the rhizomes form a matted and interwoven structure that is quite shallow in the soil, but provides great sta- bility considering the comparative height of the culms. On all the segmented parts of a bamboo, growth only occurs at the tips or from the buds, which are the points at which the cells divide. The rhizomes and culms extend in much the same fashion; each internode is wrapped in tightly overlapping sheaths that loosen as the wood they protect hardens, and either fall off the culms or rot away from the rhizomes.

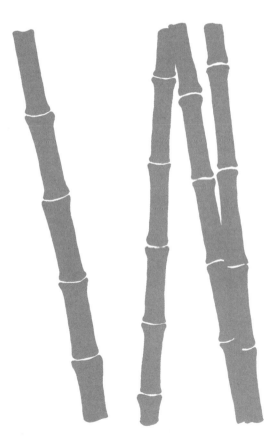

Chapter 5
Going Underground

Undoubtedly the most important part of a bamboo is the rhizome structure, which will determine the habit of the bamboo both in terms of appearance and spread. The structure of a rhizome has already been described but can be summarized as an underground culm, but instead of producing branches and leaves it develops roots and shoots. Generally a young plant will have thin rhizomes and as a result produces thin culms. With time, maturity and good culture, more and thicker rhizomes will form, which in turn produce more roots, thereby increasing nutrient and water intake, leading to bigger buds, thicker shoots and taller culms. For a bamboo to develop properly there has to be a balance between basal and top growth. For example, very large culms are only supported by rhizomes of similar proportion, in thickness or quantity. Encouraging rhizome growth should always be a priority when planting a young bamboo, so mulch regularly to keep the root system warm and the soil moist. Top growth on a young bamboo is of secondary importance to a healthy rhizome system, because the latter will always provide new replacement growth. When purchasing a young bamboo it is wise to ignore the appearance or shape on top, but always to check the state of the rhizome and freshness of the roots, as well as looking for new buds and shoots.

In my view the need to understand the importance of a developing rhizome structure in relation to top growth of bamboo is paramount. The expectations some people have of a bamboo in a five-litre pot are unrealistic. If you want a bamboo that you can carry home, expect a few thin and short culms with a suitably proportioned pot full of root and rhizome. I always tell customers that the culms are free and they are paying for the rhizome, which is the part they should look after. If a tall plant or mature specimen is your desire, the height and quantity of culms will have to be supported by an adequate rhizome system. Forget the carrier bag and the trunk of the car; take a forklift truck or a crane instead. Remember more roots that feed, equals more and thicker rhizome, equals more and bigger buds, equals plentiful thick, tall culms. The plant in the small pot is unlikely to provide thickness and height in the same year although you will not have to wait long, so why waste money on giant specimens?

There are two distinct types of rhizome structure, pachymorph and leptomorph, described as "clumpers" and "runners" respectively. There are also forms intermediate between the two, and these often develop as a result of growing conditions, climate and sometimes the health of an individual plant. It is therefore possible to have clumping runners or running clumpers. The depth of a rhizome in the soil varies considerably between growing conditions and the different genera. Most rhizomes are usually within the first 30 cm (1 ft.) of soil and rarely lower than 50 cm (1.6 ft.), unless they are in deep woodland mould where decaying leaves over many years will have increased the soil depth over the rhizome. However, a new rhizome is usually produced above an older rhizome, particularly on bamboos with a leptomorph structure; in some cases, such as *Phyllostachys*, the most viable rhizomes are in the top 15 cm (6 in.) of soil.

The root and rhizome system of leptomorph bamboos is especially suited to control erosion on steep banks or areas of deforestation, the top growth covering the same area as the extending rhizomes. Pachymorph bamboos, although generally clumping, also have rhizomes that extend beyond the culm base of the plants, much like the supporting roots of a tree. These types can also be used to stabilize soil in smaller areas, although some temporary erosion barriers may be needed until the plants establish.

Pachymorph rhizome of *Fargesia robusta*.

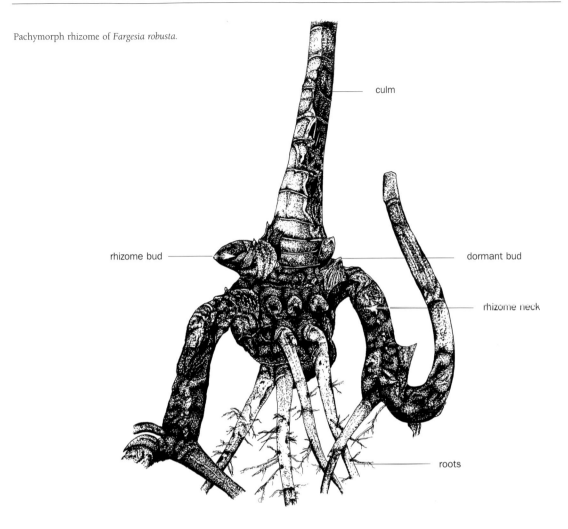

Pachymorph Rhizomes

In general these rhizomes have a sympodial habit and form tightly clumping plants that keep to their original planting area. Pachymorph rhizomes are common on many of the tropical bamboos not described in this book. *Bambusa* is perhaps the best example, but *Fargesia* and *Thamnocalamus* are very cold-hardy genera that are impressively refined in habit. *Chusquea* also produces pachymorph rhizomes that can sometimes become intermediate in habit, depending on growing conditions.

A pachymorph rhizome typically has very short segments between its nodes and is usually quite thick and solid, curving upwards to form a culm. The necks that attach one rhizome to another are very short, thereby forming a plant with a clumping habit. Additional rhizomes develop from lateral dormant buds, and the culms that arise at the rhizome tips are often thinner than the supporting rhizome. Roots are produced from the bases of the older swollen rhizomes that support the culms; newer rhizomes and culms are often supported and nourished by the older rhizome and show little root growth in the first year. For propagation purposes it is better to sever sections with some older rhizome attached that already has some roots.

Leptomorph Rhizomes

Bamboos with this type of rhizome are normally from the temperate regions and include most of the bamboos in this book. The rhizomes resemble underground horizontal culms and can extend for considerable distances, and some forms could be classed as invasive. *Sasa* is the

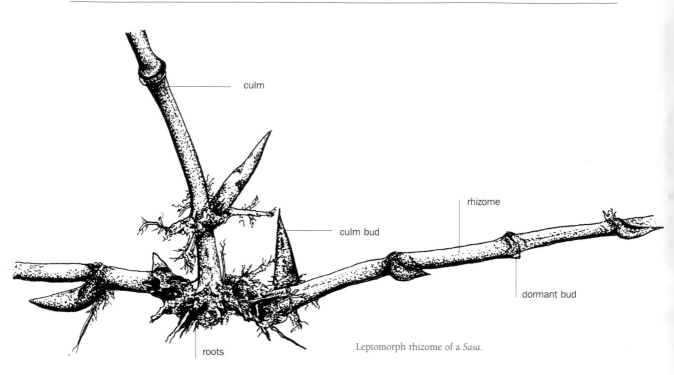

culm

culm bud

rhizome

dormant bud

roots

Leptomorph rhizome of a *Sasa*.

best example of a stable leptomorph rhizome system, providing the plant with the ability to run wild in some situations. *Phyllostachys* and *Pleioblastus* also have this type of rhizome structure but, in contrast to *Sasa*, many plants can be quite compact in cool gardens, with stunted rhizomes. In general, culms are more widely spaced when produced from leptomorph, or running, rhizomes and this open-clump habit is described as monopodial.

The dormant buds of leptomorph rhizomes have the ability to produce either new rhizomes or culms although they may only break dormancy if there is damage to the rhizome. This is a useful trait as severing the rhizomes (and removing the extension) often forces dormant buds to form culms close to the main plant, making it more clump forming. A culm can also develop at the terminal growth point of a rhizome, after which a new underground branch of rhizome arises from a dormant bud. The segmented sections of rhizomes are sheathed as they develop. The sheaths mimic those on the aboveground culms offering protection as the internodes expand. The sheaths rot quickly in the soil once the internodes have extended to their full length. Culms are usually produced on alternate

sides of the rhizome and have short thin necks that expand into culms, which are often much thicker than the supporting structure.

Roots can occur at the base of the culms, above the narrow neck, as well as from the nodes on the rhizomes. However the culm bases on a true leptomorph structure do not have any buds, so for propagation purposes a length of segmented rhizome with visible buds must be attached.

The long rhizomes of a leptomorph bamboo create a matted, interwoven structure. In an earthquake, dive for the nearest large bamboo grove; the ground is unlikely to be broken where there is a dense tangle of rhizomes. Where rhizomes are forced towards the surface, perhaps because they are growing over others or moving over obstacles or very compacted soil, they can arch out of the ground before re-entering, creating a serpentine effect.

Intermediate Rhizomes

Although technically there are only pachymorph and leptomorph rhizome systems, some bamboos display amphimorph qualities with a combination of the two. This formation is quite

Serpent-like rhizomes on a specimen of *Phyllostachys bambusoides* 'Marliacea' have a structure similar to the culms. Note the colouring that develops in good light.

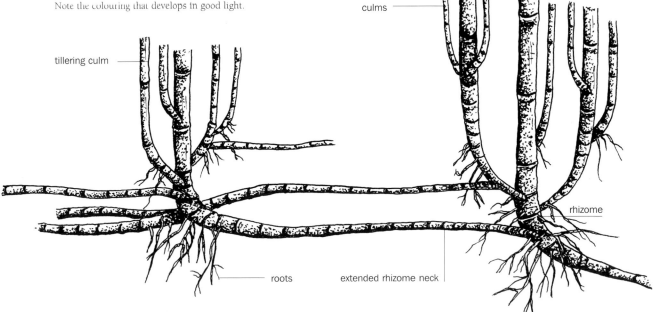

Intermediate rhizome of *Yushania*.

rare and does not apply to any of the bamboos in this book.

Some pachymorph bamboos (usually clumping) can have elongated and jointed rhizome necks producing culms that are more widely spaced. These necks act like stems between the proper rhizomes and are always devoid of roots; this makes them easy to differentiate from leptomorph rhizomes, which have roots at the nodes. An example of this type of rhizome system is *Yushania anceps,* which can be quite invasive.

Some of the taller leptomorph bamboos, notably *Phyllostachys,* are much less invasive in cool regions than in their native habitat or when grown in warm temperate or subtropical gardens. The cool climate provides a short growing season for the rhizome, which in consequence remains stunted and forms a bamboo of clumping appearance.

Roots

As growing points at one extremity of a bamboo these are not segmented, and they have the ability to elongate like the roots on many other plants. They are not sheathed or protected in any way and, in general, are of even thickness, very fibrous and concentrated around the upper layers of the newest rhizomes. The roots can store carbohydrates in the form of starch, although this is of secondary importance to the rhizomes, which act as the main storage organs. On some genera where water storage is important due to harsh growing conditions, such as freezing soil or exposure, some of the roots can be much thicker; some of the best examples are *Fargesia robusta* and *Thamnocalamus crassinodus.* Other bamboos have adapted to wet conditions, with air channels present in both roots and

Aerial roots on *Semiarundinaria fastuosa*.

rhizomes. *Phyllostachys heteroclada* is tolerant of waterlogged soils and is aptly known as the water bamboo.

Roots can sometimes be seen above ground, usually growing from the lower nodes on culms, and take on the guise of aerial roots. These above-ground roots serve no purpose other than to stabilize the culms at soil level against wind rock. Aerial roots are present on some species with thick culms that carry a great weight above a shallow rhizome system, in particular *Phyllostachys* and *Semiarundinaria* species. Unfortunately the aerial roots are often covered by persistent basal sheaths or a natural mulch around the base of the culms. In some of the *Chimonobambusa* species, notably *C. quadrangularis* and *C. hejiangensis,* root initiation can occur higher on the culms, resulting in stunted hornlike growths or short downward pointing hooks that can be vicious on thick culms.

Chimonobambusa hejiangensis, showing thorn-like upper root initials.

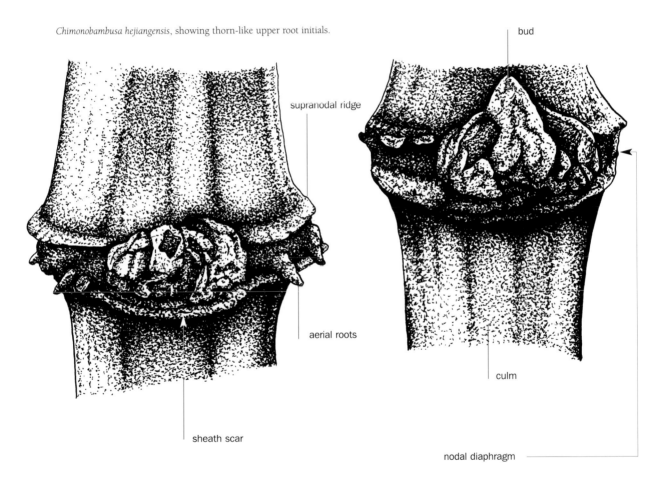

Chapter 6
From Root to Roof

For some of us the vision of a bamboo is one of large tropical-looking leaves dripping in the warm rains of a summer storm, or the silhouette of arching branches against the background of a deep blue sky. For others, a stark and satisfying culm structure and awe-inspiring emergence of monsters from the ground is the paragon of all gardening. Often a bamboo is planted to provide sound and movement in the landscape, the constant rustle of leaf on leaf never quite disturbing the silence, but often drowning out the noise of traffic and general hum of urban activity. Sitting by a bamboo, sighing in a summer breeze, while the birds sing their late evening chorus gives new meaning to peace and tranquillity.

The need to know about the visible part of a bamboo is possibly more interesting, but less important than understanding the structure of the various rhizome and root systems – a point indelibly forced upon you in the previous chapter. Unless you are growing bamboos purely to prevent soil erosion you will be mostly concerned with the above-ground parts. These, in simplest terms, consist of culms with branches and leaves. However, there are other features attached to these parts that can affect the ornamental value of an individual species. Sheaths, sulci and supranodal ridges are terms not generally associated

A very thick culm of a *Phyllostachys vivax*.

with other plants and will be explained later in the chapter, together with ligules, oral setae, auricles and blades, not forgetting the flowers. However, not all of these parts play an important role in the developing structure of the plant and some are only visual distinctions used for identification purposes.

Clump Habits and Culm Spacing

As with the morphology and description of the rhizomes there are specific terms for the culm and clump formations of bamboos. These are not often used but are worth knowing as they relate to the different rhizome types. However, the terminology for describing rhizome and clump formations given below is far from precise, as it does not take into account how a bamboo may perform in different garden conditions. It is easier, therefore, to refer to the culm formation of bamboos in relation to the rhizome types: clumpers, runners and those in between. I offer no apologies for using this simple terminology throughout the book.

Diffuse habit is applied to bamboos with culms that arise singly but are well spaced. This description would normally apply to plants with leptomorph, or running, rhizomes such as *Phyllostachys*, particularly when grown in temperate gardens. Diffuse habit can also be attributed to some pachymorph bamboos, and *Chusquea* with its well-spaced individual culms is perhaps the best example.

Running habit.

Intermediate habit.

Caespitose habit applies specifically to clumping bamboos that have the short rhizome necks of true pachymorph rhizome systems. *Bambusa* and *Fargesia* are notable examples.

Pluricaespitose habit refers to bamboos that develop individual clumps of culms well spaced from each other. Although sometimes associated with running leptomorph bamboos, this habit is more applicable to pachymorph root systems that have long rhizome necks as found in the genus *Yushania*.

The bamboos with leptomorph rhizomes and a pluricaespitose habit usually exhibit tillering culms and are called amphipodial, which means they exhibit clumps of culms from an amphimorph rhizome system. New culms from this formation of bamboo can tiller off the base of existing culms, as well as along the length of the running rhizome. Some individual species from the genera *Indocalamus*, *Pleioblastus*, *Pseudosasa* and *Shibataea* display this characteristic. The term amphipodial is also applicable to monopodial and sympodial structures. Monopodial loosely describes the culm formation from a leptomorph rhizome and sympodial for the tight culm formation from a pachymorph rhizome.

Clumping habit.

Culms

The unique character of bamboos is formed by the distinct structure of the above-ground stems, or culms. Each culm is divided into segments of nodes (solid) and internodes (usually hollow, although on *Chusquea* they are solid), similar to grasses, with the woody nodes providing the strength to keep the culms upright. The division between the node and internode is sometimes known as a culm or nodal diaphragm. The diaphragm is best seen when a culm node of a *Chimonobambusa tumidissinoda* is separated, showing two smooth and flat plates.

As with grasses and other monocotyledons the thickness of the emerging stem remains the same throughout its life. The maximum height of an individual culm is attained in one growing season, and mostly over a few weeks in the warmer months. As the culms emerge into daylight they quickly become woody, extending to

Below: A section of culm showing a node on Phyllostachys irridescens.

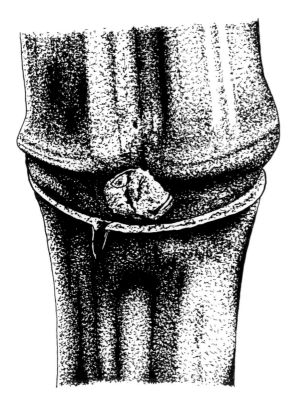

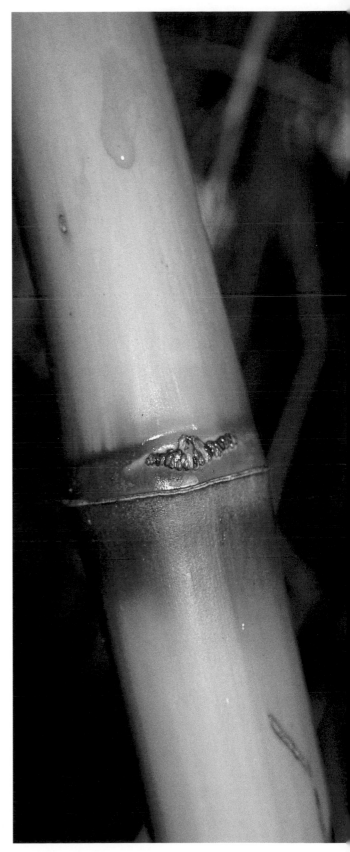

Right: A culm section of Chusquea *showing dormant branch buds.*

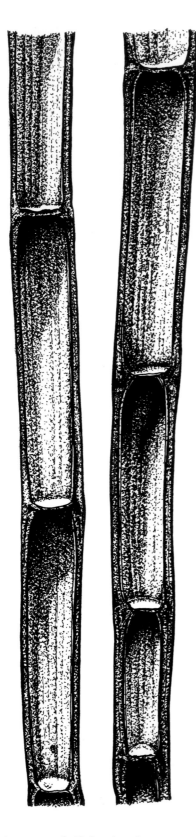

The interior structure of a *Phyllostachys* culm.

almost their full height before some species produce branches and leaves. Although the culms are not soft at this stage, they have a more brittle quality than a much older culm, and are more susceptible to physical damage than at any other time. Full culm strength is not attained until the third or fourth year – this is useful to know should you wish to crop bamboos for cane production, as older culms last longer than young ones (see chapter 2, "Harvesting and Curing"). I have found that a gale-force wind will rarely damage or topple a new culm, but a visitor to the garden who casually shakes a new culm will often be whipped round the face by an overhead section, hinging from the snap of an underdeveloped internode.

The outer surface of a culm is usually smooth and hard, often with a protective waxy finish on younger culms. The waxy bloom usually disappears with age as the bamboo wood hardens and becomes more resistant to moisture. The external structure of the culms is solid and impervious to moisture transference except where a falling sheath leaves a scar just below the node.

The internal structure of a culm is very fibrous and structured to support the huge weight of overhead branches and leaves. Without going into great scientific detail, the wood of a bamboo culm consists of nearly 90 percent supportive structure in the form of general cell tissue and structural fibres, with 10 percent devoted to the vascular bundles that conduct the flow of water and nutrients. The long structural fibres consist of lignin and silica, as opposed to lignin alone in other woody plants; the presence of silica makes the fibres stronger and more flexible. The vascular bundles are more numerous and smaller towards the outside of the culm than they are towards the centre and they become blocked with age, reducing the vigour and causing the eventual death of a culm. Young culms may not have fully developed supporting structural fibres, which, as described above, can result in brittleness. The thickness of the culm wood varies according to genus and species. Some species of *Phyllostachys* for instance have thin-walled culms, making them unsuitable for construction purposes. Others have thicker culm wood and *Chimonobambusa* species notably have thick walled culms, while *Chusquea* species are usually solid.

The life expectancy of individual culms also varies according to genera and species but is approximately ten years, by which time they will have been superseded by new vigorous culms. The old culms must be removed at this stage, or before, to keep the plant tidy. In my garden I have *Phyllostachys* culms that I inherited over seventeen years ago when they were already ten years old. Although they are not as productive in leaf as the younger culms growing alongside, it is interesting to note that they are over a quarter of a century older. *Chusquea* culms can also persist for well over thirty years. Culms on a young juvenile bamboo will not have the same life expectancy as those on a mature plant, and may only last a few years before they are replaced with culms of greater size and vigour.

Culm colour is generally green, but the outer layer of cells can contain other pigments that are affected by sunlight, exposure and seasonal variation. The genus *Phyllostachys* in particular is well known for its array of different coloured culms according to species. What better way to introduce the novice to bamboos than to liken the available culm colours to a rainbow, except much more exciting. You have a choice of golden, black, green with yellow grooves, golden with green grooves, green with black grooves, green with violet and yellow stripes, pale dusty blue, yellow with red tints, burnished orange, bloomy grey-green, green with brown blotches, green with black spots, green with dusky purple-brown stains, green with white sheaths, deep purple and green, pink tinted yellow and green striped, golden with barcode green striping, black with silver streaks, yellow-green stained and streaked with purple-black, tawny brown, and of course, green. It is even more impressive when you say it in one breath.

Culms on shorter bamboos, whether short in habit or juvenile forms of more arborescent types, usually taper uniformly from base to tip. Occasionally culms on larger-growing species can become slightly thicker than their girth at emergence before tapering towards the tip; some

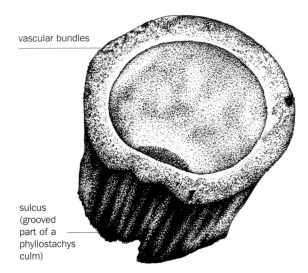

vascular bundles

sulcus (grooved part of a phyllostachys culm)

Cross section through a *Phyllostachys* culm.

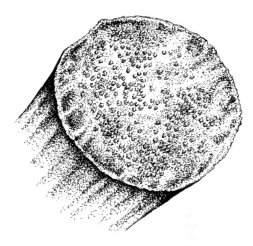

Cross section through a *Chusquea* culm, showing solid structure.

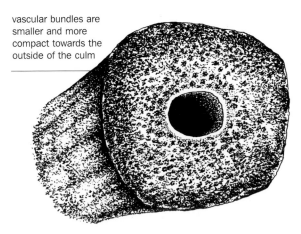

vascular bundles are smaller and more compact towards the outside of the culm

Cross section through a culm of *Chimonobambusa quadrangularis*, showing thick walls and slightly square shape.

1   2   3   4   5   6   7   8   9   9   10   11

Above: A blotched culm *of Phyllostachys bambusoides* f. *lacrima-deae.*

1. *Phyllostachys sulphurea*
2. *Phyllostachys nigra* (old culm)
3. *Phyllostachys glauca* f. *yunzhu*
4. *Thamnocalamus crassinodus* 'Merlyn'
5. *Bashania fargesii*
6. *Phyllostachys violascens*
7. *Phyllostachys nigra* 'Megurochiku'
8. *Phyllostachys nigra* 'Fulva' (new culm)
9. *Himalayacalamus falconeri* 'Damarapa'
10. *Phyllostachys nigra* (new culm)
11. *Phyllostachys nigra* 'Fulva' (old culm)
12. *Borinda albocera*
13. *Sasa palmata* f. *nebulosa*
14. *Phyllostachys aureosulcata* f. *spectabilis*
15. *Phyllostachys aureosulcata* 'Harbin Inversa'
16. *Phyllostachys aureosulcata* 'Harbin'

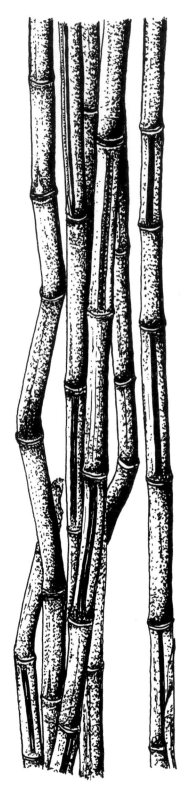

species taper gently over a long length and others are straight-sided until very close to the top.

The various shapes of bamboo culms also provide us with some interesting features. Some are completely cylindrical; *Phyllostachys* have indented sulci, or grooves, which are often coloured; one or two are almost in square cross section; and for those of you with a fondness of swellings, some species have pronounced nodes. Other species display geniculation, a zigzag formation, and there are also instances of congested nodes and internodes low down on the culms, giving a tortoiseshell effect.

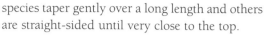

Above: Phyllostachys aureosulcata f. *spectabilis* showing culm geniculation.

Above: Congested internodes on the culms of *Phyllostachys aurea.*

Aborting culms

A developing bamboo, usually one that is not quite mature, can often produce many culms in a season and some of these may collapse shortly after emergence, turning soft and withering. Sometimes seasonal growing conditions are the cause but more likely it is due to a growth imbalance, which means that the underground parts are not able to support the over-productive top half of the plant. The previous season may have been well suited to rhizome and bud production but with insufficient energy stored to support them. Soil or air temperature, strong wind or drought, may also effect culm development, and if the conditions are not right the bamboo will naturally abort some its culms. I have noted that bamboos, the genus *Phyllostachys* in particular, also put energy into developing the thickest of the new shoots and often abort any that are inferior; this method of self selection often occurs in nature. Unfortunately aborting culms are something you will have to tolerate but, I can assure you, it is not a cause for concern.

Shooting time

There is nothing quite like the sight of emerging shoots on a giant *Phyllostachys* to impress the potential bamboo enthusiast and one I take great

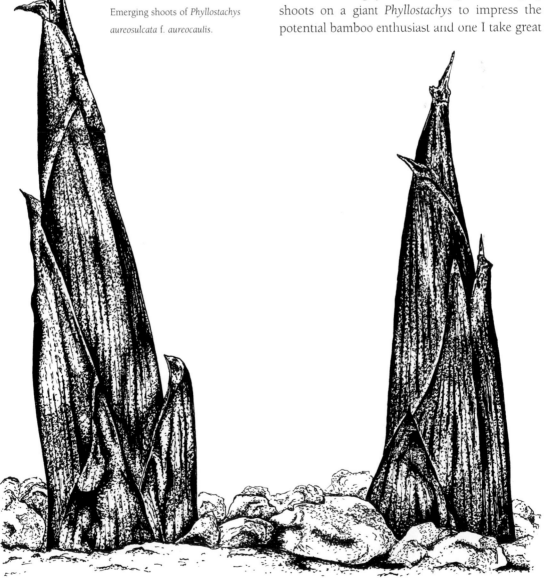

Emerging shoots of *Phyllostachys aureosulcata* f. *aureocaulis*.

delight in showing visitors to the garden. It almost guarantees addiction to this moreish plant group and I have customers who now provide me with running commentaries of their developing *Phyllostachys vivax* f. *aureocaulis* shoots each summer over the telephone.

Before writing this book I vowed I would record the sequence of each species and the time it shoots during the course of a year, but sadly this has not happened yet. However, over the years it has been noticeable that there is a distinct and uniform sequence of species and the time their shoots emerge. As an example, the first bamboo to shoot

in my locality is *Fargesia rufa*, closely followed by *Fargesia robusta*. *Sasa kurilensis* forms are next with *Phyllostachys nuda* and *Phyllostachys aureosulcata* types close behind. *Phyllostachys violascens* reliably shoots during the third week of May (at least it does here) and then a great glut of genera and species sprout forth in the early summer months, making it difficult to keep up with the delight and awe inspired by so much new growth. *Phyllostachys vivax* and its forms produce new culms that act like beacons indicating the approach of midsummer alongside the piercing vertical culms of *Semiarundinaria fastuosa* with

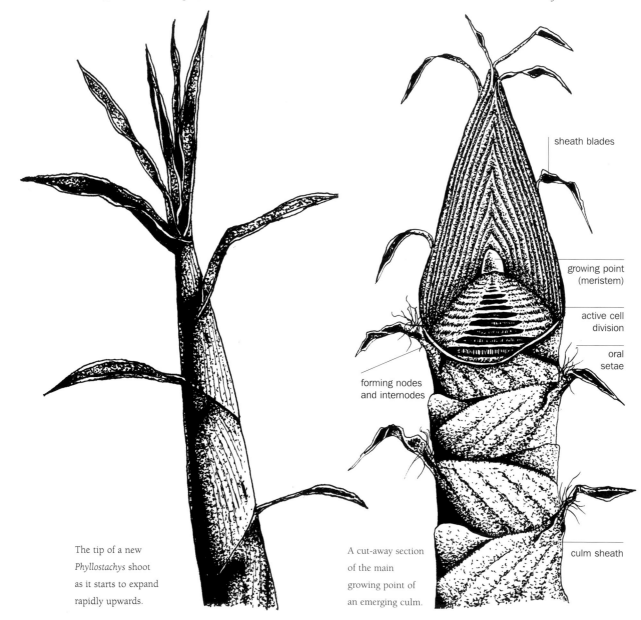

The tip of a new *Phyllostachys* shoot as it starts to expand rapidly upwards.

A cut-away section of the main growing point of an emerging culm.

sheath blades

growing point (meristem)

active cell division

oral setae

forming nodes and internodes

culm sheath

Culm production and development on a juvenile plant.

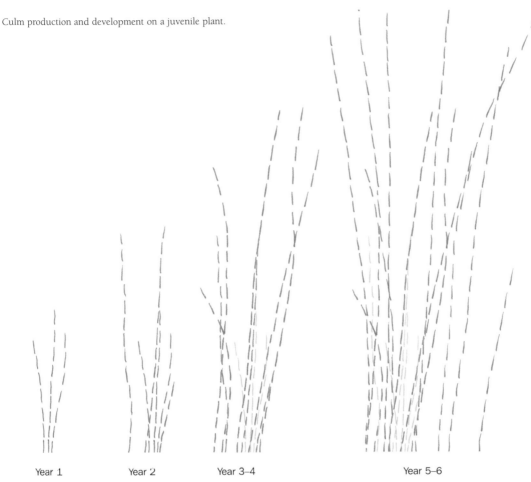

Year 1   Year 2   Year 3–4   Year 5–6

their opening sheaths. The shortening days of July are enlivened by an eruption of *Phyllostachys bambusoides* and its cultivars with culms of great thickness and speedy emergence. Last but not least, the sharp points of *Phyllostachys bambusoides* 'Marliacea' become visible in August; it is always a worry whether they will mature before the onset of cold autumn nights, but they usually manage to develop strongly during the changeable months of early autumn (September and October). *Chimonobambusa marmorea* is the odd one out, it shoots during the cold winter months and, I suppose, could take first or last place in the sequence.

There is a definite relationship to shooting time and the geographical origin of each species, in terms of latitude, climate and altitude. Bamboos originating from more northerly latitudes tend to shoot earlier and have a faster rate of development in cool temperate gardens than those from more southerly locations.

The speed of culm development varies according to species but some *Phyllostachys* are capable of growing 10 m (33 ft.) or more in only two weeks – it is possible to measure their hourly growth on warm humid summer days.

Culm production and growing up

A bamboo has two stages in life: juvenile and adult. Most bamboos are planted as juveniles and only reach maturity after a period of establishment in the garden. The need for good root and rhizome formation has been explained, but how long does it take for culms to provide the structure of a mature plant? My answer is summarized in the above figure, which shows the expected culm formation from a juvenile plant over a few years. Note that soil, climate, moisture, exposure and health of the original plant will all affect the development of the young plant and whether it produces more or less, thin or thick, and tall or short culms.

Alternatively, if you plant a segment chopped from a mature and healthy bamboo, the growth that can be expected will not usually match the existing thick culms. The rhizomes have been severed, damaged, mutilated and possibly torn in the removal process, and the rhizome buds will also be damaged. Those buds that remain will not have much supporting root structure to nurture them, and as a result new culms are likely to be shorter and thinner than those on the parent plant. The division will, more or less, revert to juvenile as a reaction to the severance and use its energy to heal the damage and produce new roots and rhizome for further culm production. The taller more woody bamboos with congested rhizome systems tend to resent disturbance, although some running bamboos thrive on being removed and replanted.

A word of caution; if you do remove a portion of bamboo and sever the roots, reduce the leaf area of the propagule in proportion. The damaged root system is unlikely to be capable of supplying the top growth with all the required water and nutrients to keep the leaves turgid and desiccation can occur. Either prune the culms back in height or remove a quantity in their entirety. Some damage to the mother plant may also be evident where a rhizome that fed culms left standing may have been removed or severed.

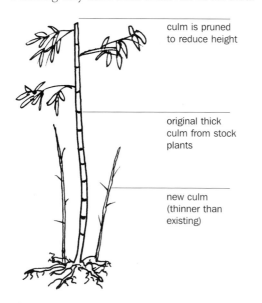

culm is pruned
to reduce height

original thick
culm from stock
plants

new culm
(thinner than
existing)

Above: Juvenile culm development from a mature section of bamboo.

Branches

Branches emerge from buds at the culm nodes, on alternate sides of a culm. Branches form at various times throughout the growing season according to genera and species, for example on *Phyllostachys* and *Semiarundinaria* they emerge as the shoot grows upwards but rarely come into leaf until the full height has been reached. On *Chimonobambusa* the branches do not develop until the culm has reached its full height. On

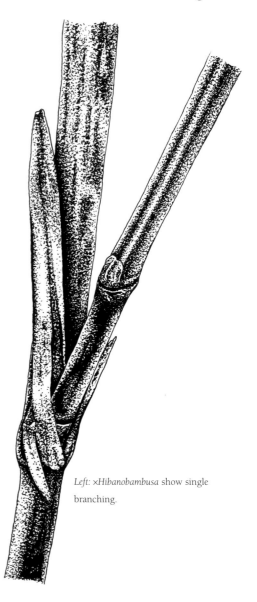

Left: ×*Hibanobambusa* show single branching.

Right: A new culm of *Phyllostachys bambusoides* 'Castillonis Inversa' with developing branches.

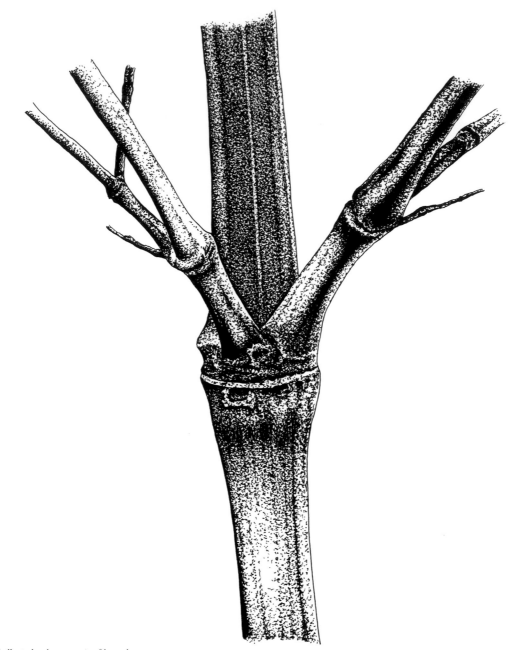

Phyllostachys have a pair of branches.

some *Fargesia* species branching does not occur until the second growing season. How the branches are formed along the length of a culm also varies between genera and species; some form from the top downwards and vice versa. *Pseudosasa* and *Sasa* are good examples of bamboos that branch only on the upper half of the culms, whereas on some *Phyllostachys* species the branches form all the way up and it is common-

place to remove the lower ones to expose the often colourful culms.

One of the most important aspects of identifying different genera within the range of temperate bamboos is the number of branches produced at the nodes. This is known as the branch complement and will be dealt with later in "Nothing but the Plants", under individual plant entries. However, to give a few examples, ×*Hibanobambusa*

Sinobambusa have three branches.

has one branch per node; *Phyllostachys* two; *Sinobambusa* three; *Fargesia* and *Yushania* three or more; *Chusquea* has multiple branching with sometimes as many as thirty or more. Secondary branching may also occur from buds on primary branches, and this is evident on the main branch of the pair on a *Phyllostachys*, sometimes giving the impression there are three branches.

The angles at which branches emerge from the buds in relation to the culm is also useful in identification but is more important in influencing the appearance of a bamboo. *Phyllostachys* branches tend to be rigid and angled at forty-five degrees from the culm, creating well-spaced layers of foliage. *Fargesia* species mostly develop branches initially held close to the culm, which is subsequently weighed down by the mass of foliage to create an arching habit.

Yushania produce more than three branches.

Leaves

The bamboo leaf is a strange affair as, unlike those on broad-leaved trees or shrubs, it does not emerge from a bud. Instead the leaves are formed from the leaf sheaths that encircle the branches and are attached to these by a strong structural projection of the leaf midrib known as the petiole. The leaf sheath has many characteristics, often similar to those of a culm sheath, and is dealt with later in this chapter under "Sheaths" (p72). The blade on a culm sheath is often superficial but still able to photosynthesize. The blade attached to a leaf sheath is the true leaf and also known as the leaf blade.

A typical bamboo leaf is lanceolate, with a pointed tip, a rounded base and an obvious central vein. Bamboo leaves always have petioles unlike their counterpart grasses, which instead have leaves that wrap around the stems

at the base. Bamboos are evergreen and the flexible petioles are necessary to ensure the leaves remain attached to the plant in extremes of weather. The upper surface of a bamboo leaf is often glossy, while the underside appears matt due to the undulations of the minute stomata that are present. The lower surface can often be faintly hairy which helps keep it dry, allowing the stomata to breath.

Leaf size and culm height are not related in any way; some very short bamboos can have large leaves in relation to their size and some of the very tall arborescent bamboos have minute leaves by comparison. Young juvenile plants, especially those grown from seed, often have much larger leaves than in maturity. *Phyllostachys edulis* for example, as a young juvenile from seed, has leaves four or five times the size of those on a mature plant and is virtually unrecognizable at an early age. The same happens with other *Phyllostachys* and *Semiarundinaria* when produced from small rhizome sections or by micropropagation. The resulting young plants are very short and leafy with almost no visible culm structure for the first two or three years, and you may need convincing they are what they claim to be.

Unlike many temperate evergreen plants, such as laurel or holly, that have thick leathery leaves, those on bamboo are generally thin and papery and do not look capable of surviving a winter blasting. Temperate bamboo leaves, however, are tessellated: they have the long parallel veins typical of grass leaves with the addition of veins running at right angles across the width of the leaf to form a grid. This cross veining provides structural reinforcement and prevents the destruction of the leaves in winter months when the sap levels fall. On some of the larger-leaved species, such as *Sasa*, the tessellation is visible and an indication of the leaves' ability to withstand a cold northerly aspect – hold a fresh, large leaf up to the light and

Right: Chusquea show multiple branching.

Below: Sasa kurilensis 'Shimofuri', with large leaves, and *Yushania anceps,* with small leaves.

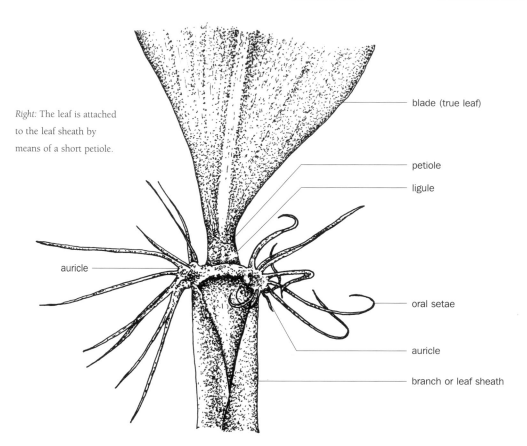

Right: The leaf is attached to the leaf sheath by means of a short petiole.

blade (true leaf)

petiole

ligule

auricle

oral setae

auricle

branch or leaf sheath

Above: Leaf tessellation on *Sasa*.

it is possible to see the grid-like venation. However, *Phyllostachys* and *Pleioblastus* are also well tessellated but this is not visible without magnification.

As culms vary in their shapes and colours, so do the leaves. The leaves and culms combine to make a landscape picture of your choice, and one with sound, whether it is the fine and elegant leaves whispering on a *Fargesia* or the deep tropical rustling of a large-leaved *Sasa*. Temperate bamboo leaves range from thin and almost needle-like to massive ashet-sized plates of green. There are some striking variegations: white, cream and yellow stripes, streaks and mottling; some with ghostly winter bleaching; pale glaucous undersides; and if that is not enough you can select from a matt or gloss finish. White and cream variegations hold their colour well in shade but the golden *Pleioblastus viridistriatus* prefers better light to show its true brightness.

1. *Sasa kurilensis* 'Shimofuri'

2. *Pleioblastus fortunei*

3. *Bashania faberi*

4. *Thamnocalamus crassinodus* 'Kew Beauty'

5. *Sasa veitchii*

6. ×*Hibanobambusa tranquillans* 'Shiroshima'

7. *Indocalamus hamadae*

8. *Pleioblastus pygmaeus*

9. *Pleioblastus viridistriatus*

Shedding time

The average life expectancy of a leaf is two years. Old leaves are gradually replaced by new ones, which develop during the growing season, although they do not always drop at the same time. Some *Phyllostachys* can shed a few leaves in early summer as new growth takes preference. The species *Phyllostachys bambusoides* and its forms shed their old foliage much later in the summer, because they shoot much later than other species in temperate gardens. *Fargesia* species tend to shed their leaves in late autumn or early winter to reduce transpiration from a large surface area in readiness for the cold season. In very harsh situations the leaves of some small-leaved bamboos can curl inwards, appearing like the fine needles on a pine, and this is another adaptation to prevent moisture loss. Leaves on some genera persist for more than two years, *Sasa* and *Pleioblastus* are examples that also show bleaching around the margins of each leaf, which reduces the area for moisture loss in the winter. Bamboos that display this bleaching, although attractive in the winter months, may need selective

pruning during the following growing season to remove some of the older, more persistent leaves. In the case of the shorter *Pleioblastus* it is easier to shear the plant to the ground, which usually has no ill effect on vigour.

In summers with record levels of heat and drought, bamboos in my garden have thrived without supplementary water or mulching. Rather than go crisp in the heat like many of the broad-leaved shrubs around them, some of the bamboos have occasionally shed a portion of their leaves to reduce the area of transpiration. This takes only a few days from when the leaves turn yellow to when they drop and is of little concern. For those new to bamboos, the very brief seasonal leaf loss can be a worry, especially when the yellowing leaves affect the visual quality of the plant. I have encountered this problem many times. A customer purchasing a *Fargesia* in early autumn will be confronted with a yellowing

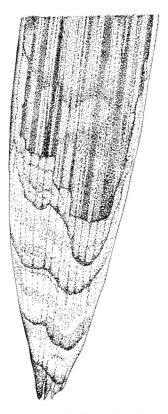

Above: Leaf bleaching on *Sasa kurilensis* 'Shimofuri'.

Left: The large, thick leaves of *Indocalamus* provide contrast to the smaller, more delicate greenery of *Thamnocalamus*.

Above: Fargesia nitida in late autumn shedding its leaves in readiness for winter. Within a week or two the yellow leaves will have dropped, leaving the plant fresh and lighter in appearance.

As proof of their evergreen qualities *Phyllostachys* punctuate the surrounding deciduous woodland with their intense greenery in the depths of winter.

plant only a month or two later. An often irate 'phone call ensues: "Why has my bamboo turned yellow?" In reply I give a lengthy explanation about "shedding time" and promise the plant will look good when it starts to grow in the spring. And it will.

As a last word on bamboo leaves, I must impress on you their most important attribute to our gardens. A lady visited my garden on the gloomiest of winter days. After some time showing her around and allowing her to touch and shake the giant culms, feel and comb the clean and glossy winter foliage, she commented on the lush almost tropical appearance of the bamboos around her. Finally, she looked up at their leafiness, blowing her fingers to warm them from the cold, damp air, "Are they evergreen?" she asked.

Sheaths

These are not the most obvious structures on a bamboo plant, but they are, perhaps, the most complicated. Sheaths can be divided into three types – leaf, rhizome and culm – and all have a protective function, although some are more visible than others.

Leaf sheaths support the leaf blades, or true leaves, as described earlier. They also protect the extending branches and the buds on the upper part of the bamboo. The sheaths are always visible and most have no ornamental value.

Rhizome sheaths are rarely observed because they protect the expanding internodes underground. They rot quickly once they have served their purpose.

Culm sheaths, sometimes known as culm leaves, are the most noticeable of the three types as they envelop the emerging culms, again to

Below: An image of a culm sheath.

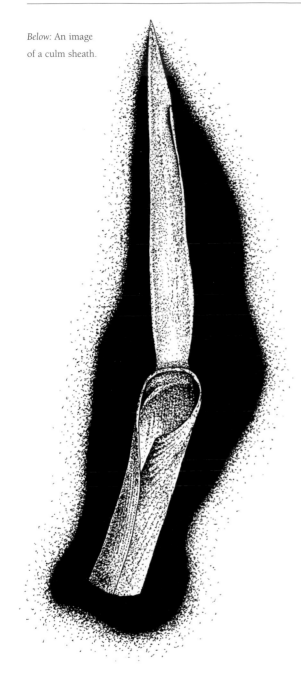

Above: The large culm sheaths, just before shedding, on an established clump of *Thamnocalamus crassinodus* 'Kew Beauty'.

offer protection. Culm sheaths usually have a blade, but much smaller than the leaf blade on a leaf sheath. Culm sheaths are often very colourful and highly ornamental. They are also used to identify certain species within a genus.

A culm sheath is generally quite hard with the texture and appearance of very tough parchment. The sheath is difficult to tear, yet flexible and strong, and gives structural support as well as protection to the soft emerging internodes until

they harden. The outer surface of the sheath is usually rough textured, sometimes hairy and can be longitudinally veined. All these features go some way towards keeping the vulnerable growing points of the culm free of moisture and safe from physical damage. The inner surface of a culm sheath is always smooth and glossy which allows the internode to rise rapidly through its casing. The waxy or powdery coating often present on a new culm also helps emergence and prevents moist air condensing on the surface, acting and appearing very much like a fine layer of talcum powder.

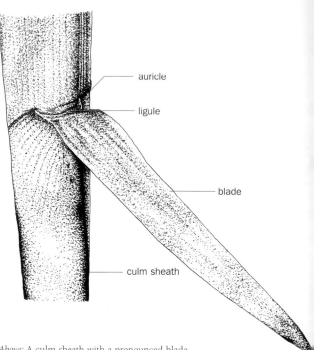

Above: A culm sheath with a pronounced blade enveloping a culm.

Culm sheaths persist on some genera such as *Pseudosasa*, while on others they are shed very quickly, as for *Phyllostachys*. Together with the annual fall of leaves, the sheaths build up a natural organic mulch around the base of a bamboo and should always be left in situ. As well as their protective quality, culm sheaths are often decorative. New sheaths of *Fargesia robusta* and *Thamnocalamus tessellatus* are almost pure white. The new shoots of the *Thamnocalamus crassinodus* forms are covered in dense layers of pink hairy sheaths. On *Semiarundinaria* they are green and have the ability to photosynthesize as they emerge. The new shoots of *Phyllostachys* are encased in the most beautiful sheathing: pale creamy green in *P. dulcis*; mottled with dark blotches in *P. vivax* species; and deep red in *P. iridescens*.

Blades, ligules, auricles, fringes and oral setae

The culm sheath has a structure at the top known as a ligule. This is normally inconspicuous and acts as a seal between the top of the sheath and the emerging culm or branch, preventing water

Above: Thamnocalamus crassinodus forms have hairy sheaths.

Right: Culm of *Chusquea gigantea* showing sheath and blade.

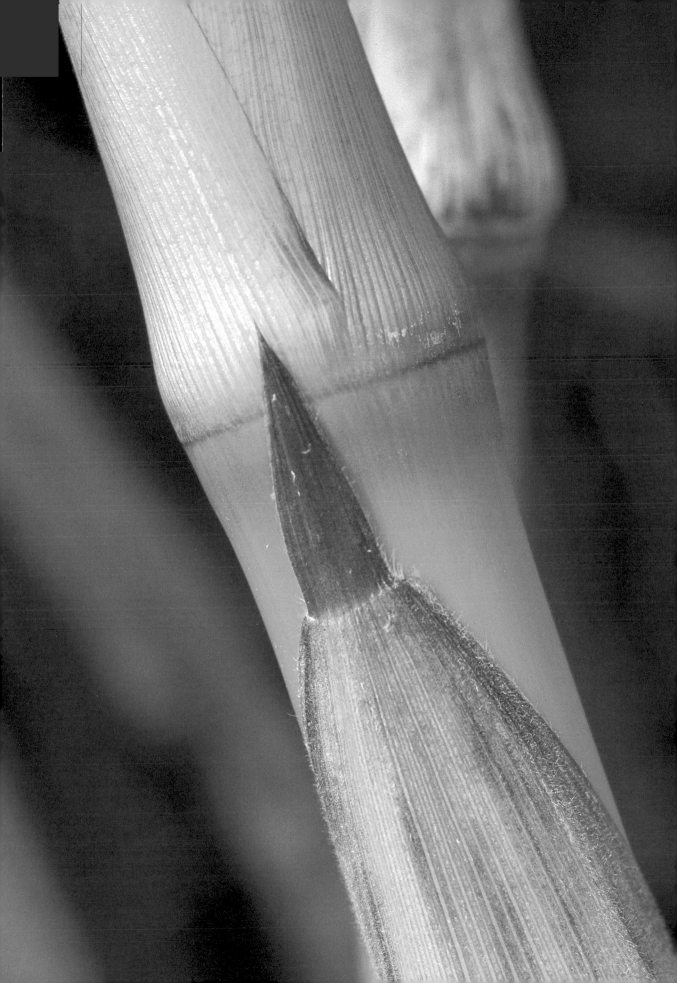

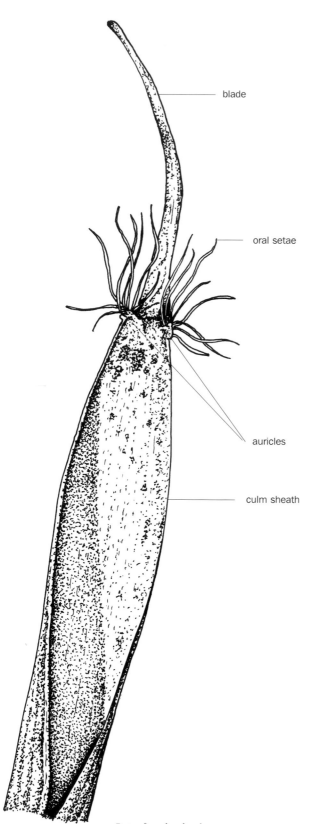

blade

oral setae

auricles

culm sheath

Parts of a culm sheath.

from running down to the developing buds and branches at the node at the base of the sheath.

The blade on a leaf sheath, as has been explained earlier, is the true leaf. A culm sheath also has a blade that extends from the ligule. The culm sheath blades are smaller than the leaf blades, and are not present in all species. The blades on culm sheaths are often much larger higher up the culm than they are nearer the ground, and at the very tip of the culm the blades can develop into true leaves, which proves their affinity with the leaf blades at the ends of the branches. Some culm sheath blades are coloured like the sheaths and can extend outward at various angles, others adhere closely to the culm and act almost as an extension to the ligule. Culm sheath blades vary in size and when large are often colourful. They range from the very pronounced, weeping and blowing in the wind, to the short and stumpy, resembling sharp points protruding from the shoots.

Auricles, as the name suggests, are short ear-like extensions on the upper part of the sheath, usually paired one either side of the blade. Oral setae, sometimes known as fimbriae, are bristly hairs that fringe the auricles. In the absence of auricles the hairs may occasionally be present on the upper margin of a sheath, when they are usually described as a fringe. Auricles and oral setae are often seen as parts of the culm and leaf sheaths, but both are absent on some species. In all cases these two parts have no function but are useful for identification purposes.

Flowers, Flowering and Seeds

This is undoubtedly a thorny subject as little is known and much surmised about the infrequent and unpredictable event of bamboo flowering. The bamboo flower is of great interest to botanists as it provides the key to the correct identification of many genera and species. The sporadic flowering, which may not happen once in a hundred years, makes this process almost impossible.

Unlike most plants in our gardens bamboos do not flower annually, and when they do the flowers are very inconspicuous. Exactly when

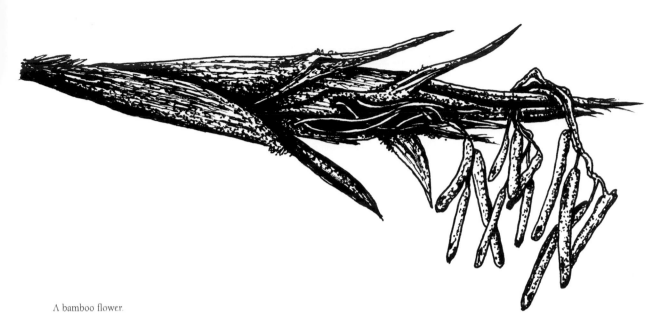

A bamboo flower.

and how often they flower is the subject of speculation, and although bamboos may die as a result of flowering, this is not always the case.

What is known is that flowering usually occurs over a long cycle, each species having a different time clock with a sudden alarm triggering its time of flowering. There is much conjecture as to what sets off this alarm and alerts the bamboo to its flowering period. Sunspots, increased predator grazing, drought and hot summers, altitude sickness and ozone levels have all been suggested, and some have been researched. In reality, we do not understand the timing. Some bamboo species have never flowered since records of their cultivation began. *Chimonobambusa quadrangularis* is proof of this. In contrast, a few species flower regularly, seemingly as part of their natural growth cycle, and survive the event, their habit and vigour apparently unaffected. When you plant a new bamboo you take a chance, not knowing if it will flower in your lifetime.

When flowering does occur it can be partial or complete, and all plants of the same clone, wherever they are growing in the world, are affected. This gregarious flowering will occur irrespective of age, cultivation differences, climate, habitat or whether a plant is cultivated or growing in the wild. Different clones of the same plant may have different flowering times as has

recently been discovered when *Chusquea culeou* flowered. In this case there were two clones of the species, from different locations and of different provenance and possibly genetic make-up, perhaps as a result of a previous cross-pollination with another clone.

When they appear, bamboo flowers are wind pollinated and produce ample pollen, which is easily trapped by the hairy stigmas. However, successful pollination usually relies on the abundance of flower from a complete flowering rather than a partial flowering, which reduces the chances of seed production. It is advantageous to avoid self-pollination and instead cross-pollinate with another plant, preferably of a different clone. This will increase the chances of a new and possibly stronger generation being produced.

Complete flowering

If a bamboo flowers completely, on all its branches, the plant is normally weakened. Leaves are replaced with flowers, culm production ceases or becomes weak and existing culms age, sometimes showing different colouration, and even new culms will flower. Photosynthetic activity is severely reduced so any food reserves are soon used up with the result that pachymorph bamboos usually die because the short rhizomes are directly linked to the individual culms. This type of flowering is known as monocarpic and confined mostly to the clump-forming bamboos.

Leptomorph plants have greater food reserves and so stand a greater chance of survival. New shoots, although sometimes weakened, often persist and produce culms that do not flower, and the plant may eventually recover. Reversion to type forms or mutations into different cultivars can occur when leptomorph bamboos flower. *Phyllostachys bambusoides* 'Kawadana' was a mutation from flowering plants of *Phyllostachys bambusoides* 'Castillonis' many years ago, but 'Castillonis' also survived as a cultivar. Bamboos with extended pachymorph rhizomes, such as *Yushania,* also have the ability to survive and regenerate slowly from a dying colony over many years, as happened with *Yushania anceps* a few decades ago.

Partial flowering

This is more common than complete flowering and there are many instances where a single branch of an isolated bamboo has produced flowers with no ill effect to the plant's health or vigour; *Phyllostachys aureosulcata* f. *spectabilis* is a recent example. Some bamboos can flower partially and regularly over a reasonably predictable period of time. Sometimes their growth is set back for a year or two, and at other time they are completely unaffected by the flowering cycle. Seed can be produced on a plant that does not die, which is a bonus, enabling us to produce new clones by cross-pollination, which may bring about new or stronger forms.

After flowering

To try and lay down a few rules may seem futile considering all the uncertainties of flowering, but should you be witness to complete flowering of a loved one, then follow these simple guidelines. It would be unwise to remove the root system of a pachymorph bamboo immediately after flowering. Leave it for a few years, as it has been observed that regeneration is sometimes possible. Never cut a flowering bamboo down. Wait and see if it is going to produce valuable seed; most monocarpic flowerings should be productive. If you see seed being formed, protect the plant from birds and stop them getting to it first.

Seeds

Bamboo seeds vary in size and are rarely larger than a grain of cereal. Usually they drop from the plant as soon as they are ripe. In general, seed is usually ripe for collection four or five months after the pale, hanging anthers are seen. Sometimes cutting off the dying culms just before the seeds are expected to ripen will prevent any loss to the birds. Store the culm in a cool and dry building wrapped loosely in a sheet to catch the falling seeds.

Most species germinate easily, especially if seeds are sown immediately after collection. Seeds that have been stored for any length of time may require a period of cold to break their dormancy and soften the hardened casing. This can be done by sowing in the winter months or putting the seeds in a refrigerator for a few weeks.

Chapter 7
The Hostile Environment

Much has already been said about the habitats of bamboos and the regions they inhabit in the wild. The main area of concern for most people is how suitable a particular species is for their garden and whether it will survive. Each indi-vidual plant has its limits for tolerating cold, heat, drought and wind exposure. Details of such likes and dislikes are described in the main plant descriptions that follow in "Nothing but the Plants".

USDA Plant Hardiness Zone Map

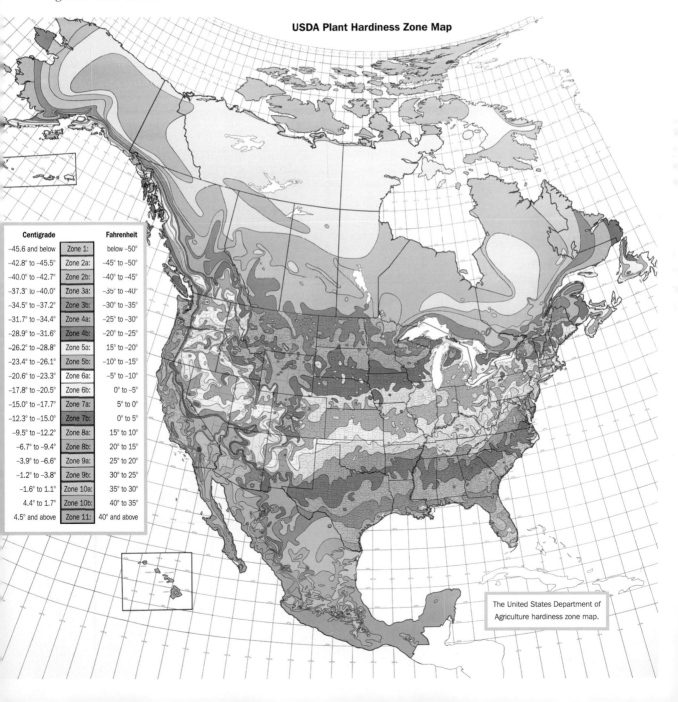

Centigrade		Fahrenheit
−45.6 and below	Zone 1:	below −50°
−42.8° to −45.5°	Zone 2a:	−45° to −50°
−40.0° to −42.7°	Zone 2b:	−40° to −45°
−37.3° to −40.0°	Zone 3a:	−35° to −40°
−34.5° to −37.2°	Zone 3b:	−30° to −35°
−31.7° to −34.4°	Zone 4a:	−25° to −30°
−28.9° to −31.6°	Zone 4b:	−20° to −25°
−26.2° to −28.8°	Zone 5a:	15° to −20°
−23.4° to −26.1°	Zone 5b:	−10° to −15°
−20.6° to −23.3°	Zone 6a:	−5° to −10°
−17.8° to −20.5°	Zone 6b:	0° to −5°
−15.0° to −17.7°	Zone 7a:	5° to 0°
−12.3° to −15.0°	Zone 7b:	0° to 5°
−9.5° to −12.2°	Zone 8a:	15° to 10°
−6.7° to −9.4°	Zone 8b:	20° to 15°
−3.9° to −6.6°	Zone 9a:	25° to 20°
−1.2° to −3.8°	Zone 9b:	30° to 25°
−1.6° to 1.1°	Zone 10a:	35° to 30°
4.4° to 1.7°	Zone 10b:	40° to 35°
4.5° and above	Zone 11:	40° and above

The United States Department of Agriculture hardiness zone map.

Cold Hardiness

When I discuss a new bamboo with friends and associates the first question that comes up is how hardy is it in terms of its ability to withstand cold. In some cases this can only be found out by growing the plant or from listening to the experiences of others who have already done so. Looking at the native environment of the plant should also help; how high it grows in the Himalayas, and whether it is from mountains or woodland. Many bamboos have been grown for many years across the world and these are tried and tested, so we can be quite specific about the extremes of cold they will tolerate. In the plant descriptions each bamboo has been given a minimum temperature at which it will be on the borderline of survival, together with a zone number from the widely accepted standards for cold hardiness used in the United States and Europe.

Heat Tolerance

In some cases a bamboo can tolerate extremes of cold but not a long hot summer, which may have a detrimental effect on a plant originating from a region of low annual average temperature. In a continental climate of cold winters and scorching summers, some of the larger-leaved bamboos may not perform well, their leaves rolling and shrivelling in blistering sunlight.

Some of the highland, or montane, bamboos, a few fargesias and *Thamnocalamus crassinodus* forms in particular, have tiny leaves. In areas with high summer temperatures and intense sun, whether continental or maritime, these bamboos may also not show their true worth. However, there is no rule to say that they cannot be grown. Provision of shade or humidity, such as a cool woodland situation or container culture, may allow such plants to flourish in an area not usually classed as suitable.

Microclimates

There are always examples of plants growing outside of their boundaries and the phrase "Well, I

Snow resting on the culms of the very hardy *Phyllostachys aureosulcata* f. *spectabilis*.

manage to grow it" is common among bamboo enthusiasts. What they do not tell you is that their special plant has a special situation. The importance of shade and humidity for plants growing in extreme heat has been mentioned, but what about encouraging plants that need warmth to develop a fine structure in cold areas?

A particular *Phyllostachys* may perform well in an average temperate garden, and taken to its cold extremes it may remain healthy, but might not put on the large culms of your dreams. I have seen many devices for forcing a plant beyond its capabilities, usually to speed up maturity from the juvenile state. Black polythene pegged to the surface of the soil to warm up the roots and rhizome for early development; constant drip feeding and watering during the summer months; and special structures to encase a plant in its own warm environment. They may prove successful but they are not often aesthetically appealing. I believe that trying to grow a plant outsides its known boundaries may be feasible for a collector but for the average gardener, growing one that suits the conditions gives much more pleasing results. Sometimes patience and time is all that is required to get the best results, and in some instances no amount of forcing will speed up the development of a bamboo.

There are simple measures that you can take to aid a plant on the borderline of hardiness. The shelter and warmth of a walled garden or walls of a building can often provide a suitable microclimate, where the temperature a degree or two higher than the open garden will give an early start to spring growth. Walls may also give protection from wind, the greatest dwarfing agent. Clearings in dense woodland have a similar effect and also town gardens, which benefit from the residual heat from an urban environment to raise the average minimum temperature. Sometimes a generous mulch of organic matter is enough to protect a plant, particularly when young. The mulch will conserve moisture and warmth in the soil, insulating the rhizomes and buds from the winter cold, as well as providing the plant with a regular nutrient supply. Growing plants in pots and then offering winter

protection is an artificial form of gardening and mature plants are rarely produced, but it may be the only way to grow a choice subtropical *Bambusa* and rare untested *Fargesia*.

Irrespective of any measures taken to increase a plant's chance of survival, it is when it is young that it is most at risk. A newly planted juvenile specimen may have culms killed outright in a mean winter or blazing summer, but a plant that has been established for several years, of greater stature and maturity, will have a much better chance of survival.

Hardiness in the United Kingdom

Being an island with a climate mostly under maritime influence enables British gardeners to grow most of the bamboos in this book. Those who garden in the north will be able to grow a wide range of bamboos, distinct in colour and habit, but slower to establish than in the south and some may never reach their desired stature. In the warmer south, many bamboos will perform as we expect them to in temperate gardens, or as well as can be expected outside of a warm temperate region. We know what *Phyllostachys* are capable of in the south of France or in their homeland China, and realize that similar growth is impossible here. However, most of us are happy to put up with less luxuriant growth as we do not have gardens large enough to cope with anything of forest-like proportions. In the warm coastal regions of the southwest of England, the protected microclimates of cities and possibly the counties of the west influenced by the Gulf Stream, it is often possible to grow the bamboos, which just tolerate zone 9, although they are better suited to higher zones. It as important not to forget factors other than cold that can affect the success of a bamboo; exposure and altitude, regardless of latitude, will also have some effect on your plants.

The low sun of a summer morning lights up the hairs on the new culms of *Thamnocalamus crassinodus* 'Lang Tang', which comes from a group suited to cool temperate gardens.

Hardiness in the United States

Take two extremes from this large continent where bamboos are grown and it is easy to see the difficulties that American gardeners have in selecting the correct plants for their climatic zone. Much of New England, for example, could be classed as zone 4, with few of the bamboos listed tolerating the cold temperatures. However, many bamboos listed as zone 5 or higher grow there, although it is widely accepted that they will never reach their maximum height. In the worse case scenario of long periods of below average temperatures, some bamboos may lose their top growth but respond much like an herbaceous plant and shoot afresh the following year. If the following winters are not as hard, the plant may continue to develop greater maturity so that any subsequent hard winters will tend to have a less detrimental effect on the plant as it ages.

At the opposite climatic extreme, on the west coast of California, for example, a discussion I had with a nursery owner from Santa Cruz was most enlightening. The giant cane bamboos, mostly *Phyllostachys* and some *Bambusa,* were the types generally grown, not just by demand but also because of their suitability to the climate. There was some wariness about trying many of the montane forms because of their susceptibility to heat, and also because of their low commercial value. Giant bamboos were more in demand and performed best in gardens; the montane bamboos were grown by enthusiasts or experienced gardeners but not available for general sale to the unwary. The ethics of offering success with a product, rather than the chance of failure, is both noble and sensible.

For Americans in the south and southwest states, there is the chance to grow some bamboos within the range of a cool temperate garden, as well as many of the genera outside it. Most of the plants in this book are suitable for hardiness zones 4 to 8, and if you wish to grow *Bambusa, Dendrocalamus, Gigantochloa* and *Guada,* you will have to move property or invest in a very large temperate house. The hardiness zones for the United States are more precise than the European ones, and unless you know someone who has successfully grown a particular plant it is wise to refer to the hardiness zones when making your plant selections.

China

If a map of China is superimposed on one of the United States it covers roughly the same area. However, the terrain and climate are very different. The plant listings that follow include an abundance of bamboos that are Chinese in origin and in some descriptions provinces have been named as the natural habitat or main area of cultivation. China is broadly divided into the mountains and valleys of the west, with their unique pockets of microclimate, and the low plains of the east, often with great seasonal temperature differences. As well as this great variance of longitude,

there is also a great distance from north to south penetrated by river valleys with rich flood plains. Knowing the native habitat of a plant and the climate and geography of the region may help us understand whether it is suitable for our gardens.

Soils

Bamboos are very versatile and will adapt to many different types of soil, unless they are very dry and desert-like, or in water. Lessen the extremes to very dry sandy soils and soils that waterlog occasionally and you have the range in which bamboos can survive, but some improvement will be beneficial. In a dry soil, the addition of organic matter and mulching will add life and increase the moisture-holding capacity. In wet conditions certain species are more tolerant of waterlogged conditions than others, and these

Above: The Provinces of China.

Right: The rare *Phyllostachys nigra* 'Fulva' with tawny colouring

are listed later in chapter 10, "Specific Qualities". Bamboo rhizomes will penetrate clay soils without a problem, as long as they have a good start with a carefully worked planting hole. Fine silty soils that slip and slide on steep banks can be stabilized and bound by the creeping rhizomes of many leptomorph bamboos.

Bamboos tolerate a wide range of pH. I garden on chalky boulder clay with a pH of 7.1 and all the bamboos perform brilliantly. Close by are very acid areas but plants supplied from the nursery have proved equally at home. They are a slightly richer green in their colouring and shorter in stature, but happy and very ornamental. In cases of very acid or very alkaline conditions, the pH can be modified by the addition of certain nutrients or compounds or replacement soil of more suitable quality brought in, but these are extreme measures in any type of gardening. The best indicator of whether a soil is suitable is that where few other plants grow successfully, neither will bamboos.

In many of the plant descriptions I have explained how an individual plant grows according to whether the soil is wet or dry. Often a bamboo will be more rampant in a dry soil because it has to travel to obtain water. A bamboo in a moist location with a high water table does not have the same need to search and can often be much more compact. This is a generalization from my observations over the years and not a strict rule. One or two of the *Sasa* species, for example, will not be confined by a moist soil and go rampantly forth regardless. Some of the most beautiful bamboos I have seen grow on dry soils. They have probably suffered severe stress on occasions throughout their life, but have grown strong and with great character nevertheless.

From left to right, starting top left
Phyllostachys iridescens
Phyllostachys nigra 'Megurochiku'
Thamnocalamus crassinodus 'Merlyn'
Phyllostachys aureosulcata 'Harbin Inversa'
Phyllostachys nidularia
Phyllostachys aureosulcata f. *spectabilis*
Sasa palmata f. *nebulosa*
Thamnocalamus crassinodus 'Gosainkund'
Phyllostachys aurea
Fargesia rufa
Phyllostachys nuda
Phyllostachys bambusoides 'Castillonis'

Nothing but the Plants

Chapter 8
The Chosen Few

The following alphabetical list describes in detail those bamboos well suited to the cool temperate garden within the hardiness zones 4 and 7, which specifies an average annual minimum temperature from -34°C to -12°C (-30°F to 10°F). There are a few plants included for zone 8, but only because I consider it is worth taking a risk to enjoy their particular beauty. Where a species is suitable for zones 4 to 7 but its forms and cultivars are not, this fact has been clearly indicated in the text. Plants suitable for zones 8 and above and which do not succeed in cool gardens are listed separately in chapter 9, "Close to the Edge".

The situation preferred by a bamboo is given in terms of sun and shade and is self explanatory, but the height will vary according to where the bamboo is growing, for example plants in cold northern gardens are often shorter than those growing in warmer regions further south. Spread

A selection of culms and leaves showing the variety found within the temperate bamboos.

also varies with local conditions but is mostly affected by the rhizome structure. Bamboos with leptomorph rhizomes are referred to as running, while the more compact pachymorph rhizome system results in a tighter clump. A grove is a massed colony of culms, which can either be densely packed or open and well spaced apart. Habit is influenced by the spread but in the following pages I have described the overall look of the mature plant under this heading.

The size, colour and characteristics of the culms and leaves are the essence of a bamboo and infinitely varied. For each main plant entry the culm diameter and leaf dimensions are listed as a guide. I have also suggested various uses for a particular bamboo, which in my experience work well, but all sorts of other enchanting possibilities are for you to discover.

Bamboos that merit particular attention have their own entry with all this information detailed, but many of them have forms or cultivars that are similar and I want to draw your attention to these under the heading "Others". In some cases they may be very rare or have flowered, or their true identification is under question.

My garden
At the beginning of the book I mentioned this is an account of my own experiences with bamboos and I often refer in the following pages to how a particular plant has performed for me. To set the record straight, here is a description of my garden conditions. The soil has a pH of 7.1 and often bakes hard in summer with substantial cracking (you could lose your arm down some of the cracks). It is a chalky boulder clay with some flint and in some areas the chalk bedrock is close to the surface. In winter parts of the garden flood temporarily as the water table is variable, the ground low lying and drainage into ditches is slow. I would describe the soil fertility as poor to average, but the nutrient and humus content is increasing with the decay of the natural annual mulch of leaves from broadleaved trees and other vegetation. Apart from a thin but tall shelterbelt of broadleaved trees, the site is open on all sides to the "flatlands" and the wind that blows in from all directions. The garden has never been irrigated and no artificial nutrients or mulch of any kind have been added.

Peter Addington's garden
I also refer frequently to Peter's garden at Stream Cottage, where many of my plants originated and where my love affair with bamboos began. His garden had a high water table and a pH that ranged from slightly acid to neutral. The rich soil had almost a broadleaf woodland profile with good organic content and nutrients. Mainly it was a silty loam with an alluvial look to it, but there were occasional areas of clay. The garden was very sheltered by the surrounding woodland and a running stream flowed close by. Unlike me, Peter used to mulch his garden occasionally and provide some rotted mature for his bamboos.

Now the explanations are done, on to the most important part of the book: the plants.

1. *Bashania faberi*
2. *Phyllostachys vivax* f. *aureocaulis*
3. *Chusquea culeou*
4. *Indocalamus hamadae*
5. *Semiarundinaria fastuosa*
6. *Pseudosasa japonica* 'Akebonosuji'
7. *×Hibanobambusa tranquillans* 'Shiroshima'
8. *Phyllostachys aureosulcata* f. *spectabilis*
9. *Pleioblastus shibuyanus* 'Tsuboi'
10. *Sasa veitchii*
11. *Thamnocalamus spathiflorus*
12. *Phyllostachys bambusoides* 'Allgold'

Bashania

A small genus similar in appearance to *Arundinaria* (see chapter 9, "Close to the Edge") and *Pleioblastus* but far more inspiring, although it has only a few species to its name. It is native mainly to central China, mostly in the mountainous areas among forests. A very hardy genus, it is tolerant of extremes and develops a leptomorph rhizome system. In gardens, plants have a sturdy appearance.

Bashania faberi

Hardiness: min. -13˚C (9˚F), zone7
Aspect: sun or light shade.
Height: 2–3 m (6.5–10 ft.), average 2 m (6.5 ft.)
Spread: 1–2 m (3.3–6.5 ft.) in 10 years, open, slightly running.
Habit: dense branching, shrubby and tufted.
Culms: 0.75 cm. (0.3 in.) thick, deep green.
Leaves: medium, broad for their size, 15 x 2.5 cm. (6 x 1 in.), often bleach at the tips in winter.

The various synonyms confuse the identity of this plant and often its recognition in gardens. It is better known in the United States than in Europe. My own plant was a gift from Roy Lancaster, who thrust in my arms – possibly an act of desperation – a brown leafless specimen in a large clay pot. I assume he thought I could save it and although not a holy figure I would indeed have to perform a miracle. As a tribute to my skills or more likely this bamboo's resilience it sprang back to life within weeks, although it was another three years before I risked lifting a piece for Roy as thanks for his original gift.

Bashania faberi is native mainly to the Western Sichuan and Gansu Provinces of China where it occurs at elevations between 2,600 and 3,400 m (8,500–11,000 ft.), making it perfectly hardy and essential panda food. The arching tufts of quite broad leaves give the plant a distinctive appearance and are so dense that on a well-grown plant the culms are only visible at the base. Regular thinning of old culms however, will give a more polished appearance. This is best done in early spring before new growth starts. If the average height of 2 m (6.5 ft.) is exceeded the plant can be pruned and the cuts will eventually be covered by the dense clusters of leaves, making it a possible candidate for a low hedge.

The most outstanding feature is the winter bleaching on the leaf points. As the nights grow cold and draw in, the ends of the leaves turn to a creamy

ochre with only the very tips blackening. The effect is difficult to describe but it is worth growing the plant for this alone.

Uses

For underplanting taller bamboos or broad-leaved trees. Low hedge or screen, or a background for colourful winter-stemmed dogwoods or willows. Suitable for growing in large tubs and pots.

Bashania fargesii

Hardiness: min. -25˚C (-13˚F), zone 5
Aspect: sun or shade.
Height: 5–10 m (16.5–33 ft.), average 6 m (20 ft.)
Spread: 2–10 m (6.5–33 ft.) in 10 years, open, usually running.
Habit: grove forming, bold, vertical and rigid branching.
Culms: 2.5–5 cm. (1–2 in) thick, silvery grey.
Leaves: medium, long, to 15 x 2.5 cm. (6 x 1 in.), glaucous.

Just to prove we all have something to learn, here is a brief story of why I call it my "mistake plant". My first view of this species was at Stream Cottage, that wondrous garden of Peter Addington's, where it formed a tight, tidy, almost statuesque clump that could be viewed from all sides, the almost ghostly grey culms seemed to catch every bit of light in its shady home. I had no idea of the age of the plant or its potential when I was allowed to take a large chunk. After careful division I made several smaller plants, one for the garden and the rest ending up as near-hospital cases in the nursery. However, the injured soon pulled through and some were sold. What could I say to the customers who asked me how it would perform when, in truth, I could not find any information on this rare *Bashania* – no reference in books or the internet, my only knowledge was of Peter's plant. Since then I have discovered the following. The plant in my garden did not disappoint and took well to its new home, forming a strong clump in a very much more open and drier situation than in Peter's garden. Five years on and it had romped through the border most impressively and gained superiority over everything in its way, as well as obliterating the view from the house. Quite a beast compared to my original vision, but the same plant. I had also given pieces to two other bamboo eccentrics: one of the plants remains tight(ish) to this day, but the other has exceeded its boundaries and become the most

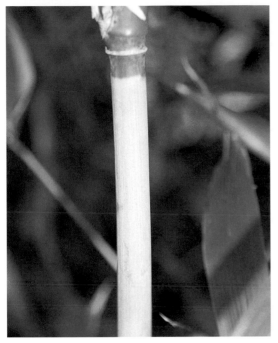

A silver-grey culm of *Bashania fargesii*.

dominant plant in the garden. Why such a difference between divisions from the same parent and in such a short time? The plant remains tight where the water table is high, but on stony arid ground it has spread outward and upwards, conquering all in its path. The difference is all due the available moisture and I have never witnessed any other bamboo react to different conditions so spectacularly.

Some years ago my wife gave me strict orders to choose between a *Chusquea culeou*, which dominates one side of our house and now also keeps our bedroom window clean with its buffeting in the wind, and my bashania on the other side, romping aimlessly towards the driveway. I chose to remove the bashania, and this is the interesting part; having never destroyed a bamboo before. I pruned the whole plant hard to 1 m (3 ft.) above the ground in the autumn, leaving just enough leaf on to justify its existence as a plant. It looked quite appealing at this point and I made an instant plea for a stay of execution, but was immediately overruled. The following spring when new leaf and culm flushed, I sprayed it heavily with the most eco-friendly systemic weedkiller I could find, which checked it to the point that all growth stopped. During the summer the bamboo looked withered and sad and so it was pruned to the ground again. Apart from some wispy, juvenile offerings which have never been menacing it has given up, the matted rhizome is still there, slowly decaying which makes further planting difficult, but nonetheless total eradication within twelve months was almost unheard of. If ever you have to eradicate a bamboo, please don't expect the same, I think this was more luck than judgement.

Enough of the tales. Regardless of its aspect this bamboo, which grows at altitudes well over 1,000 m (3,280 ft.) in the wild, does show some uniformity in its physical features. It is slightly deeper rooted than many bamboos and is extremely tolerant of drought and wind. It usually shoots in May (late spring) when an army of pointed new culms rise uniformly from the soil and soon the whole plant has a grey-green lustre. On close inspection this is due to the pale silvery stained culms, a coloration unique among temperate bamboos. The leaves are glaucous on the underside and catch the light as the wind blows. The very thick culms are long lasting when cut. Most importantly it is one of the top twenty cold-hardy bamboos.

Uses

A stiff screen or windbreak; for stabilizing soil or banks; for a large grove. Good for culm production.

Bashania qingchengshanensis

Hardiness: min. -20°C (-4°F); zone 6
Aspect: sun or half shade.
Height: 2.5–4 m (8.2–13 ft.), average 3 m (10 ft.)
Spread: 1– 2.5 m (3.3–8.2 ft.) in 10 years, open, slowly spreading grove.
Habit: slightly arching due to the weight of leaves.
Culms: maximum diameter 1 cm. (0.4 in.), green with pale yellow-green waxing below the nodes.
Leaves: medium to large, 20 x 3 cm. (7 x 1.25 in.), deep green with bleaching in winter.

A recent addition to the fold, with few mature plants to judge as yet. Nearly equal in hardiness to *B. fargesii* but of smaller stature, deeper colour and less rigid in growth. It is probably not the most ornamental bamboo but its reliability, speed of establishment, and ease of propagation, should make it a popular landscape plant.

The winter bleaching is untidy on close inspection, but *en masse* and viewed from a distance, it makes a good effect, and ideal for those Capability Brown moments. Very early to shoot, usually by mid spring, which is surprising for a plant of low elevation, at a maximum of 1,000 m (3,280 ft.) compared to the mountainous habits of *Bashania fargesii*. The early shooting makes it suitable for mid to late summer pruning.

Uses

As a foil or background to taller, giant culm bamboos. Municipal landscaping or low hedging.

Borinda

A confused genus with a close affinity to *Arundinaria*, *Fargesia*, *Thamnocalamus* and *Yushania* and in fact most species have been transferred from these genera to the *Borinda*. Differences cited between these genera include, for example, the fact that *Borinda* has more branches in the first year than *Thamnocalamus* and a different rhizome structure to *Yushania*; *Borinda* flowers are more like those of *Yushania*; all are important factors in correct identification. The hardiest borindas are often deciduous in their native Nepal and Yunnan, so should defoliation occur in more temperate regions there is no need to worry because fresh growth returns quickly in spring. Out of more than a dozen species identified, there are only three available: *Borinda albocera*, *B. boliana* and *B. fungosa* (see *Fargesis fungosa*). *Borinda albocera* is perhaps the most attractive and robust, and likely to become widely available. We can hope that more will come on the market in the future in Europe and the United States.

Borinda albocera

Hardiness: min. -13˚C (9˚F), zone 7
Aspect: light shade.
Height: 3–4.5 m (10–13 ft.), average 3.5 m (11.5 ft.)
Spread: 0.8 m–1.5 m (2.6–5 ft.) in 10 years,
tidy and clumping.
Habit: lax in youth but gracefully arching in maturity.
Culms: maximum diameter 2 cm. (0.8 in.), pale and bloomy, sky blue when young becoming yellow with maturity.
Leaves: small to medium, 15 x 1 cm. (6 x 0.4 in.) long, narrow and willow-like.

When it first became available in the United Kingdom those who were fortunate enough to access this plant were dubious about its hardiness. It resembled a form of *Thamnocalamus crassinodus* and was originally classified in the genus *Fargesia*, and in the knowledge that both these genera develop into strong plants very quickly, such scepticism was surprising. Young plants do need support and patience because although new culms appear profusely, they often rot back. However, given time and preferably shelter, this species will prove worthy of a place in the garden. Its profuse branching gives it the flexibility to be pruned, and a carefully manicured plant will reward you well.

The stunning pale blue, bloomy culms and hairy

A culm of *Borinda albocera*, showing a pale blue internode emerging from the hairy culm sheaths.

sheaths are unsurpassed and close inspection may also reveal a crimson felted ring, sometimes present just below the nodes. Young culms lose their bloom in subsequent years, turning a soft yellow and contrasting with the newer culms and pale, glaucous leaves. Old culms must be thinned regularly as they become heavy with leaf and can look very ragged.

Borinda albocera covers a wide and variable area of the Chinese province of Yunnan, at a maximum elevation of 2,800 m (9,180 ft.), and it is thought there may be different clones, so beware. The given minimum temperature is the lowest you can expect this plant to tolerate without protection. Different forms of this species have recently been introduced and are described below under the Yunnan bamboos.

Uses

Place as a specimen among other established bamboos, trees or large shrubs; it contrasts well with shorter bold-leaved plants such as *Fatsia* or *Mahonia*. Planting against a wall will show off its finery to maximum advantage.

The Yunnan bamboos

The very fruitful province of Yunnan in China, particularly the valleys and hills of the northeast, have made good collecting grounds for many new species. Out of the many expeditions in the past, the Southwestern Forestry College 1993 Yunnan Bamboo Expedition, in particular, yielded some new bamboos to cultivation as Yunnan 1 to 6. There are likely to be more but numbers 1 to 6 are the ones currently being grown, having been imported to Europe by Jos van der Palen in the 1990s. They have since been distributed to the United Kingdom and are now finding their way to North America. Most are from the genus *Borinda* and all look potentially hardy, given their geographical origin, although none are fully tried and tested as yet.

Yunnan 1, 2, 3A and 3B are all clones of *Borinda albocera*. Yunnan 1 and 2 have particularly good culm colour, and Yunnan 3A and 3B have the added bonus of very small leaves and an elegant habit.

Yunnan 4 was introduced under the name *Borinda edulis*, but is now thought to be *B. lushuiensis*. This species may have a limited cold tolerance compared to the others, but is already growing in Cornwall, England, to 10 m (33 ft.) high with thick glaucous culms and contrasting dark red-brown sheaths.

Yunnan 5 has been identified as a strange half-climbing species (possibly of *Yushania*) with red-tinted, sharply curving but stiff branches. This grows strongly in my East Anglian nursery, in pots under cold polythene, but has not yet been tried outdoors.

Yunnan 6 is *Borinda perlonga* (possibly a *Fargesia*) and is certainly hardy in the southwest of England, but it is yet to be confronted with extremes of weather to put it to the test. The whole plant is a fresh pale green, including the culms, which arch elegantly to the ground on mature plants.

Chimonobambusa

A genus with a general reputation for vigorous spreading, however, if you have a large enough garden for these plants they can look sumptuous when allowed to wander as nature intended. Apart from *Chimonobambusa marmorea*, which is the subject of debate as to whether its origins are Chinese or Japanese, all other species have their home in China and Taiwan. The majority do not exceed an elevation of 1,600 m (5,250 ft.) and usually inhabit forest floors where the air is cool and moist, this at least should tell us what their favoured requirements are in temperate gardens.

The leptomorph (running) rhizomes of some species produce late season and even early winter shoots, a trait

A Chinese image of *Chimonobambusa tumidissinoda*.

of many tropical bamboos, so there was some initial trepidation about their robustness. These fears have now been allayed, as the versatility of *Chimonobambusa* and the ease with which they adapt to their surroundings has been noted. They also respond well to judicious thinning as maturity is reached, removing older culms to expose the fresh new growth. Nodes on all species are prominent, some more than others to the point of bulging, as with *C. tumidissinoda*. Most also have small spines or aerial roots arising at the lower nodes.

There are some twenty species known but few of these are in cultivation in the West. In China some of the unavailable species can reach 10 m (33 ft.) and are used for timber; one species is the staple diet for the giant panda and others are used in domestic cooking. One of the most recent introductions is *Chimonobambusa hejiangensis*, which although, having performed well so far, has not yet been put to the test in a vicious winter. The few species grown in Western gardens vary widely in appearance and should be better used.

Chimonobambusa macrophylla f. intermedia

Hardiness: min. -20°C (-4°F), zone 6
Aspect: semi-shade.
Height: 1–2 m (3.3–6.5 ft.), average 1.5 m (5 ft.)
Spread: 1–2 m (3.3–6.5 ft.) in 10 years, slowly running.
Habit: low, slightly arching with the weight of leaves.
Culms: maximum diameter 1 cm. (0.4 in.), rich green with prominent nodes.
Leaves: small to medium but larger than most other Chimonobambusa species, 15 x 2.5 cm. (6 x 1 in.) rich green.

Introduced in the 1980s, plants have sporadically flowered in various locations. This has resulted in some production of seed, which has germinated readily to the delight of nurserymen, and with the result that plants should now become more widely available.

The dense tufts of leaves at the top half of the culms are its main attribute. In my experience, the leaves scorch in the dry air of my locality and although the appearance is acceptable in winter it is not so desirable during the lush summer months so I thin the plant regularly. It performs better in areas of higher humidity and high rainfall.

Uses

In woodland plantings or mixed with the large-leaved *Sasa palmata* f. *nebulosa* or in isolated groups for architectural effect.

Chimonobambusa marmorea

Hardiness: min. -20°C (-4°F), zone 6
Aspect: light shade.
Height: 1–3 m (3.3–10 ft.), average 1.5 m (5 ft.)
Spread: 1.5–3 m (5–10 ft.) in 10 years, runs evenly but speedily.
Habit: usually low and billowing with foliage.
Culms: maximum diameter 1.5 cm. (0.6 in.), with purplish, spotted sheaths, darkening with age.
Leaves: long and thin 10 x 1 cm. (4 x 0.4 in.)

The stigma attached to this bamboo of being untidy and unpredictable in its growth and vigour I think is unfair, as it performs brilliantly in my garden and gives much satisfaction. It rarely exceeds 1.5 m (5 ft.) and grows well in the heavy clay soil in full sun. It is now profuse in its production of new, initially leafless, culms in mid and late autumn when little else is happening. These new culms rarely die back even during a harsh winter, though I have noticed that culm production is less in the moister warmer west of the United Kingdom, and often with dieback. In China this species yields heavily in the cooler regions making it a popular choice for garden culm production and making strong carrying handles and straps. The culms are also very thick walled, which gives them a long life if cured correctly.

Chimonobambusa marmorea was one of the earliest bamboos to be introduced into Europe and receive a common name. It is often referred to as the "marbled bamboo" because the new shoots are spectacularly blotched purple and cream. The branches appear first at the top of the naked culms in the following summer with a tuft of fresh, narrow green leaves. Branching on the lower nodes occurs in subsequent years, so pruning back any damaged top growth just means a shortened but still leafy culm. I do this regularly because I have to – it grows by a path often used by my wife – but the shortened stumps soon leaf and cover the cut so she only gets wet below the knees from brushing by the foliage. To my delight the bamboo has travelled under the concrete path and appeared at the other side.

Marbled culm sheath on
Chimonobambusa marmorea.

Chimonobambusa marmorea borders a path and is pruned regularly to reduce its height.

Uses

As ground cover and underplanting or in shady raised beds where not too dry. Try it on the edge of pond with a few carefully placed rocks for an ethereal effect. Apart from successfully edging a path, my plant grows at the base of the red-barked *Acer palmatum* 'Sango-kaku' which erupts impressively from the fresh greenery.

Chimonobambusa marmorea 'Variegata'

Hardiness: min. -20°C (-4°F), zone 6
Aspect: sun or light shade.
Height: 1–2.5 m (3.3–8.2 ft.), average 1.5 m (5 ft.)
Spread: 1–2.5 m (3.3–8.2 ft.) in 10 years, slightly invasive.
Habit: low, slightly stiffer than the species.
Culms: maximum diameter 1 cm. (0.4 in.), pale yellow with occasional green striping. They turn orange-red in full sun.
Leaves: small to medium, 10 x 1 cm. (4 x 0.4 in.), with a few white stripes.

Overall this cultivar is slightly more diminutive than the species and not quite as rampant. The foliage although less luxuriant than *Chimonobambusa marmorea* does have some faint white striping, but you will have to look closely (an occasional complaint comes from customers dreaming of some bold irregular markings). It is identical in all general botanical characteristics to its parent but from a horticultural point of view, it is more versatile. It colours well in full sun where the leaves can be paler but the culms are more notable and burnish to an iridescent orange-red, especially so on a mature plant. I have seen some of the best examples of this bamboo growing in raised beds or large pots, where this vivid colouring can best be appreciated. One noticeable fact about the species and its cultivar is that they both prefer a rich soil with balanced nutrients. Without this they quickly show signs of chlorosis, so pot on frequently when using containers, and do not forget they can be pruned to suit your required height.

Uses

As for *Chimonobambusa marmorea* and also for pots, tubs and raised beds. Try it in a cool conservatory with palms and aspidistras for a Victorian ambience.

Chimonobambusa quadrangularis

Hardiness: min. -15°C (5°F), zone 7
Aspect: light or deep shade.
Height: 3–7 m (10–23 ft.), average 4 m (13 ft.)
Spread: 1.5–6 m (5–20 ft.) or more in 10 years, invasive.
Habit: Long straight lines of vertical culms.
Culms: maximum diameter 3 cm. (1.2 in.), grey-green, the whole plant has a matt appearance.
Leaves: medium, 15 x 1.5 cm. (6 x 0.6 in.)

Known as the square bamboo because on mature plants the tall, thick culms are noticeably four sided, most pronounced at the base. The branches and leaves are on the upper nodes and the lower nodes produce thorn-like hooks, actually aerial roots, which can be quite sharp. Culms are usually produced very late. They are edible and very succulent.

This is naturally a woodland plant and benefits from the shelter of surrounding trees and large shrubs. In the open it can look dishevelled, as wind quickly shreds the leaves and blows the vertical culms in all directions, loosening them from their rhizomes.

It has gained the reputation for preferring moist, cool soil and of dubious reliability in dry soils. This is nonsense. One of the finest stands of *Chimonobambusa quadrangularis* grows in the driest part of England in the extensive gardens of the late Mr. Maurice Mason, in dry, flinty earth in Norfolk, England. The twenty-five-year-

Adventitious root formation on a culm of *Chimonobambusa quadrangularis*.

old grove is overhung by pines and the rarest of broadleaves, and wandering between *Arbutus* and lofty *Eucalyptus* this bamboo knows no bounds. The mature trees rise above it and the whole effect is one of symmetry, not the raggle-taggle eyesore often associated with this plant. Long straight lines of rhizome and culms criss-cross the ground. The matt culms appear to absorb the light and the drooping, papery leaves move fluidly in the breeze. I believe the success of this grove is due to its long life, for it is a bamboo that never shows its true colours as a youngster. Most of all, this particular plant has made use of surface moisture, the soil is covered in a natural mulch of leaves from the surrounding trees which keep temperature and moisture uniform. The rhizomes are shallow, allowing them to benefit from the lightest rainfall. Normally shallow rooting would make a plant weak, lacking in structural stability, but this example somehow manages to break the rules and, with plumb-line accuracy, forms narrow columns of cascading leaves.

I have seen it grown successfully in a large pot, but great devotion is needed to create beauty, it quickly starves and is all too keen to dry out. Pruning is not an option because of the high leaf canopy, it is reluctant to branch low down.

Uses

Where there is plenty of space as an open woodland grove or, should you wish to control it, a dense, congested clump which will require annual thinning and supplementary feeding. One of the finest plants for controlled Japanese gardening, where selection of the best culms and careful use of stone and gravel becomes an art form.

Chimonobambusa quadrangularis 'Suow'

Hardiness: min. -11°C (12°F), zone 8
Aspect: light or half shade.
Height: 2.5–6 m (8.2–20 ft.), average 3 m (10 ft.)
Spread: 1–4 m (3.3–13 ft.) in 10 years, runs slowly.
Habit: columnar culms form an open grove.

Culms: maximum diameter 2.5 cm. (1 in.), soft yellow randomly striped green.
Leaves: medium, long and narrow, 15 x 1.5 cm. (6 x 0.6 in.), slight variegation.

A worthy cultivar with subtle culm colouring, particularly if allowed to thrive in shade with moisture provided for establishment. The soft yellow incandescence against an almost essential dark, leafy background can be enhanced by pruning out old culms and some of the lower branches, thereby encouraging vigour in rhizome production and new culms. Generous mulching and supplementary feeding would also benefit a congested plant that shows reluctance to expand outwards. Not quite as hardy as the species and with reduced vigour, this cultivar quickly recovers from any winter damage to the leaves.

Both this cultivar and the species are difficult to propagate from mature plants in the open ground because of the lack of root growth on the newer, more accessible culms. Divisions taken from juvenile specimens using a sharp saw are more viable. I have known 'Suow' revert to green at this propagation stage and any such plants are unlikely to form yellow culms. However, once a good selection has been planted it rarely reverts unless the main crown is damaged. 'Suow' is gradually becoming more available in the trade and should certainly be on the wish list of the most avid collector.

Uses

In shady areas. It associates well with low, dark evergreen ferns such as *Polystichum polyblepharum*. Stand containers and pots on shady patios or under pergolas.

Others

Chimonobambusa hejiangensis appears similar in stature to *C. quadrangularis* but so far is much less rampant. The finely structured culms have obvious swollen nodes with large buds, as well as the downward pointing blunt hooks. The leaves are large and a dark, glossy green giving that just-drenched jungle look. Still very rare, this medium-sized bamboo should prove to be a winner in this genus when its numbers are increased.

Chimonobambusa quadrangularis 'Nagaminea' was given to me by Tony Pike, an enthusiast with an eye for good gardening, who told me it may not be as hardy as 'Suow'. I have yet to find this out, as my plants are growing in pots for propagation purposes. Culms have a green stripe above each branch and, so far, older culms have turned a rusty, ochre yellow. It is certainly distinct.

Chimonobambusa quadrangularis 'Tatejima' is a last

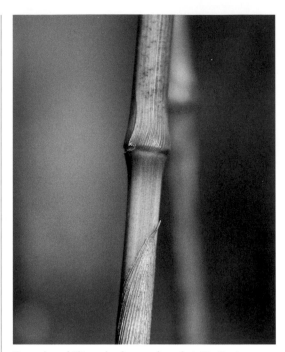

New culms of *Chimonobambusa quadrangularis* 'Tatejima'.

minute addition to the book, purchased from a nursery friend who obtained plants in France. It is more like 'Nagaminea' than 'Suow' with very obvious green striping on the culms, which in the depths of winter are suffused with pink, an effect most noticeable on younger culms. This may be due to growing conditions at the place of origin, but to date the colour still holds. The leaves appear to be of a darker green and the variegation is more noticeable. Watch this plant.

Chimonobambusa quadrangularis 'Yellow Groove' is listed by the American Bamboo Society and is similar to the species but with a yellow sulcus, or groove, on the culm internodes.

Chimonobambusa tumidissinoda

Hardiness: min. -13°C (8.5°F), zone 7
Aspect: light shade.
Height: 3–6 m (10–20 ft.), average 3.5 m (11.5 ft.)
Spread: 3–10 m (10–33 ft.) in 10 years, very invasive.
Habit: impressive and intent on marching, delicately arching culms.
Culms: maximum diameter 3 cm. (1.2 in.), rich green paling with age.
Leaves: long, to 10 x 1 cm. (4 x 0.4 in.), thin and papery.

Emerging branches of *Chimonobambusa tumidissinoda*.

This is still known in China as *Qiongzhuea tumidinoda*, about which there has been much discussion. To cut a long story short, the original but incorrect publication of the species did not satisfy taxonomists and as this is the only spring-shooting *Chimonobambusa* it may deserve the status of a separate genus. Regardless of the name it is a very beautiful plant. But beware, it is also one of the most vigorous temperate bamboos you could wish for, nevertheless well worth growing if you have space.

As well as personally being indebted to Peter Addington for my introduction to bamboos, the rest of the world also has Peter to thank for bringing this mouth-watering offering to our shores in 1987. The Yi people of Sichuan in China guarded this plant with their lives; their centuries old trade in walking sticks of this bamboo was unique and secretive. This tale was also told to me by Roy Lancaster, and we have never been sure how Peter obtained this plant. Relations with the Yi may have changed over the years because this plant is now sometimes exported from China to European nurseries.

The rich green culms have obvious saucer-like swellings at the nodes, and the leaves are long and dainty, hanging artistically from the upper branches. The only untidy plants I have seen are those too exposed to the sun and wind, or ones that have never been thinned of their old culms.

When I first saw this bamboo in Peter's garden it could not have been planted more than a few years but had already started to move in straight lines toward the stream on the boundary of his property. It was a nightmare to dig up, very little root attached to the rhizome and culm, I had more success from rhizome sections buried in compost. I know of many other plants in England and they all vary slightly from relatively refined groves to aggressive colonies. My favourite is in the garden of Tony Churly, in Norfolk, England, where it has established quickly yet in a respectable manner and is now 3 m (10 ft.) high, covering a grassy edge to the garden. It has expanded towards the light, away from

other bamboos and the woodland behind it, but staying quite dense and not swarming into the local town as we all expected. However, I do use it as a stock plant, and this may be the reason its spread is checked.

A plant in Tony Pike's old garden in Surrey, England, was restricted between a conservatory and workshop in a narrow alley. It had dramatically mushroomed upwards to the light, the thick nodal swellings visible from ground to well above eye level, the foliage arching like parachutes overhead. This plant had culms twice as thick as the one in Norfolk, but both had equal beauty. Tony Pike's plant was the only bamboo I ever threw down my spade to in defeat; the rhizome was matted and woven in layers, making it virtually impenetrable. It had even romped over and away from the thick barrier in place to prevent it spreading. The plant in Tony Pike's garden was much drier and had a much warmer aspect than the Norfolk specimen, and these factors together with the restriction may have helped it to mature more quickly.

If you do not have room for the beast, you can tame it. I grow *Chimonobambusa tumidissinoda* in large containers for exhibition, and although they remain juvenile, never reaching the true height and thickness of a garden plant, the shape and form are still apparent. I recommend moving container plants under cold glass or polythene for the winter to avoid the rootball freezing and the foliage desiccating. Failing this, be prepared to control its spread in the garden by physically chopping back the rhizome, as barriers do not work with this bamboo.

Uses

This is a bamboo of solitary beauty, so do not congest it with other plants. Apart from impressing your friends pronouncing its names and its novelty value, you can grow it in pots or anywhere there is space. You have been warned of its vigour.

The culms of *Chimonobambusa tumidissinoda* in silhouette.

Chusquea

Botanically, *Chusquea* is a relatively modern genus as it is native to the largely unexplored plant paradise of the Andes in South America, where many cool temperate plants abound. Representatives of the genus can be found at sea level and upwards to 4,270 m (14,000 ft.). However there are other species that expand the boundaries of altitude and latitude, from Mexico, from lowland areas in Central America and Argentina, and from the tropics of South America.

Although this book is primarily concerned with the montane, or highland, *Chusquea*, it is worth digressing briefly to describe the requirements of the lowland species; for there is an intense desire to try these, particularly in the United States and the coastal areas of Northern Europe.

Of the known species most are not cold hardy and only suitable for the warmer parts of the United States. Their requirements are very specific in keeping with their endemic status in an isolated environment. Examples include *Chusquea circinata*, *C. coronalis*, *C. cumingii*, *C. foliosa*, *C. quila*, *C. uliginosa* and *C. valdiviensis*, and a few of these will be described in more detail in chapter 9, "Close to the Edge". Most of these species grow well in the warmer months, but they are only just frost hardy and can be severely checked when cold weather arrives; many are suited to a Mediterranean- type climate, although some also have a need of higher rainfall and humidity.

Highland and low-latitude Chusquea

These species either inhabit the moist cloudy uplands of the Andes or the southern beech (*Nothofagus*) forests of the Valdivia and Chiloe Provinces in Chile, where the climate is also cool and rainfall high. Some of the highland species have to tolerate daily temperature fluctuations from below freezing to over 20°C (68°F), although seasonal temperatures hardly change. Many of these high-altitude plants suffer in constant warm nights and high average soil temperatures and because of this they are better suited to gardens in maritime or low alpine climates that experience less seasonal temperature fluctuations and usually higher rainfall than the climatic extremes of a continental interior. The continental climate in the United States covers huge tracts of land thousands of miles from the sea, whereas few places in the United Kingdom are more than a hundred miles from the coast.

Main characteristics

Nearly all *Chusquea* have solid culms, making them more suitable for cutting than any other bamboo. Florists beware, hollow-culmed bamboos dry out within hours of cutting whereas *Chusquea* last for some days. *Chusquea* also have a unique branching system and form multiple branch buds around the nodes. One of these

buds may be dominant as in *C. gigantea*, but in general the broader radiating branch system gives the culms an unequalled bottlebrush or foxtail appearance, particularly on *C. culeou* where the main branch does not take precedence. Multiple branching also occurs in other bamboo genera, but of a more congested appearance due to secondary branches arising from the base of the original primary branch.

All montane *Chusquea* species have pachymorph (clumping) rhizomes. However, they can appear very open in habit compared to a congested *Fargesia* due to the fact that the rhizome necks of *Chusquea* are longer than in other clumping genera. New culms appear evenly around and within the main plant and are not wildly incursive. Once plants have sight of maturity and emerge from a sometimes lengthy juvenile phase in a garden, they will grow quickly and strongly producing many culms annually, sometimes shooting twice in a season, although late arrivals may be damaged in the oncoming winter. It is perhaps just as well that we cannot duplicate their exact growing conditions in the high Andes because they are great opportunists, quickly colonizing any open space from felling or natural woodland decay.

Chusquea andina

Hardiness: min. -15°C (5°F), zone 7
Aspect: sun or light shade.
Height: 1–1.5 m (3.3–5 ft.), average 1 m (3.3 ft.)
Spread: 50–80 cm. (1.6–2.6 ft.) in 10 years, clumping.
Habit: tidy and vertical.
Culms: maximum diameter 1 cm. (0.4 in.), old culms turn pale olive green.
Leaves: small and narrow, 10 x 0.8 cm. 4 x 0.3 in.), on short upright branches.

Very rare in cultivation but worthy of mention because it is tolerant of long cold spells and drought. Culms are very stiff and vertical with shortened branches when compared to *Chusquea culeou*, each culm almost wary of touching its neighbour and all ranged in near regimental precision. Very difficult to propagate because it is slow growing, compact and resentful of disturbance.

Emerging multiple branches on *Chusquea culeou*.

Chusquea culeou

Hardiness: min. -18˚C (0˚F), zone 6
Aspect: sun or light woodland.
Height: 4–7.5 m (13–24.5 ft.), average 6 m (20 ft.)
Spread: 75 cm.–1.5 m (2.5–5 ft.) in 10 years, open but clumping.
Habit: bold but tidy, slightly arching U-shaped clump.
Culms: maximum diameter 3 cm. (1.2 in.), deep green paling to olive yellow, young canes often purple tinted.
Leaves: narrow varying in length between clones, on average 10 x 1 cm. (4 x 0.4 in.), deep green.

The most variable species of *Chusquea* because of its wide distribution and range, from high tree line to low forest and open grassland. As such, one specimen can look quite different from another, and some will appeal to you more than others.

This species is easily distinguished from other chusqueas because the array of multiple branches, which extend most of the way around the node, lacks any one being dominant. Tall, initially vertical, and pale sheathed culms appear leafless at first. In my garden some of the culms stay this way for the first year except for a few tufts of leaves and branches. The following season the sheaths are split by the emerging branches, and on a warm late spring day you can hear and witness them crack. The sheaths darken by the end of the second season from their pale parchment colouring to a mottled straw brown, most of them dropping and some persisting for another year. Take time to pull these off for the benefit of appearance. Sometimes the sheaths are split at the node as the new buds swell before forming the branches.

Young culms often colour a rich plum purple where they rise through the sheaths, this coloration varies between clones and also position; plants in good light often colour the best. I have also seen specimens in very exposed situations produce good colour on older culms, with subtle flushes of amber, orange and scarlet suffusing the pale yellow-green. As the leaves and branches develop, the outer culms and tops of the taller new ones arch slightly with plume-like grace.

Sheath splitting on *Chusquea culeou.*

The original generation of *Chusquea* that came to Europe in the 1920s was raised from seed and distributed throughout the large gardens and estates. Unfortunately nearly all these plants and their numerous division have recently flowered and died, with copious amounts of seed being produced. Decades later, other batches of seed arrived and plants produced from these are still alive, giving credibility to the importance of provenance and the many clonal variations within this species.

I have seen many fine plants of *Chusquea culeou*, all so different from each other that it would be easy to fill a garden with nothing else. A form with distinction, collected in South America by Michael Wickenden of Cally Gardens, southwest Scotland, matured at a rapid pace; the Gulf Stream may have evened out the temperature and the rich, well-cultivated soil of the walled garden could have a been a bonus, but it grew majestically and speedily upwards, above the high walls to dominate one of the boundaries. Conversely, a plant bought by Tony Churly from a specialist nursery for his East Anglian garden in the more extreme climate of eastern England is short, stout, has fans of stumpy leaves but is so indefatigably gorgeous that I have tried three times to dig a piece for myself, without luck.

This is a good time to tell you that division of old, mature specimens is almost impossible. *Chusquea culeou* has an infuriating habit of keeping its outer rhizomes deep, and curving back sharply towards the main crown, often with little or no fibrous root attached. Propagation on the nursery is by division of young juvenile plants, which unfortunately take their time to mature. Now that young plants are available from seed, it is pot luck as to what you will get. Suffice to say, every *C. culeou* is a thing of beauty, and speed of maturity from seed production is usually quicker than division.

My pride and joy

Fortunately my *Chusquea culeou* was not one of the original generation which flowered and it was obtained by pure hard graft, having been offered the smallest of divisions from a plant I had long admired. Success came second time around, probably more luck than

The exceptional form of *Chusquea culeou* in Tony Churly's garden in Norfolk, England.

judgement as the first piece failed. Many customers comment on the beauty and form of the plant as I did when I first saw its parent. I always tell people about how it has developed over the last fourteen years in slightly exaggerated terms, in the hope that they can smile and at least remember what to expect when they purchase a young *C. culeou* for the first time.

My solitary mature culm as it was, when first dug, was pruned down to only a few branches and put in isolation, but in good, free draining soil at the front of the house. This was only after I sold the lawn for use in a landscaping job and realized that I had better do something with the bare earth, before my wife spotted the lack of greenery. Sulking in retaliation to being severed from its mother, the tiny piece grew a few wispy juvenile shoots that flagged and flopped in the sun and the wind. For five years, similar growth continued to appear, some of it thicker and taller, but not by much. The first of the thin culms by this time were exhausted and browning, so out they came, leaving only a few culms that justified their existence. Another year or two on, and I had a plant that looked healthy but of no great stature, the tallest culms struggling to 1.5 m (5 ft.).

One sultry, early summer morning I stood viewing the plant in frustration, it had shown little reward for all the care and respect I had given it, so I went indoors to make a brew, as we Lancashire folk say. Mug in hand, I returned to the chusquea, pondering over the next action to encourage the growth I knew it was capable of.

And there they were. Glistening points of pink and green emerging provocatively from the earth, new shoots a plenty, and thicker, much thicker! They rose quickly in a matter of weeks to increase the height by a third. Every year since, new culms have exceeded the previous years by a minimum of 30 cm. (1 ft.) to create the 4.5 m (15 ft.) specimen that it is now. The advice here is not to worry or overfeed and water because you think it needs it; leave it alone, it will only do what it wants when it is

ready. There is a definite need for this plant to strengthen its root and rhizome before it is able to support the heavy, solid culms it produces. As you can not see what is happening down below soil level, you will have to have faith.

Recently my wife grumbled at the lack of daylight in the house, so I removed over 50 percent of the culms in November, all old ones, carefully and evenly thinned. The result I can recommend, it looked like a different plant and did not show any reaction to this butchery. This season I have noticed as many new culms rising through the centre of the plant as around the edge. The light, warmth and moisture having penetrated into the crown and probably encouraging dormant buds to sprout forth, either that or I have not noticed them trying to fight through the original dense greenery before.

Uses

As a solitary specimen or plant in a triangle for a dense, long term screen. I have rarely seen a good specimen in a pot; they quickly become chlorotic, and it is difficult enough to provide saleable plants that do not show signs of stress unless seed raised.

Others

Until all plants of *Chusquea culeou* 'Tenuis' flowered in the 1990s, this was distinct from the species in its shorter and more spreading habit. Production from seed has proved difficult and from the few plants raised it is too early to say whether it has remained true to type.

New culms of *Chusquea culeou*.

Chusquea gigantea

Hardiness: min. -18˚C (0˚F), zone 6
Aspect: sun or light shade.
Height: 6–16 m (20–52 ft.), average 10 m (33 ft.)
Spread: 2–5 m (6.5–16.5 ft.) in 10 years, very open, vigorous clump.
Habit: bold vertical culms, with strong arching branches.
Culms: maximum diameter 6 cm. (2.4 in.), sea green foliage, paling to olive yellow. Old culms often tinted yellow and red.
Leaves: long and narrow 12 x 1 cm. (5 x 0.4 in.), sea green.

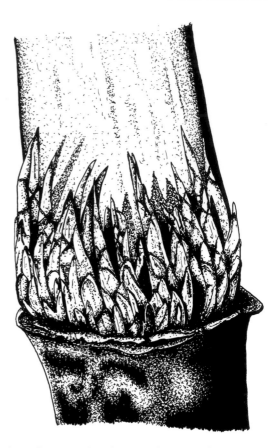

The newly emerging branches on a culm section of *Chusquea gigantea*.

Chusquea gigantea is the name now widely accepted in Europe but in the United States the plant is known as *Chusquea* aff. *culeou*. Confused? You will be when I tell you that in Europe it was first known as *C. culeou* 'Tenuis' (see p101) and then *C. breviglumis* (which by the way, is the common synonym for the true *C. culeou* in the United States). I suggest you put your trust in a reputable collector or nurseryman when looking for the correct plant, and take heed of the following description.

Bolt upright and very tall, it is a true giant positively thriving in a windswept oceanic climate. The rhizome system, although pachymorph (clumping), is long necked and expands rapidly but evenly. The branch system is very distinct, with between one to three primary branches at the centre of the subsidiary ones, the central branch often maturing at a length of well over 1 m (3.3 ft.), sometimes giving a rather tangled, jungle-like effect which is very convincing on a mature specimen. This central primary branch is the key feature you should look for to identify this plant. Culms will eventually be tall and thick turning pale olive green. The young shoots are a deep, blood-stained shrimp pink and grow rapidly upwards; measure them daily if you have nothing better to do. The sheaths are persistent for a season or more, and add a light and dark effect to the culms that gives scale and perspective when viewing the bamboo from afar. A specimen of *Chusquea gigantea* at the Royal Horticultural Society's Garden, Rosemoor in Devon, England, is on an exposed fork between two paths and has incredible colouring on many of the culms. Blends of pale orange, red and yellow in with the green are the result of exposure and sunlight; the plant is very healthy so the coloration it is not due to any nutrient deficiency.

The rhizome is deep on this species, and for any plant established longer than a few years, I suggest dynamite or heavy earth moving machinery to aid propagation. I had the dubious pleasure of removing Michael Hirsh's plant from his previous garden in Lincolnshire, in the east of England; Michael was the founder of the European Bamboo Society (EBS Great Britain). It took so long, two of us ended up working by torchlight to complete the task. Disappointingly only three pieces survived, and from these I have a plant in my own garden and managed to build up only enough stock to sell one or two plants a year. It should always be propagated from pot-grown juvenile stock. Even then it does not stay young and divisible for long and is therefore still quite rare.

My first experience of this species was again at Peter Addington's Stream Cottage where he had cut a narrow swathe through his large plant and put down stepping stones so it could be admired from within. My plant is still a youngster by comparison, planted out for three years after being kept in a large pot for many years. It had been used for exhibition and was starved and stressed to the point of leaf drop. In fear of losing the

Leaf shadow on the sheathed culms of *Chusquea gigantea*.

The stark upright habit of *Chusquea gigantea* is highlighted by the low underplanting of a flowering shrub.

plant, I made an exact hole in the lawn, dropped it in, disposed of the displaced soil elsewhere and covered the surface of the rootball with the sods of turf. This was done in late autumn and for three years it has never been fed, watered or mulched; the grass now burns off at the base of the plant because the *Chusquea* takes all the moisture. The resulting growth from this half-dead plant has been staggering, it has trebled in height and girth in repayment for the disrespect I have shown it. Quite the opposite to my *Chusquea culeou*, which was pampered to the extreme but took many more years to provide results.

Uses

Needs isolation, for example as a large lawn specimen, so it can be viewed as an individual stand. The best plant association I have seen is where this *Chusquea* is planted against a high wall, so the culms are framed by brickwork. A bright variegated ×*Hibanobambusa tranquillans* 'Shiroshima' one side provides contrasting colour, leaf shape and habit to the overhanging *Chusquea* branches, a combination that would be the dream of many a garden designer.

Chusquea macrostachya

Hardiness: min. -18˚C (0˚F), zone 6
Aspect: sun or light shade.
Height: 3–6 m (10–20 ft.), average 4 m (13 ft.)
Spread: 75 cm.–1. 5 m (2.5–5ft.) in 10 years, reasonably compact and clumping.
Habit: tidy, forming an elegant arching shape.
Culms: maximum diameter 3 cm. (1.2 in.), deep green, pale older culms.
Leaves: narrow, smaller than Chusquea culeou, 7 x 1 cm. (3 x 0.4 in.), deep green.

A much sought after species because of its exquisite habit of arching culms and branches rising from a refined clump. As with *Chusquea* gigantea there is a dominant primary branch produced from the whorl of buds around the nodes although this is not as long. Young plants are lax, ungainly and will test your patience but as with all good things it is worth the wait.

Many plants sold under this name are actually *Chusquea culeou*, so take care to ascertain the true identity before buying.

Uses

Prefers solitude, but try planting a *Vinca minor* (lesser periwinkle), preferably one of the white-flowered forms, around the base. The wandering shoots of the periwinkle will snake between the culms and light up the crown in spring with a starlight effect.

Chusquea montana

Hardiness: min. -18˚C (0˚F), zone 6
Aspect: sun to half shade.
Height: 1–3 m (3.3–10 ft.), average 2 m (6.5 ft.)
Spread: 75 cm.–1.5 m (2.5–5 ft.) in 10 years, clumping.
Habit: tidy, compact and upright.
Culms: maximum diameter 1.5 cm. (0.6 in.), turning yellow-green as they mature.
Leaves: narrow and short to 7 cm. (3 in.), fresh green.

Many plants sold in Europe under this name are selected short forms of *Chusquea culeou* raised from seed. In the United States, *C. nigricans* is the widely accepted synonym for *C. montana* but many plants grown as *C. nigricans* are in fact dwarf forms of *C. culeou*.

The true *Chusquea montana* is easily distinguished on account of its swollen nodes and very short

branches. It is very delicate in appearance but extremely robust. In its native environment of Southern Chile it is at home in the higher altitude boundaries of the cool misty southern beech (*Nothofagus*) forests.

Uses
On well-drained sloping rock gardens or in open borders, to provide contrast in shape and texture to other plants. Alternatively plant at the edge of a path where its form and character can be best appreciated, it will take away the monotony of the usual flatness of this position. If you are feeling bold, surround it with low weeping sedges and a vivid background of red *Crocosmia*.

Fargesia

An important genus that may contain species yet to be renamed within *Borinda*, and others only known in China and yet to grace our gardens. Seventy-eight species are listed in *A Compendium of Chinese Bamboo* (China Forestry Publishing House), many of which are unequalled in their appearance and should considerably increase the range of temperate bamboos. Together with *Thamnocalamus*, *Fargesia* are the only reliable clumping (pachymorph) bamboos that are not subtropical or tropical. They inhabit the vast uplands of central China, mainly from Gansu and Sichuan between 900–4,200 m (2,950–13,780 ft.), making them some of the most cold-hardy bamboos.

Cold hardiness is usually measured by the temperature at which damage is done to mainly evergreen foliage or cell damage to wood. However, some fargesias can be classed as deciduous, as they frequently defoliate during winter in their natural environment. In the United States and Northern Europe we are not prepared for this leaf fall, but I have had young specimens suffer from winter cold, and more mature ones from drought, losing their leaves but nearly always recovering the following spring.

There is considerable variation in the location and requirements of different species. Some are endemic to a small area, with specific needs that are difficult to replicate in gardens; others are widely distributed and more adaptable. There has been some success in

The new culms on *Fargesia robusta* appear early and are very ornamental.

growing *Fargesia murielae* and *F. nitida* in parts of Canada and Scandinavia where temperatures regularly drop below -29°C (-20°F). In continental areas high temperatures are of greater concern. Some fargesias suffer from excesses of sun and daytime heat, together with long periods of drought but, where shade and moisture are provided, results can be impressive. The winter cold is rarely a problem unless long and excessive. In maritime climates, most fargesias thrive and also tolerate higher light levels. However, there is much yet to be learned about each species and its tolerances, to heat in particular.

The culms are cylindrical, but usually thin and flexible. Some of the new culms are quite colourful and grow rapidly once they have pierced the soil. A minimum of four or five short branches develop at the nodes, and one or two species exceed this allocation with eight to fifteen branches. Branches are evenly spaced, anything up to halfway around the nodes, staying close to the culms before emerging at a maximum angle of 45 degrees and usually remaining short. Leaves are fine and tessellated, but robust and plentiful; the weight of foliage arching the culms of some species including *Fargesia utilis*. In contrast to the tree-like *Phyllostachys*, the genus *Fargesia* is more shrubby with plentiful thin culms reaching on average 3–5 m (10–16.5 ft.).

Fargesia angustissima
Hardiness: min. -9°C (15°F), zone 8
Aspect: half or light shade.
Height: 4–7 m (13–23 ft.), average 5 m (16.5 ft.)
Spread: 75 cm.–1 m (2.5–3.3 ft.) in 10 years, clumping.
Habit: tall and delicate with arching culms.
Culms: maximum diameter 2 cm. (0.8 in.), bloomy, purple new shoots.
Leaves: very slim, 5 x 0.5 cm. (2 x 0.2 in.)

A species mainly grown in the United States and not properly tried and tested in Europe. Native to Sichuan in China, it needs exact growing conditions similar to the evergreen broad-leaved forests of this region. It is not as hardy as many other species and is on the borderline for inclusion in this section, but I believe this *Fargesia* has the potential to adjust to new habitats. New culms are vividly sheathed purple and emerge covered in a powdery white bloom, later lost as they age and develop their loose canopy of ultra-slim leaves.

Uses

This species is best suited to a sheltered courtyard, walled garden or rich woodland, with initial shelter from other plants to help it establish.

Fargesia denudata L1575

Hardiness: min. -23˚C (-10˚F), zone 6
Aspect: sun or half shade.
Height: 3–5 m (10–16.5 ft.), average 4 m (13 ft.)
Spread: 75 cm.–1 m (2.5–3.3 ft.) in 10 years, densely clumping.
Habit: tidy and stately, slightly weeping.
Culms: maximum diameter 1.5 cm. (0.6 in.), paling to rich yellow.
Leaves: short but broad in relation to length, 5 x 1.5 cm. (2 x 0.6 in.), pale green.

The original form was introduced by Roy Lancaster and I am lucky to have one of the original plants from his garden, hence it is described here. There appear to be different forms in cultivation, so it would be worth finding one with the collectors number L1575 and checking its history and movement through the nursery trade.

It comes from the Sichuan and Gansu Provinces in China, growing at altitudes between 1,800 m (5,900 ft.) and 3,400 m (11,150 ft.) in mixed forest among shrubs and into the subalpine levels. On first impression it is similar to the graceful *F. murielae*, but the leaves are smaller and more delicate in their arrangement on the masses of shorter branches. The whole plant has a pale yellow-green colouring but is certainly not languid as you might expect from this description. The old culms

particularly ripen to a rich burnished yellow in full light and provide background for the constantly flickering leaves in the breeze. This species is very reliable in cool conditions and quickly forms an imposing specimen, staying tightly clumping and is easy to recommend. Do not be put off by the lax habit of a juvenile plant; a mature specimen is unequalled in appearance and will develop in a short time.

Uses

As a solitary specimen in a lawn, or the foreground of a large border. In large gardens try placing in sizable, well-spaced groups by ponds or on sweeping grassland, associated with compact, dark pines and the ghostly white stems of *Rubus cockburnianus* and *R. biflorus*.

Fargesia dracocephala

Hardiness: min. -23˚C (-10˚F), zone 6
Aspect: sun or light shade.
Height: 2.5–5 m (8.2–16.5 ft.), average 3 m (10 ft.)
Spread: 70 cm.–1 m (2.3–3.3 ft.) in 10 years, tight clumping.
Habit: tidy, rigid broad V-shaped clump.
Culms: maximum diameter 1.5 cm. (0.6 in.), deep green paling to yellow-green, sometimes red-tinted in the sun.
Leaves: narrow and layered, thicker than most Fargesia species and tapered at both ends, 10 x 1.2 cm. (4 x 0.5 in.), deep green.

This species is very strong growing in its native China and is food plant for the giant panda. However, it is usually sold as a short and leafy, juvenile container plant that does not have the hallmarks of a mature specimen, and in most gardens it is a slow starter. I have seen few plants in the United Kingdom that exceed 3 m (10 ft.). My own plant seems to have matured at just over 2 m (6.5 ft.) but it grows against the wall of the house facing northeast. It is a dry, unforgiving aspect with only early and late sunshine, all of which may account for its short stature. Most other woody plants of similar height would probably look gaunt and haggard in the same position but somehow this bamboo thrives in its cheerless surround, with fresh, dark greenery and a strong, stout culm structure. Its spread of branch and foliage at the top is four times that of the clump at ground level and the culms radiate evenly from the crown to create an obvious fan shape. The stiff leaves do not curl when under stress as with many *Fargesia* species and apart from the annual moult of leaves, usually in late autumn, the plant always looks content.

Nearly all cultivated plants are from German seed distributed in the 1980s and there is a chance of clonal variation, which may be another reason for the shorter plant in my garden. *Fargesia dracocephala* 'White Dragon' is a selected seedling in the United States with white-flushed spring foliage.

Uses

A low screen or dense hedge. Use with the more structural timber bamboos such as *Phyllostachys vivax* or *Phyllostachys bambusoides* 'Castillonis' for the perfect complement. Ferns, twisted *Arbutus* and giant lilies (*Cardiocrinum*) with this rigid flat-topped fargesia would be an essential mix for a planting of primeval mood.

The elegant leaves of *Fargesia ferax*.

Fargesia ferax

Hardiness: min. -10°C (14°F), zone 8
Aspect: light shade.
Height: 3–5 m (10–16.5 ft.) estimated.
Spread: 75 cm.–1.5 m (2.5–5 ft.) in 10 years, clumping.
Habit: leafy and arching.
Culms: maximum diameter 1.5 cm. (0.6 in.), matt green, bloomy when young.
Leaves: long and very narrow, 10 x 0.75 cm. (4 x 0.3 in.), matt green.

Although little known in the West, this species is worthy of mention because of the distinct lanceolate leaves, which hang elegantly from the multiple branches. Its performance has not yet been properly assessed and the minimum temperature is a guess. It has survived lower temperatures in the east of England in a pot under cold polythene but is likely to be deciduous outdoors in a hard winter. This delicate looking bamboo has a very narrow distribution in Sichuan, China, at an elevation of 2,500 m (8,200 ft.) and, as such, may be fussy in gardens.

Uses

Suitable shelter should be provided until more is known about how this plant performs: against a lightly shaded wall with moisture from a down pipe would be ideal, or the dappled shade of sheltered woodland.

Fargesia frigida

Hardiness: min. -23°C (-10°F), zone 6
Aspect: sun or light shade.
Height: 2–3.5 m (6.5–11.5 ft.), average 2.5 m (8.2 ft.)
Spread: 50 cm.–1 m (1.6–3.3 ft.) in 10 years, clumping.
Habit: elegant and wispy, deciduous in winter.
Culms: maximum diameter 1.5 cm. (0.6 in.), persistent culm sheaths tinted red, with yellowing culms.
Leaves: thin and tiny, of delicate appearance, 2.5 x 0.5 cm. (1 x 0.2 in.), green.

This species is listed as *Borinda frigidorum* in the United States and also known as *Fargesia frigidorum*. A promising plant because of its cold tolerance but unfortunately it is deciduous. (However we do grow magnolias, deutzia and other spring and summer delights that have little to offer in the winter, so why not this bamboo?) A true evergreen bamboo would be the first choice of most gardeners, so I suspect this will always remain a collector's item. Although the summer glory of the foliage and late crop of colourfully sheathed culms are enough to make most fanatical plant enthusiasts part with their hard-earned cash.

Uses

Plant among other bamboos or central to a border where it is not too obvious in winter.

Fargesia fungosa

Hardiness: min. -10˚C (14˚F), zone 8
Aspect: sun or light shade.
Height: 3–6 m (10–20 ft.), average 3.5 m (11.5 ft.)
Spread: 75 cm.–1.2 m (2.5–4 ft.) in 10 years,
tight clumping.
Habit: very leafy, with foliage forming dense layers.
Culms: maximum diameter 2 cm. (0.8 in.),
new shoots red with sheaths covered in black hairs,
old culms blush red in full sun.
Leaves: distinct and fingered, quite large with hairy
undersides, 10 x 1.5 cm. (4 x 0.6 in.)

In the United States this species is now classified as
Borinda fungosa. Originally distributed as seed from
Yunnan, where it flowered gregariously in the early
1990s at altitudes between 1,800 and 2,600 m (5,900
and 8,530 ft.). Young seedlings need protection until a
good quantity of culms is produced before planting out.
Once established plants are comparatively heat tolerant
because of the large (for *Fargesia*), robust and hairy
leaves. It may also be quite cold hardy, the minimum
temperature given above is quite conservative, and
plants in the United Kingdom have performed well in
various locations.

With the combination of bold foliage, persistent
culms and their reddening, this a quite a colourful and
well presented bamboo. It will undoubtedly grow much
shorter in gardens than in its native China, where the
culms are used for weaving and the shoots eaten.

Uses

Against a plain background or wall where its shape and
distinct leaf formation can be admired.

Fargesia murielae

Hardiness: min. -29˚C (-20˚F), zone 5
Aspect: sun or light shade.
Height: 3–4.5 m (10–14.8 ft.), average 4 m (13 ft.)
Spread: 75 cm.–1.2 m (2.5–4 ft.) in 10 years,
very dense clump.
Habit: tidy, umbrella-like shape.
Culms: maximum diameter 1.5 cm. (0.6 in.), olive yellow.
Leaves: narrow, 8 x 1 cm. (3 x 0.4 in.), soft green.

Discovered by Ernest Wilson in 1907 and named after
his daughter Muriel. Plants were first propagated at the

Royal Botanical Gardens at Kew, England in 1913. This
is perhaps one of the most important plant introductions
of the twentieth century and one of the most cold hardy
of all bamboos, surviving well in exposed parts of
Scandinavia, Eastern Europe, and the central and north-
eastern United States. It originates from the home of
many good garden plants, the Hubei Province in China,
at elevations up to 3,000 m (9,850 ft.).

Unfortunately all plants that derived from Wilson's
collection flowered and seeded, starting late in the 1970s
and throughout the next decade. There are few reports of
plants having survived but the seeds were profuse in their
germination and there are already semi-mature plants in
gardens from these seedlings, and many different forms
have also appeared. A clone collected by the Sino-
American Botanical Expedition, given the title SABE 939,
also flowered. It was reputedly even more cold hardy and
the seedlings will therefore offer interesting comparisons
to the existing clone, and new cultivars are likely.

The slowly spreading, dense mass of culms from
Fargesia murielae form a stout column at the base and
support the mass of breezy foliage. The whole plant has
great density and makes an effective screen. To my surprise
it is often confused with *F. nitida*. At the juvenile stage from
seed or by young division they can look similar, but on
maturity the plentiful culms of *F. murielae* emerge bright
green and later turn a matt yellow-green, whereas the
young culms of *F. nitida* are nearly always brown-purple. In
addition the leaves of *F. nitida* are more glaucous than the
fresh pale green foliage of *F. murielae*, whose branches also
form much earlier. The ultimate shape of *F. murielae* is that
of a billowing fountain being blown in the wind, but the
common name of umbrella bamboo is more often used
and fountain bamboo applied to *F. nitida*.

The various cultivars of *Fargesia murielae* are all
akin to the general appearance of the species; some
shorter in stature, others more robust but all having
similar texture and colouring. The many forms and
clones of *F. nitida*, however, vary more widely and show
great individuality that makes identification of their
forms much simpler.

My *Fargesia murielae* flowered late in the 1980s and
died. The birds must have collected the seed for, apart
from a few that germinated as meagre seedlings around

the base of the dying plant, I was left with nothing. Fortunately specimens in my locality were plentiful and I could often be found ferreting around the base of dead plants with a seed tray and trowel.

Uses

There are many uses for this elegant species, which accounts for its popularity. It provides a foil for most other bamboos, a screen, windbreak or baffle for noise reduction. It is the ideal lawn specimen and, because of its cold tolerance, prized for container growing. Plants in pots that suffer desiccation in the winter recover very quickly the following spring.

Others

Fargesia murielae 'Leda' was a variegated form of the old clone and flowered alongside the species; it was particularly beautiful when grown in light shade. To the best of my knowledge we have not been blessed with a reliable variegated clone of *F. murielae* yet to replace 'Leda'.

Fargesia murielae 'Weinhenstephan' was a vigorous clone also now lost in cultivation. This now has an alternative in 'Jumbo', which has broader leaves than the species and is speedy in maturing with a taller, more open habit.

Fargesia murielae 'Simba'

Hardiness: min. -29°C (-20°F), zone 5
Aspect: sun or half shade.
Height 2–3 m (6.5–10 ft.), average 2 m (6.5 ft.)
Spread: 50–80 cm. (1.5–2.6 ft.) in 10 years, tight clumping.
Habit: solid and dense but very elegant.
Culms: maximum diameter 1 cm. (0.4 in.), very pale green.
Leaves: narrow, 7 x 1 cm. (2.75 x 0.4 in.), pale green.

Some of the first *Fargesia murielae* to flower in the late 1970s were at Thyme's nursery in Denmark and 'Simba' was the most notable cultivar from a selection of seedlings. It is short, stout and full of character, being essentially a very compact form of the species but when planted side by side, 'Simba' is usually a paler green. Young plants often sold as 'Simba' are sometimes juvenile forms of *F. murielae*, so beware and check for the paler, more gentle colouring often evident even on a young plant.

My plant of 'Simba' has finally matured after fifteen years and reaches just over 2 m (6.5 ft.) and stands

Fargesia murielae 'Simba', approximately seven years old, growing in open woodland.

proud in the garden with *Yushania maculata*, much more glaucous in colour as a background, and the large leaves of *Sasa palmata* f. *nebulosa* fluttering on one side. These three completely different bamboos are the perfect representation of the plant group, offering great variety for something so green, yet simple and rewarding.

In 2003 we suffered the highest daytime temperatures on record with a drought to accompany them. With the removal of some large shrubs close to my 'Simba' the previous winter and possible disturbance at the roots, it looked sad during most of the late summer and early autumn: leaves closed and curled, many paling to yellow and shedding, the pale undersides looking ghostly in the glare of the sun. It would have been sensible to water it. I have never watered established bamboos in the garden and so as not to break my belief, I left it alone. As I write in the depth of winter, after the usual murk and drenching, it now looks almost defiant of its summer basting, the beacon of fresh, pale greenery pierces the gloom of an English mist.

Uses

An invaluable plant for small gardens or pot culture. Associate as described above, with other bamboos; or use in front of darker greenery to bring out the intensity of the pale foliage.

Others

Fargesia murielae 'Bimbo' is a recent cultivar, short in stature and airy and light above. 'Harewood' is similar and was produced alongside 'Simba' in Denmark, as was 'Thyme', which is intermediate in size at 1.5 m (5 ft.).

Fargesia nitida

Hardiness: min. -29˚C (-20˚F), zone 5
Aspect: light or half shade.
Height: 3–4 m (10–13 ft.), average 3 m (10 ft.)
Spread: 60 cm.–1 m (2–3.3 ft.) in 10 years, clumping.
Habit: squat and vertical, always tidy.
Culms: maximum diameter 1.5 cm. (0.6 in.), dark purple.
Leaves: short and slim usually 5 x 1.5 cm. (2 x 0.6 in.),
grey-green.

This species and its forms are all useful plants for cold regions, being introduced in the late 19th century, the original form, in particular, has been well tried and tested in many gardens and aspects. It is native to a large area in central China, growing in forests on the northern slopes of mountains up to an altitude of 3,400 m (11,150 ft.), where it is used extensively for weaving baskets and light fencing.

There are many cultivars and also clonal variation within forms; therefore two plants in different gardens may be labelled *Fargesia nitida* but can contrast greatly in their presentation. Climate, locality, soil and all the other variables sometimes play a part in this variance of habit, and forms are often labelled with their garden of origin. It is not unusual to be hunting around the nurseries of the southwest of England and finding a young plant of *Fargesia nitida* Glendurgan form, or *Fargesia nitida* ex-Endsleigh, and so the list goes on.

Some older plantings of the true species are flowering and there are reports of some seed, yet my plant shows no signs, although there is still time. It is hoped the complete flowering as happened with *Fargesia murielae* will not occur because of the many different clones of *F. nitida* and its broad distribution in the wild. However it would be sensible to seek out the next generation of seedlings, which includes some choice forms, as insurance against a complete flowering.

Fargesia nitida is a very refined plant, with a dense column of dark purple culms that holds aloft the great mass of frothy blue-green foliage arching lightly outwards on the wispy branches. The general appearance, although graceful, is slightly stiffer than the many cultivars with smaller leaves and more weeping habit. On all forms, the new culms remain leafless until their second year and rise vertically through the mass of existing foliage. *Fargesia*

nitida is usually recommended for part shade where it will keep its distinct, dark culm colouring and the fine leaves will not be affected by direct, hot sun. An open or exposed plant will always have the best culm colour but the leaves will curl inwards to the central veins in extremes of heat, cold and wind; although this curling is not unattractive, some leaf scorch can occur. Plants in deep shade never develop the purple colouring on the culms and appear paler with the more persistent blue-grey bloom.

Fargesia nitida was the first bamboo I planted and is easy to grow once it has established its roots. It matures quickly and provides great interest and beauty. It is controlled and refined in its habit and needs little attention or aftercare. Indisputably it deserves a very high ranking among bamboos.

Uses

Very versatile. It can form a screen or windbreak, make a fine lawn specimen, grace a woodland garden or grow in pots. Like the many forms of this plant, the possibilities are endless.

Others

In keeping with the more vertical, rigid appearance of the true species I have an unnamed clone, *Fargesia nitida* tall, which erupts through the shade of a congested border with a mass of more open, thicker culms with good blue colouring and persistent straw-coloured sheaths. The leaves are also larger.

Fargesia nitida 'Chennevieres' is rare, as upright as the species with narrow leaves.

Fargesia nitida 'Ems River' has reliable purple culm colouring and also smaller leaves, and is very vertical in habit.

Fargesia nitida 'Wakehurst' is similar in strength and vigour, and a plant that has impressed me recently with its robust and plentiful dark culms.

New introductions from Gansu and Sichuan

In 1995 Jos van der Palen of the Netherlands named two bamboos collected in the south of Gansu Province in China by an employee of the Shanghai Botanic Gardens as Gansu 95-1 and Gansu 95-2. After studying them in various locations in Europe, Gansu 95-1 was identified as *Fargesia rufa*, described later, and Gansu 95-2 as a form of *F. nitida* now simply called *F. nitida* 'Gansu'. This plant is well worth growing having smaller leaves than the species massed on the hanging branches causing the culms to arch widely, more akin to *F. nitida* 'Nymphenburg'. The culms are a rich blue-purple that shows even in shade and shoot very early, some new culms branching late in the same season. The leaves quickly close with exposure, so a light woodland setting is suggested for this plant. 'Gansu' was collected from a cold area at relatively high altitude, it is short, to only 2–3 m (6.5–10 ft.) and so ideal as a small, elegant garden plant. With few other bamboo species in its

New culms of *Fargesia nitida* 'Jiuzhaigou 1'.

native locality and isolated from the main stands of *F. nitida* in China, 'Gansu' is likely to be a separate generation from the original seedlings introduced in the late nineteenth century.

Fargesia nitida seedlings have been collected from Jiuzhaigou Park in northern Sichuan since 1986 by three different people and are numbered 1 to 10 with the occasional cultivar name appearing now in Europe. Numbers 1 and 2 are the best known and are both very distinct. *F. nitida* 'Jiuzhaigou 1' is a pure delight with a narrow upright habit to 3 m (10 ft.), and good sheath and culm colouring. The deep green culms emerge from the dusky pink-purple sheaths and age to red-purple and eventually pale orange-yellow, creating a kaleidoscope of colour. Leaves are small and bunched, hanging lavishly from the thin branches; some light overhead protection from hot sun is best to stop the leaves closing.

Fargesia nitida 'Jiuzhaigou 2' was collected by M. Laferrere of France, and although I have not seen this as a mature plant I am told it is short and stocky to only 2 m (6.5 ft.) with more open, vertical culms. It does have very small leaves, although young plants on my nursery originated abroad, possibly from meristem culture, which could be the reason for this. It lacks the colour of 'Jiuzhaigou 1' but looks very promising with its unusual habit and fine foliage; another selection which would benefit from light shade.

Fargesia nitida 'Eisenach'

Hardiness: min. -29°C (-20°F), zone 5
Aspect: light shade.
Height: 3–5 m (10–16.5 ft.), average 4 m (13 ft.)
Spread: 75 cm.–1 m (2.5–5 ft.) in 10 years, clumping.
Habit: bold but tidy, slightly arching.
Culms: maximum diameter 1.5 cm. (0.6 in.), dark purple-brown.
Leaves: smaller than the species, 4 x 1 cm. (1.6 x 0.4 in.), dark green.

A cultivar that has justified its status within this species. It has been planted widely in various locations and shown to have a polished appearance and grows more slowly than the species. The vertical culms colour beautifully to a dark red in the sun and can bifurcate at the base as they curve upwards. Leaves are small and dark green on elegant, nodding branches. The leaf size would indicate its preference for some shade but in a moisture-retentive soil it performs well except when exposed to a dry wind. Usually taller than the true species, noted particularly on plants grown in the United Kingdom, although in colder continental locations it will be much more compact.

Uses

Good when planted in a north or east-facing aspect, away from direct sunlight, with low ground cover plants around the base. Pale-leaved pulmonarias and low evergreen rushes highlight the colour of the dark culms; *Pulmonaria longifolia* 'Ankum' and *Luzula sylvatica* 'Aurea' are my favourites.

Others

Fargesia nitida 'De Belder' is a speedy, robust cultivar which can often be wider than it is high because of its prolific culm production. The canes curve upwards and away from the clump, giving the distinctive broad anvil-shaped habit. The culms have similar dark colouring to 'Eisenach' except in shade, and the leaves are also small but less likely to curl in hot sun.

Fargesia nitida 'Nymphenburg'

Hardiness: min. -29°C (-20°F), zone 5
Aspect: light shade.
Height: 3.5–5 m (11.5–16.5 ft.), average 4 m (13 ft.)
Spread: 75 cm.–1 m (2.5–3.3 ft.) in 10 years, tight clumping.
Habit: stiff and upright at base with a weeping crown.
Culms: maximum diameter 1.25 cm. (0.5 in.), silver-blue with pale sheaths.
Leaves: narrow and long varying in size to a maximum of 9 x 1 cm. (3.5 x 0.4 in.) but usually smaller, grey-green.

A mature specimen of Fargesia nitida 'Nymphenburg' in the author's garden.

If I had to select just one form of *Fargesia nitida* for my garden, this would be it. I have it planted in one of the most uninviting places, particularly for a bamboo. In a narrow border between the house and a path, it has less than a metre (about 3 ft.) to grip, and the soil is shallow with clinker and rubble for drainage. Although light overhead, it only sees the sun early and late in the day which, given the soil conditions, is probably its saving grace. The overall silvery green lustre to this plant lights up the red brick of the house and lends a cosiness to the property.

The culms are usually paler and rarely show the dark purple of other forms, however, the new culms emerge from the sheaths a gleaming pale, powdery blue. The branches high up are angled tightly to the culm top and splay evenly outward under the weight of the leaves.

Shade is usually recommended for this plant and I would not normally argue with this, but there are fine examples of 'Nymphenburg' locally in drier soil, full sun and open to the wind. One in particular is as old as my plant of twelve years and equally magnificent, but only half the height. It rarely shows signs of stress unless the summer is very dry, when most *Fargesia nitida* forms will close their leaves in unison.

Uses

It can be tried almost anywhere. Plants need to be of reasonable size to show well in a container as young plants can be quite lax. With its strength and vigour 'Nymphenburg' would make an impressive hedge or broad screen and can be mixed successfully with some of the more refined *Phyllostachys* species, such as the black *P. nigra* or very rigid *P. rubromarginata*.

Others

Fargesia nitida 'Anceps' is becoming well known for its open growth habit and delicate appearance, although quite tolerant of climatic extremes and is notably heat hardy.

Fargesia nitida 'McClure' is very strong and eventually grows taller than most *F. nitida* forms but does prefer shade and needs tidying regularly, as it generates such a mass of often top-heavy growth.

Close up of the culms of Fargesia nitida 'Nymphenburg'.

Fargesia robusta

Hardiness: min. -18°C (0°F), zone 6
Aspect: sun or light shade
Height: 4–6 m (13–20 ft.), average 5 m (16.5 ft.)
Spread: 75 cm.–1.5 m (2.5–5 ft.) in 10 years,
open, but clumping
Habit: strongly vertical and stately
Culms: maximum diameter 2.5 cm. (1 in.), deep green with white culm sheaths and red branch sheaths.
Leaves: narrow, 13 x 2 cm. (5 x 0.75 in.), dark green, rarely bleaching.

The array of seasonal colours have already earned this recent introduction a good reputation. The best way to describe this plant is from the bottom up. Until the introduction of *Fargesia rufa* this was the first bamboo to shoot in my garden with dark shiny shoot tips evident in early spring and expanding rapidly by mid spring, whatever the weather. The pointed and hairy culms push through the soil like a battery of missiles emerging from their armour and quickly pale to a luminescent lime green and crimson, the dark hairs holding the dew and catching the sunlight. As the shoots expand upwards the sheaths pale to complement the lush, grass green culms emerging through their protection. By midsummer all the new culms, which radiate around the tight base to this plant, have matured to their full height and started to branch, the sheaths at this point are regimentally spaced and still firmly attached to the nodes. As energy goes into branch and leaf production the sheaths turn a ghostly matt white that appears to absorb all light, and at this point *F. robusta* is easily the most stunning plant in the garden. After a few weeks the sheaths drop first from the uppermost nodes and then downwards in sequence. At the onset of the dormant season the short branches, angled at 45 degrees, and leaves strengthen and the small papery sheaths around the base of the branches, just above the nodes, turn a rich crimson which lasts well into the following season. Combine these colourful qualities with a plant that is quick growing, vertical, clump forming and dependably evergreen and you will insist on including it in your collection.

A colleague in the industry once told me that this

The pale sheaths on the culms of *Fargesia robusta* in midsummer (July).

New culms of *Fargesia robusta* shoot very early with good colouring.

A developing culm of *Fargesia robusta* 'Red Sheath' displays an impressive culm sheath blade.

species would be the next *Fargesia murielae* after its demise through flowering. *Fargesia murielae* exists after its regeneration, but *F. robusta* is better. Whichever form you choose, I believe it lives up to its species name and is extremely robust, possibly tolerating temperatures lower than shown.

Uses

Place this bamboo in a prominent position where it can be appreciated through the seasons. The summer sheaths will lighten up the darkest of plantings. It can take exposure, so is useful for screening and makes a dense hedge. I have specimens for exhibition that remain in pots and stay very fresh as long as older culms are occasionally removed to reduce the leaf area; this makes them less top heavy and require less moisture.

Others

Fargesia robusta is native to Sichuan Province in China. There may be variation within the species, possibly due to the provenance of each collection.

The sheaths of the same *Fargesia robusta* a few weeks later, as they begin to loosen from the culms.

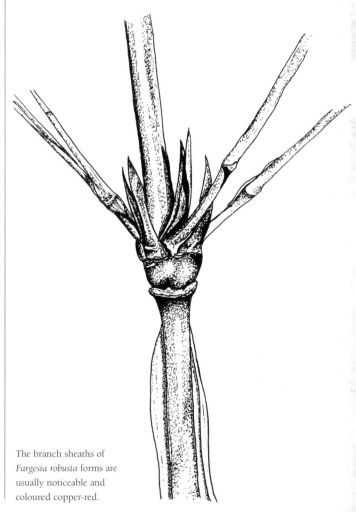

The branch sheaths of *Fargesia robusta* forms are usually noticeable and coloured copper-red.

The rich colouring on the branches of *Fargesia robusta* 'Red Sheath'.

Fargesia robusta 'Red Sheath' (previously listed as ex-Ming) is a form I named in collaboration with Michael Brisbane over one of the best home-made Chinese meals I have ever had. This cultivar has much larger leaves and is more open in habit than the species. The branch sheaths are also greater in size and as a result their red colouring is more noticeable. Maturing plants of 'Red Sheath' and the species planted next to each other are dissimilar and 'Red Sheath' produces by far the better colour during the winter.

Fargesia robusta 'Wolong' is best known in the United States and was collected in Wolong, Sichuan, in 1996. It has larger leaves than the species and may be similar to 'Red Sheath'. Oprins Plants, of Belgium, offer *F. robusta* 'Pingwu' with a description similar to the species. Pingwu is also in Sichuan. I have only seen photographs of these plants so it would be unwise of me to speculate further.

Fargesia rufa

Hardiness: min. -20°C (-4°F), zone 6
Aspect: sun or light shade.
Height: 2–3.5 m (6.5–11.5 ft.), average 2.5 m (8.2 ft.)
Spread: 75 cm.–1.5 m (2.5–4 ft.) in 10 years, broad clumping.
Habit: short, squat, arching at the edges but delicate in appearance.
Culms: maximum diameter 1 cm. (0.4 in.), orange-red or dark shrimp pink culm and branch sheaths, depending on soil type.
Leaves: narrow, wavy, 8 x 0.75 cm. (3 x 0.3 in.) pale green.

Formerly this was known as *Fargesia* Gansu 95-1, mentioned earlier under *F. nitida*, one of two new plants sent from China for identification. Propagation has been rapid, and it is becoming more widely available and proving to be one of the most valuable introductions for some time due to its short, tidy habit and quick development. Its origins are in the shrubby forests of Gansu and Sichuan at altitudes of 1,000–2,500 m (3,280–8,200 ft.) and further north than most bamboos. The average annual temperature in the collection area was 8°C (46°F), with a low winter minimum and high summer maximum temperature indicating its suitability for cold, continental gardens.

This species supersedes *Fargesia robusta* as the earliest bamboo to shoot, at least in my garden. The short culms

The coloured sheaths on new culms of *Fargesia rufa*.

Fargesia rufa with colourful sheathing on the branches.

are often fully developed by late spring (May) and a few later ones appearing in summer. It generates a prolific quantity of culms each year, and a young plant supplied as a division with five or six culms will have nearly ten times this number within three years. Its ability to regenerate from heavy thinning or hard pruning is also a likely reason why it is one of the feeding plants for the giant panda.

Mature plants are usually wider than they are tall and, although clumping, they move uniformly across the soil with reliable culm production and long-necked rhizomes. New culm sheaths are lightly tinged pale orange-red or shrimp pink. This coloration is often brighter on plants growing in containers or alkaline soil than on those in rich neutral or acid soil. The nodes and culm sheaths are similarly coloured. Foliage can be quite dark on plants that are well nourished but normally it is pale green, similar to *Fargesia murielae* 'Simba', and leaves point neatly down from the many branches at each node.

It is possible plants under this name are hybrids between *Fargesia dracocephala* and *F. rufa*, and the true *F. rufa* may not yet be in cultivation.

Uses

It provides a contrast to a tall bamboo. Plant in drifts in woodland clearings or mid border for winter structure. Use as a path edging or a low dividing hedge. Probably the best bamboo for a container; it fills the pot quickly and requires little maintenance except feeding, water and selective thinning.

Fargesia utilis

Hardiness: min. -18°C (0°F), zone 6
Aspect: sun or light shade.
Height: 4–6 m (13–20 ft.), average 4.5m (14.8 ft.)
Spread: 75 cm.–1.2 m (2.5–4 ft.) in 10 years, clumping.
Habit: tight at the base with a huge crown.
Culms: maximum diameter 2.5 cm. (1 in.), pale green darkening with age, very dark red in sun on young plants that are thinned.
Leaves: narrow, 9 x 1.5 cm. (4 x 0.6 in.), pale green

A mature plant is a sight to behold. Delicate branches cascading with fine greenery take the shape of a mushroom cloud caused by an atomic explosion. A young or even semi-mature plant shows no evidence of this, but has its own appeal. Young plants are less congested, and in sun the culms are a glowing claret red on their upper reaches. Occasionally culms will generate secondary branching, a characteristic of *Thamnocalamus*, which adds to the weight at the top. Culms are quite late in shooting. They are freely produced and have persistent straw-coloured sheaths. In its native Yunnan the tough flexible culms are matted to produce flooring.

Uses

Not recommended for a small garden because of its enormous crown. It needs a solitary position where its habit can be fully appreciated at distance. I have large plants in containers which are thinned regularly and they last well, confined and with little food. A few strong culms appear annually which arch lightly at the top and display the deep red colouring; they are always thin in leaf as the old culms are removed to prevent congestion.

Fargesia yulongshanensis

Hardiness: min. -29°C(-20°F), zone 5
Aspect: sun or light shade.
Height: 4–7 m (13–23 ft.), average 5 m (16.5 ft.)
Spread: 50 cm.–1.2 m (1.6–4 ft.) in 10 years, clumping.
Habit: tall and graceful with a delicate appearance.
Culms: maximum diameter 3 cm. (1.2 in.), a pale-blue bloom when young turning pale yellow-green with age.
Leaves: small and narrow, 6 x 0.5 cm. (2.4 x 0.2 in.), pale fresh green.

A mature specimen of *Fargesia utilis*.

Native to Yunnan Province in China, it grows at 3,050–4,200 m (10,000–13,800 ft.), the highest elevation for a Sino-Himalayan bamboo. Although scarce in cultivation it shows great promise because of its cold tolerance. The new culms initially resemble those of *Thamnocalamus crassinodus* cultivars and are covered with a waxy bloom after the sheaths have dropped. The ring of red-brown hairs sometimes visible at each node is a key to correct identification, but can be confused with the similar feature on *Borinda albocera*. Culm sheaths are also colourful with their tints of pink and purple. The leaves are small, narrow and relatively sparse, held high on the gracefully arching culms.

Unfortunately there are very few mature plants, so it is difficult to judge the ultimate shape and habit. There are also plants in the trade that carry this name but are in fact a different, unidentified species with similar looks and apparently quite hardy.

Uses

Well suited to parks and large gardens and tolerant of full exposure.

Newly emerged culm of *Fargesia yulongshanensis*.

xHibanobambusa

A bigeneric hybrid between *Phyllostachys nigra* f. *henonis* and *Sasa veitchii*, both of which flowered simultaneously on Mount Hiba in Japan at the beginning of the twentieth century. The genetic qualities of both parents are evident and combine to make a very distinct bamboo suitable for gardens. xHibanobambusa has a leptomorph rhizome system but without the rampant vigour of many *Sasa* species. The single branch per node, developing into two or three during following seasons, is also a character of *Sasa*. From *Phyllostachys* it inherits the grooved internodes and reliably stout culm structure. There is one species and one cultivar.

xHibanobambusa tranquillans

Hardiness: min. -22°C (-7°F), zone 6
Aspect: sun or half shade.
Height: 3–5 m (10–16.5 ft.), average 4 m (13 ft.)
Spread: 1–3 m (3.3–10 ft.) in 10 years, usually compact but some plants have well-spaced culms.
Habit: tidy dense bush, usually as wide as it is high.
Culms: maximum diameter 2 cm. (0.8n), green in all their parts, quite glossy.
Leaves: large and broad, 25 x 5 cm. (10 x 2 in.), fresh mid green.

It is difficult to predict the final habit of this bamboo. I have seen plants spread far and wide and those that are frustratingly slow and congested. It is extremely tolerant of dry soils, where the rhizomes are deep and difficult

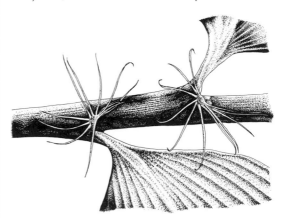

A branch section of *xHibanobambusa tranquillans*, showing the obvious oral setae.

to remove, and it does tend to spread more in these conditions. A plant that is well controlled by thinning and keeping it in check, forms a large rounded dome of lush greenery. The leaves rarely bleach, unlike *Sasa*, and reflect the light as they wave in the wind. In shape the leaves are more like those of *Sasa palmata* f. *nebulosa* than *S. veitchii*, its parent. It may need some control if planted in a border with other plants.

Uses

This is a bold landscape plant for open ground and good light. In a pot it looks floppy and unkempt, and the leaves can scorch at the first sign of water shortage. However, I have seen it grown successfully in large raised beds, where it forms a dense block of tidy foliage. Regular thinning is required in this situation to reduce congestion.

x Hibanobambusa tranquillans 'Shiroshima'

Hardiness: min. -22°C (-7°F), zone 6
Aspect: sun or half shade
Height: 2.5–5 m (8.2–16.5 ft., average 3.5 m (11.5 ft.)
Spread: 75 cm.–1.5 m (2.5–5 ft.) in 10 years, usually dense, occasionally well-spaced culms.
Habit: bold, often flat-topped dense bush.
Culms: maximum diameter 2 cm. (0.8 in.), pale green.
Leaves: large and pointed, brightly variegated, striped green and cream giving a silvery effect from a distance.

One of the loveliest, most versatile and weather-tolerant bamboos with the brightest leaves of any of the variegated bamboos, I cannot sing its praise enough. It looks good almost anywhere, and unlike many variegated woody plants it does not lose its stark colouring in shade. In general it is less vigorous than the species, however its habit is so variable according to its situation and growing conditions that it is impossible to predict its exact height or spread. I know of two plants in the same garden, one of which is well thinned and grows on quite moist soil with a deep gravel mulch. It is the best specimen I have seen and in keeping with the habit of a compact *Phyllostachys*. The other is almost uncontrollable and romps through anything in its path. It grows in the same soil but has its rhizomes heavily mulched with organic matter and is watered by seep-hose irrigation. This plant has provided me with good stock during many attempts to remove it, but with the

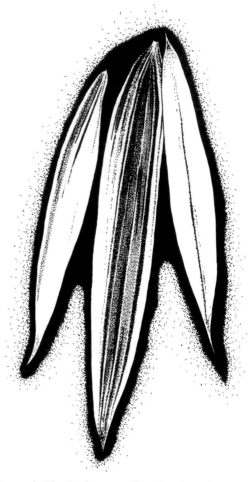

Leaves of ×*Hibanobambusa tranquillans* 'Shiroshima' showing variable amounts of variegation.

cheeky habit of a *Sasa*, it continues to appear in the garden where you least expect it.

In contrast a fifteen-year-old plant in very dry, flinty soil in Norfolk, England, covers an area over 8sq. m (26sq. ft.). It is short, with few culms exceeding 2 m (6.5 ft.), and has overtaken some sasas planted at the same time. My plant is the complete opposite. Only ten years old, it has culms reaching 5 m (16.5 ft.) and forms a compact clump nearly 2 m (6.5 ft.) wide with only a single wayward shoot escaping from the tight rhizome mass. This grows in quite moist, heavy clay and has never been disturbed or thinned, and looks better from a distance where its stature can be admired.

In a container 'Shiroshima' is usually shorter and brighter, and has the ability to survive for a year or two without extra food. However some leaf scorching can occur. I have found that the secondary branches that form from the original single branch at the node will cover any careful pruning; thus the plant can be shaped and thinned at leisure to provide a very fine specimen.

The bright green, strong culms are only a feature on tall plants; usually they are hidden by the mass of

New culm and sheath of ×*Hibanobambusa tranquillans* 'Shiroshima'; the culm sheath can often be variegated like the true leaf. Note the very bright blade at the end of the sheath.

An established clump of ×*Hibanobambusa tranquillans* 'Shiroshima' grows next to a very large *Chusquea gigantea*, with long overhanging primary branches.

pointed foliage. The bold cream-striped leaves vary considerably. Some are evenly striped and others have irregular markings with shades of green or cream dominating. As the whorls of new leaves form, the variegations spiral and can be tinted deep pink as they unfold in sunlight.

Uses

Try it by the side of a tall *Chusquea culeou* for a complete contrast in leaf, culm and habit. In a mixed border combine it with *Geranium* 'Johnson's Blue' for a vivid foreground of summer colour and red-stemmed dogwoods for winter spectacle. Quite by accident my plant is invaded by the white-stemmed winter bramble, *Rubus cockburnianus* 'Goldenvale', with soft yellow leaves in the summer. The dark red flowers of *Persicaria amplexicaulis* complete an unusual but worthwhile combination. There is also a fine specimen on the nursery which we use in many different planting themes at shows, usually in a bright blue or red ceramic pot, and it never fails to impress.

Indocalamus

A genus of twenty-six species from China and one from Japan, many of which, given their distribution in the wild, should be hardy in our gardens but only five of these species are available so far. The genus covers a broad area in China, growing as far north as Shaanxi Province, east to Shandong and Jiangsu, south through Sichuan and Hunan to Guangdong and coastal Hong Kong. Most grow at relatively low altitude, with only one or two species found above 1,000 m (3,280 ft.), and occur on low hillside slopes or as an understorey to broad-leaf forests.

The genus *Indocalamus* was originally grouped with *Sasa*, to which it has similarities, particularly in the broad leaves, small bushy stature and the few, but quite large branches. Nodes are less prominent than on *Sasa*

The veining on the large leaves of *Indocalamus* is very noticeable.

and give rise to a single branch except near the top of the culms, where there may be up to three, all of which can be as thick as the culms. The leaves of *Indocalamus* are more linear than those of *Sasa*, at least four or five times longer than wide. The leaves have a more polished appearance than *Sasa*, especially in winter, showing little or no bleaching at the tips and margins. All *Indocalamus* species are classed as spreading with leptomorph rhizomes but their habit is more refined than *Sasa* and I have seen some species stay within bounds for many years with no signs of aggression.

Their tropical appearance belies their cold hardiness and they grow well in most cool temperate gardens as long as they have some shade from burning sun.

Indocalamus hamadae

Hardiness: min. -20°C (-4°F), zone 6
Aspect: half shade.
Height: 2–5 m (6.5–16.5 ft., average 3 m (10 ft.)
Spread: 75 cm.–1.5 m (2.5–5 ft.) in 10 years, open, slightly running.
Habit: bold and erect with the leaves hanging down.
Culms: maximum diameter 1.5 cm. (0.6 in.), lustrous deep green in all its parts.
Leaves: long and narrow, to 60 x 8 cm. (2 ft. x 3 in.), deep glossy green.

Although properly classed as moderately invasive, this Japanese plant native to Kyushu rarely runs amok and is usually statuesque once established, with rigid culms and the largest leaves of any temperate bamboo. A young plant can take time to establish and will look ragged at first, but improves with age, particularly if older leaves and branches are removed together with any weak or old culms which tend to flop.

My plant grows in the dry shade of a walnut tree and after six years is only just beginning to earn its place in the garden. The massive leaves are developing as the plant gains strength and hang rigidly downwards as if hiding their undersides.

Uses

Plant with the shorter *Pleioblastus fortunei* at its base for contrasting leaf size and colour, or grow against a wall where the foliage will be framed by a plain background. Use the leaves in the traditional way for serving sushi, or for holding chicken drumsticks and ribs at a barbecue.

Indocalamus latifolius

Hardiness: min. -20°C (-4°F), zone 6
Aspect: light shade.
Height: 1.5–3 m (5–10 ft.), average 2 m (6.2 ft.)
Spread: 75 cm.–1.5 m (2.5–5 ft.) in 10 years, runs or clumps.
Habit: vertical and tidy with leaves splaying outwards.
Culms: maximum diameter 1 cm. (0.4 in.), green, new shoots often dark with red tints.
Leaves: long and narrow, 30 x 5 cm. (12 x 2 in.), deep glossy green.

Native mainly to the eastern provinces of China, this species is a good performer in temperate gardens. It has great presence even as a young plant and generates height and large glossy leaves quickly, eventually forming a bold, erect stand. It is likely to wander in a dry soil but where there is adequate moisture it tends not to stray as much. When the rhizomes do run, they to do so in long straight lines and are usually quite shallow. If they are not allowed to establish for too long these extensions can be pulled out of the soil and severed close to the main plant. Regular removal of escaping rhizomes will encourage more bud and culm formation around the main plant and with determination a strong tight clump can be created.

Uses

I have *Indocalamus latifolius* growing in a dark corner where it is well protected by two walls and, apart from a few old culms and leaves which should be thinned, it always looks very fresh. A matching pair would give a formal effect planted either side of an entrance gate. Plants could also be used to edge a large driveway.

Others

I have a form collected from a garden locally called *Indocalamus latifolius* 'Hopei'. Its original source has been forgotten, but may have been brought from Germany. It is distinct on account of the bright, ruby red stain on new shoots and darker leaf colour, the habit also appears shorter. I have no other reference to this name; however there are the Hubei and Hebei Provinces in China, and the name 'Hopei' could be a derivative of one or other. If it came from the Hebei Province, which is quite northerly, it would be a very hardy selection.

Indocalamus hamadae has the largest leaves of all the temperate bamboos.

Indocalamus solidus

Hardiness: min. -20˚C (-4˚F) zone 6
Aspect: sun or shade.
Height: 1–2.5 m (3.3–8.2 ft.), average 1.5 m (5 ft.)
Spread: 1–2.5 m (3.3–8.2 ft.) in 10 years, dense, evenly spreading.
Habit: rigid with leaves and branches held stiffly.
Culms: maximum diameter 1 cm. (0.4 in.), turn purple-grey in sun, pale sheaths.
Leaves: distinct in arrangement, 20 x 4 cm. (8 x 1.5 in.), matt green.

There is no reference to this in *A Compendium of Chinese Bamboo* (China Forestry Publishing House) and it could possibly be another species, *solidus* being descriptive of the thin, hard and solid culms. Some species of *Indocalamus* are widely distributed in China, often cultivated in the eastern provinces for making chopsticks and matting, and there are some that match the description for *I. solidus*, with its solid inflexible culms and regenerative habit, which make it suitable for cropping.

Plants sold under this name make fine ground cover, spreading evenly without being wildly invasive. The darker culm colouring and more rigid, sometimes horizontal, leaf arrangement gives it distinction from other known *Indocalamus* species. Occasionally the tips and margins of the leaves will bleach in a hard winter, this at least is done uniformly and can have an effect similar to that of the more invasive *Sasa veitchii*.

Uses

Useful in large-scale urban landscapes or parks because it can be strimmed to the ground every few years to tidy and freshen its appearance, and will grow back strongly. Also good planted as a lower level filler between trees, shrubs or other bamboos. It has proved to be very hardy in pots.

Others

Indocalamus longiauritus is a garden worthy, vigorous species of similar height with leaves more like those of *I. latifolius* but narrowly pointed and is reputedly more tolerant of sun.

Indocalamus tessellatus

Hardiness: min. -25˚C (-13˚F), zone 5
Aspect: sun or shade.
Height: 1–3 m (3.3–10 ft.), average 1.5 m (5 ft.)
Spread: 75 cm.–1.5 m (2.5–5 ft.) in 10 years, slowly spreading.
Habit: usually short and distinctly weeping.
Culms: maximum diameter 0.6 cm. (0.25 in.), thin and matt green with thin brown sheaths.
Leaves: very large, 45 x 8 cm. (18 x 3 in.), matt deep green.

This is by far the best bamboo to provide a tropical look in a cold garden. The large, sometimes twisted, heavily veined leaves weigh down the thin culms and form an impenetrable mop. The pale creamy green central vein and the new growth spiking through the previous year's foliage add substance to the broad greenery. There is usually some marginal leaf bleaching in winter and, if uniform, this is appealing. The older culms can be thinned out as new ones develop.

I have seen this plant in many gardens and rarely exceeding 1 m (3 ft.), which is by far the best height for viewing the foliage. The light casts shadows between the overlapping leaves and highlights the prominent veins.

The dark, lustrous leaves of *Indocalamus tessellatus*.

Uses

Used superbly at the Royal Horticultural Society's Garden, Rosemoor in Devon, England, where a fine clump is backed by a dramatic explosion of golden culms belonging to *Semiarundinaria yashadake* f. *kimmei*. *Indocalamus tessellatus* associates well with many plants including strong woody bamboos. For a contemporary look mix it with *Yucca gloriosa* and tall grasses such as *Miscanthus sinensis*. It grows well in pots as it is very cold tolerant, and can also be used successfully in cold conservatories.

Phyllostachys

Without doubt this is the most important genus for gardens, with the greatest variety and some of the most ornamental and versatile of bamboos. *Phyllostachys* are also an important commercial and cultural crop used worldwide. The woody culms are utilized in hundreds of products and crafts, and the new shoots of some species are eaten. Some species have been cultivated for cane and shoot production in China for centuries and their translocation through this vast country because of these qualities is now widespread.

The genus contains some of the most northerly cold-tolerant bamboos, particularly of those types that are noticeably woody and arborescent in structure. *Phyllostachys* are widely distributed throughout the temperate and semitropical zones in eastern Asia, with the majority from lowland eastern China. They are adapted to the hot summers and cold winters of continental influence but do relocate well in other climes. In the Azores, *Phyllostachys aurea* is profuse and grows with such vigour that it marches across the hillsides, whereas in eastern England it is one of the tightest clumping species.

The key identification feature of *Phyllostachys* is the indented sulcus, or groove, that runs longitudinally down each culm internode on alternate sides. This characteristic is

Some of the culms of *Phyllostachys* can be distorted or have congested internodes. This example is *Phyllostachys aurea* 'Holochrysa'.

Phyllostachys produce strong and often colourful culms; this is *Phyllostachys bambusoides* 'Allgold'.

also seen on the larger branches and occasionally on large rhizome pieces. ×*Hibanobambusa* and some *Semiarundinaria* species also have this trait but are easily distinguished from *Phyllostachys* by other features. *Phyllostachys* usually have two branches per node, one stronger than the other. Nodes on many species are often pronounced with a waxy bloom or a scar where the culm sheath was attached. On very thick culms there is often an absence of branches low down and this results in the lack of a sulcus, which confuses identification. However, most very thick culms in temperate gardens belong to *Phyllostachys*, which should allay any doubts. The sheaths that protect the emerging culms are shed very quickly as the culms rise and harden, leaving them clean.

"Shooting time", or emergence of new culms, is a revered phenomenon in the circle of bamboo enthusiasts and with *Phyllostachys* provides a long period of delight, all summer in fact. Some species shoot very early, usually in mid spring, such as *P. aureosulcata*, *P. bissetii* and *P. nuda*. Others shoot very late, *P. bamusoides* and *P. sulphurea* are examples, with many more in between times. The natural habitat has some bearing on the time different species initiate their shoots: the early developers usually come from higher latitudes than those which shoot later in the year. This aspect of latitude also reflects on the speed of maturity of one species against another, and on potential culm thickness. For example, *P. aureosulcata* types come from the more northerly provinces in China, will mature quickly but never have extraordinarily thick culms, but annual culm production is plentiful. In contrast *P. bambusoides* is from much further south and shows great variation, extending well into the semitropical zone. It shoots much later in temperate gardens, producing fewer culms, but eventually much thicker and of greater height.

Most species are from the provinces that either surround the Yangtze River or are further north. *Phyllostachys bambusoides* and *P. sulphurea* occur south of this region although they have been cultivated further north. Do not be deterred by this; the more southerly species are some of the most impressive and are perfectly hardy, they just may take longer to mature in a cool temperate garden.

Identification of many species is still fraught with difficulty, especially between the many green forms, which may be distinct in their native environment but in temperate gardens develop a more refined habit and appear similar. The new shoots and culm sheaths, with their unique colouring, patterns and structure, play an important part in the correct identification of a plant. Some botanical knowledge is necessary to identify the oral setae, ligules, auricles and culm sheath blades, and a good magnifying glass is essential.

Leaves of *Phyllostachys* are lanceolate, with a fine point and noticeably tessellated. They vary in size according to the species but always have the same shape and are nearly always five to seven times longer than

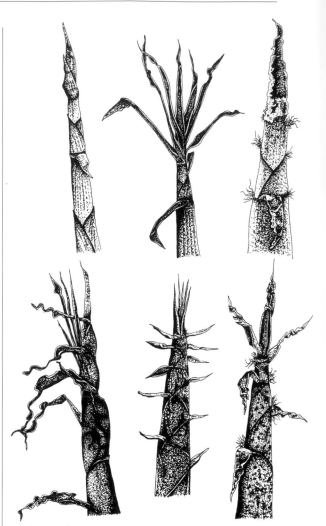

A selection of *Phyllostachys* shoots, clockwise from top left: *P. mannii* 'Mannii', *P. glauca*, *P. dulcis*, *P. praecox*, *P. edulis*, and *P. nigella*.

they are wide. Young plants tend to have larger leaves than mature plants, and leaves are often larger towards the base of the branches.

The metamorphosis of a young nursery plant into a mature specimen varies according to species and all the variables of aspect and climate, but the emergence of a new shoot and its development is a vision to behold, and is, without doubt, the main reason to grow a *Phyllostachys*.

Growth habits of individual *Phyllostachys* also vary widely, but all are arborescent, with mighty stature, good culm colour, elegance in leaf and branch, and truly evergreen. In areas with long warm summers and some moisture they can show their true leptomorph habit, with large well-spaced and rapidly developing culms. This open, almost forest-like habit, is typical of their development in their Chinese homeland. However, in colder areas with shorter summers they are usually better behaved, and form tight clumps with good culm colour and foliage held high, providing some of the most exciting bamboos to grow in temperate gardens.

For this large genus, where the form or cultivar is similar to the species it is described under "Others" at the end of each description. Cultivars that merit particular attention are described individually, in a separate entry.

Phyllostachys acuta

Hardiness: min. -18˚C (0˚F), zone 6
Aspect: sun or light shade.
Height: 4–8.5 m (13–28 ft.), average 6 m (20 ft.)
Spread: 1–2 m (3.3–6.5 ft.) in 10 years, open, but usually clumping.
Habit: bold and vertical.
Culms: maximum diameter 6 cm. (2.4 in.), dark green when young paling to yellow-green with age.
Leaves: medium, 10 x 2 cm. (4 x 0.75 in.), green.

Introduced to the United States from Zhejiang Province, China, in 1984, it is not known in Europe. The specific name refers to the sharp pointed new shoots. The emerging culms are enclosed by burnished green sheaths, edged and blotched with dark brown. As they develop the young culms are dark, fresh green with purple-tinted nodes. Older culms fade with age to a pale yellow-green. This species is harvested for bamboo shoots in China.

Uses

Essentially a collector's item, unless you can distinguish the taste of one bamboo shoot from another. The new shoots look quite colourful but could prove painful if you meditate next to this plant at shooting time.

Phyllostachys angusta

Hardiness: min. -25˚C (-13˚F), zone 5
Aspect: sun or light shade.
Height: 3.5–6.5 m (11.5–21.3 ft.), average 4.5 m (14.8 ft.)
Spread: 75 cm.–1 m (2.5–3.3 ft.) in 10 years, usually clumping.
Habit: tidy and rigid at first, more arching when mature.
Culms: maximum diameter 3 cm. (1.2 in.), greyish culms, very pale sheaths.
Leaves: narrow and long in proportion, 15 x 2 cm. (6 x 0.75 in.), green.

Typical formation of *Phyllostachys* leaves on *P. vivax*, with the early morning sun casting crisp shadows from behind.

This species is wrongly given the common name of stone bamboo, correctly applied to *Phyllostachys nuda* because of its hard, thick-walled culms. *Phyllostachys angusta* is usually quite compact and rigid in habit until it decides to mature and then the taller shoots will have greater flexibility. It is a very pale bamboo in general appearance, with older grey culms and bright whitish, blue-purple veined sheaths covering the new shoots. *Angusta* means narrow, and refers to the width at the apex of the culm sheath and its parts. The rigid culms also have short branches and, therefore, narrow crowns of foliage.

The distribution is along the eastern seaboard provinces of Fujian, Jiangsu and Zhejiang, but *Phyllostachys angusta* is also cultivated further inland for cane production. In addition, this edible species is used in weaving and for fishing rods.

Uses
It contrasts well with other dark green bamboos, such as *Phyllostachys bissetii*.

Phyllostachys arcana

Hardiness: min. -20°C (-4°F), zone 6
Aspect: sun or light shade.
Height: 4–8 m (13–26 ft.), average 5 m (16.5 ft.)
Spread: 1–2.5 m (3.3–8.2 ft.) in 10 years, usually an open grove.
Habit: very variable, but usually tidy.
Culms: maximum diameter 4 cm. (1.6 in.), green and powdery at first and then grey-green, occasionally with black spots in sunlight.
Leaves: narrow, 15 x 2 cm. (6 x 0.75 in.), green.

Most plants I know of this species are quite congested and lack maturity. However in warmer gardens it has the capacity to grow tall with well-spaced culms. Culm sheaths are yellow-grey with purple-brown longitudinal striae and the shoots emerge fresh green with powdery rings below the prominent nodes. Old culms age to grey-green and are sometimes flecked with black spots in full sun. Branch buds on the lower nodes are mostly dormant so the foliage is held high, showing the new culms and shoots to good effect.

Uses
The strong culms are good for cutting and make useful garden canes; in China they are split and used for weaving mats. Overall it is pale so plant it against a dark background.

Others

Phyllostachys arcana 'Luteosulcata' is a golden grooved cultivar of greater ornamental value than the species. In my garden it lightens up the shade cast by a Scots pine. It has started to spread after only a few years because of its dry aspect, but is providing good stock.

Phyllostachys arcana 'Luteosulcata' is often underrated but has good culm colour.

Phyllostachys atrovaginata

Hardiness: min. -22°C (-8°F), zone 6
Aspect: sun or light shade.
Height: 5–8 m (16.5–26 ft.), average 6 m (20 ft.)
Spread: 1–2.5 m (3.3–8.2 ft.) in 10 years, open but evenly spaced.
Habit: thick tapering culms with narrow columns of foliage.
Culms: maximum diameter 6 cm. (2.4 in.), deep green ageing to grey-green.
Leaves: 12 x 1.5 cm. (5 x 0.6 in.), green.

This green *Phyllostachys* with its unique habit has always been a favourite of mine. A quick developer from a young plant, the eventually very thick culms taper rapidly towards the top making the whole plant appear short for its girth. New culms are a lush green, and pale to a matt, creamy grey-green with occasional rusty tints in full sun. The mostly high branches are sharply ascending, splaying slightly from the culm, so a plant with well-spaced culms resembles a series of congested columns; for this reason its previous name of *Phyllostachys congesta* was very apt.

This species has an adaptation for growing in wet or boggy conditions, with air canals present in the rhizomes and roots. It also emits a sandalwood-like scent from the new culms, particularly when they are touched, and has the common name of incense bamboo in the United States.

Uses

A fine selection for landscaping because it matures at great speed with a very individual habit. It is best planted in isolation so its form can be appreciated from afar. This bamboo is a good choice for boggy ground.

Phyllostachys aurea

Hardiness: min. -20°C (-4°F), zone 6
Aspect: full sun.
Height: 4–8 m (13–26 ft.), average 6 m (20 ft.)
Spread: 1–3 m (3.3–10 ft.) in 10 years, clumps or runs.
Habit: bold and vertical with a mass of high foliage.

Culms: maximum diameter 4.5 cm. (1.75 in.) often with congested internodes at the base, bright green ageing to a pale creamy yellow-grey.
Leaves: 13 x 2 cm. (5 x 0.75 in.), pea green.

Well known and widespread in cultivation, this is a very variable species. In cold areas it grows congested and tight, while in very warm areas it is almost rampant. Its main requirement is full light, as it grows weakly in shade and prefers to dominate its surroundings.

As one of the best examples of how a bamboo species can vary from one place to the next I will compare *P. aurea* in the Azores with the one in my garden. This bamboo was introduced to the Azores, either for ornamental purposes or cane production, and has escaped, possibly from a previous flowering and seeding. Whatever the reason for its introduction, it billows dramatically forming huge forests rampaging up the hillsides. In complete contrast the *P. aurea* in my garden is such a tight clump that it is impossible to put a spade between the culms to divide it. The width at the base is less than 1 m (3 ft.), yet it stands proud at nearly 6 m (19.5 ft.) and is very stately with a dense V-shaped habit. It is not so rigid as to be unmoving and does wave in the wind.

Golden bamboo is the most misused common name for this species, which is correctly known as fish-pole bamboo, on account of its usage as fishing rods and walking sticks in China and Japan. The bamboo is essentially a very lush green all over and only paling to yellow with age or starvation. (I have seen plants shown at exhibitions that are almost pure yellow in leaf with very pale culms; this is as a result of starvation in pots and they looked very lacklustre.) A mature plant has a profusion of culms that are congested at the base as if they have been concertinaed together, producing misshapen nodes and swelling; also there is a pronounced swelling below each node. The congested section of culm is very woody and makes a useful grip on a fishing rod or handle for a walking stick. Other traits of this bamboo are the very pronounced grooves, or sulci, along the internodes and persistent sheaths at the very base of many of the culms. The foliage is light

Congested internodes on a culm of *Phyllostachys aurea*.

and airy on young culms becoming denser with age, which produces the elegant crown. It is referred to in some parts of the east as *hotei-chiku*, the bamboo of fairyland, but I prefer the direct translation of *taibo-chiku* which means phoenix bamboo because it does rise from the ground and hold itself high with great dignity.

Uses

Makes a fine individual specimen and mine greets all visitors at the gate with its proud stance; low horizontal black fencing frames the base of the culms. *Phyllostachys aurea* is especially suited to a minimalist setting, combined with a few boulders or uncluttered architecture. Place it in pots at your peril as it will soon starve and become top heavy; better to use a very broad shallow container for stability and feed heavily once established.

Others

Phyllostachys aurea 'Flavescens Inversa' has pale green culms with golden sulci. It is a slow, tight, remarkably congested plant in my garden and does not reward. It grows in the shadow of a large weeping willow and although this cultivar is more tolerant of shade than the species, I think lighter shade would be preferred. However, I have seen many fine specimens, mostly all tight in habit with good culm structure and colour. Some lower branch pruning is required to appreciate the culms and, as with all *P. aurea* cultivars, it produces the crowded nodes at the base of some culms.

Phyllostachys aurea f. *takemurai* is only known in the United States as far as I am aware. It is reputed to be more vigorous but lacks the compressed internodes of the other forms. I have a plant named *P. aurea* f. *formosana* which may well be the same.

Phyllostachys aurea 'Variegata' (syn. 'Albovariegata') had delicately marked variegated leaves, and a short stout habit. Unfortunately all plants have flowered and died, and the resulting seedlings always form all-green plants; a great shame as this cultivar was quite breathtaking with its subtle cast of silvery white.

Phyllostachys aurea 'Holochrysa'

Hardiness: min. -20°C (-4°F), zone 6
Aspect: sun or very light shade.
Height: 3.5–6 m (11.5–20 ft.), average 4 m (13 ft.)
Spread: 1–1.5 m (3.3–5 ft.) in 10 years, usually clumping.
Habit: tidy V-shape, with a good head of foliage.
Culms: maximum diameter 4 cm. (1.5 in.), butter yellow becoming more vivid in direct sunlight.
Leaves: 13 x 2 cm. (5 x 0.75 in.), pea green.

Worthy of individual mention because this cultivar has reliable golden culms and is the true golden form of *Phyllostachys aurea,* the badly named golden bamboo. ('Holochrysa' is sometimes called golden golden bamboo.)

New culms are a pale, bloomy turquoise-green, those of previous years are butter yellow, while some of the oldest culms are a rich rust stained old gold. The various culm colours combine well in a tidy plant of great ornamental value. The tidiness is partly due to the very rigid and uniform branch structure, but unfortunately the lower part of the culms have few dormant buds and the low branches produced will need to be pruned after leafing so the colourful culms can be appreciated.

Generally this bamboo forms a tight V shape, and is shorter than the species. My plant has this refined appearance, spreads very little and is extremely colourful in full sun, but is young at ten years. I have seen a few plants well over twenty years old and these are quite stately, more vertical and with greater height, with an occasional running rhizome forming a new clump a short distance away. All the very large plants I have seen lack the bold colouring this plant is capable of and I believe it is better suited to a cold and dry climate where culm colouring will be more vivid.

Uses

When it is short and compact it makes a fine accent on the corner of a border or at the centre of a raised bed. I have some impressive specimens in pots; with a little thinning and branch removal, they become an art form.

New culms of *Phyllostachys aurea* 'Holochrysa' emerge blue-green before turning butter yellow.

Phyllostachys aurea 'Koi'

Hardiness: min. -20°C (-4°F), zone 6
Aspect: sun or light shade.
Height: 3–6 m (10–20 ft.), average 4 m (13 ft.)
Spread: 75 cm.–1.5 m (2.5–5 ft.) in 10 years, usually tight clumping.
Habit: usually short, rigid cone-shape.
Culms: maximum diameter 3.5 cm. (1.4 in.), yellow with a soft green sulcus.
Leaves: 13 x 2 cm. (5 x 0.75 in.), pale green often with a slim white stripe.

Phyllostachys aurea 'Koi' in close up.

Phyllostachys aurea 'Koi'.

One of my favourite bamboos and well suited to a cold dry eastern England climate. My plant is at the edge of the garden facing the northeasterly winter winds blowing across open fields. Its exposed position has prevented it from reaching much above 3 m (10 ft.). Its slow, but sturdy, development has been a delight over twelve years, never producing any weak or floppy growth, and is always tidy, with robust culms that taper abruptly towards the tip. New culms emerge blue-green and take most of the first growing season to change to a pale butter-yellow with a wash of pale green in the internodal grooves. Older culms turn a richer gold in time but at this point may need removing as the branches start to die out. Regular thinning of culms and low branches is essential to prevent congestion and aesthetically improve the appearance of plant. Light shade is advised as full sun can bleach the green of the sulcus, although the yellow culms will be richer in colour.

Uses

In colder areas this is a fine plant for containers but it does have a very top heavy cone shape so choose a broad, shallow pot. It should be viewed as an individual specimen, so do not let taller plants compete with it too closely. Plant it in front of a dark background, in front of a wooded or other shady area where the midday sun cannot reach, but keep it clear of overhanging branches.

Phyllostachys aureosulcata marching across a light, woodland floor. This habit is usually only seen on very dry soils, where the bamboo travels in search of moisture.

Phyllostachys aureosulcata

Hardiness: min. -26˚C (-15˚F), zone 5
Aspect: sun or half shade.
Height: 4–9 m (13–30 ft.), average 6 m (20 ft.)
Spread: 1.2–3 m (4–10 ft.) in 10 years, evenly spreading.
Habit: vertical when mature, vase shaped when juvenile.
Culms: maximum diameter 4 cm. (1.6 in.), matt green with soft yellow sulci.
Leaves: long and narrow, 17 x 1.5 cm. (6.5 x 0.6 in.), darker green than most Phyllostachys species.

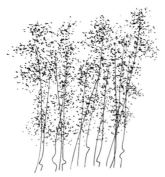

Grown widely in the United States for some time, it is a relatively recent introduction to Europe. It is native to the cold eastern provinces around Beijing in China and has proved itself to be one of the more cold hardy bamboos. As with many plants tolerant of extreme cold it can have a completely different appearance in warmer areas. The heights listed are attained in a temperate garden but in the south of France, in a Mediterranean climate or Californian type of climate, *P. aureosulcata* easily exceeds 15 m (49 ft.). It usually tends towards a roaming habit in very warm areas, but plants in a cold exposed garden in the north of England, rarely move beyond the tight clump of a juvenile plant. Most plants in relatively dry and cold areas also remain quite compact, but there are examples of this species growing in dry sandy soil that stroll across the ground in straight lines looking for moisture. There is no reliable method of predicting the spread so it would be wise to consider it as a well-behaved runner.

One of the most outstanding features of this species and its variants is the geniculation (crookedness or zigzagging) on the lower sections of some culms that can be well pronounced. New culms emerge vertically and then some bend sharply outwards, usually for a day or two, before turning in the opposite direction and finally to vertical again. There is no explanation for this phenomenon.

New, dark green culms with bright yellow sulci emerge from colourful sheaths that are pink tinted, pale green with creamy streaks. Culms are rough to the touch for the first year with a coarse pigskin texture but they become smoother with age and paler in colour. Foliage is always dark, lush and plentiful, held evenly on a short and rigid branch complement. Congested juvenile plants can get top heavy, particularly in the rain, as culms are thin at this stage and arch annoyingly, requiring some attention in the form of thinning or tying in to other more rigid culms. However once the plant has sight of maturity it does put on vertical culms with more strength and, as soon as there is a dominance of these, all the old juvenile culms can be removed completely. It shoots very early in the year, indicative of its northerly latitude in the wild.

Uses

Ideally suited as a boundary hedge or screen where, with luck, the lines of culms will go the way you want. A light background or free-standing position will show off the zigzag culms to best effect.

Others

Phyllostachys aureosulcata f. *pekinensis* is a vigorous cultivar with green culms lacking any colouring in the sulcus. It is vertical in habit and the kinks in the canes are usually abundant; it also has a tendency to spread in long straight lines.

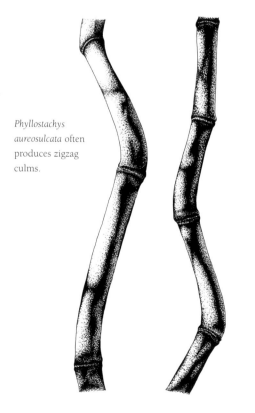

Phyllostachys aureosulcata often produces zigzag culms.

New culm of *Phyllostachys aureosulcata*; note the colourful sheath and the yellow sulcus beginning to form.

Phyllostachys aureosulcata f. aureocaulis

Hardiness: min. -26°C (-15° F), zone 5
Aspect: sun or light shade.
Height: 4–7.5 m (13–24.6 ft.), average 5 m (16.5 ft.)
Spread: 1 cm.–2m (4–10 ft.) in 10 years, loose clumps.
Habit: tidy, quite rigid, rarely a nuisance.
Culms: maximum diameter 4 cm. (1.6 in.), golden often tinted red.
Leaves: 17 x 1.5 cm. (6.5 x 0.6 in.), fresh green, occasionally thinly striped yellow.

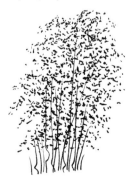

A strong shoot emerging from a small plant of *Phyllostachys aureosulcata* f. *aureocaulis*.

This very elegant bamboo is usually referred to as the golden crookstem which describes it adequately. The culms are indeed golden but can also be tinted a deep crimson-red, especially on the sunny side of new growth. Cold nights during the growing season and late in the summer can also enhance the reddening, so much so that a single culm can be bright red on one side and pure golden on the other. On some of the lower internodes sporadic green striping may develop, usually on the rounded part of the culm and not in the sulcus. The culms can also geniculate, or zigzag, although not as prolifically on this form as some of the others. New culms emerge a ghostly creamy yellow, in striking contrast to the darker older culms.

In cooler regions with shorter summers this bamboo rarely has the vigour of the species and can be trusted to behave, confining itself to its planting area and not wandering afar. *Phyllostachys aureosulcata* f. *aureocaulis* is perhaps the most versatile of bamboos with golden culms, tolerating just about any aspect or region. Customers from the east of Scotland speak highly of its cold hardiness, tidy manner, speedy growth to maturity and its ability to lift the gloom of a grey misty day.

Uses

Performs well almost anywhere, and should always be in full view and never crowded. The bright culms show well against a dark wall or fence. A low carpet of dark ivy (*Hedera*), blue periwinkle (*Vinca minor*) or spreading juniper around the base of the canes will give you all-year-round pleasure.

Others

Phyllostachys aureosulcata 'Lama Tempel' is a refined cultivar, still very rare, similar to f. *aureocaulis* but with a richer golden, more burnished culm colour. New shoots have much paler pink colouring than other golden forms of this species. Green striae are more prevalent on the lower internodes and the culms are generally stocky, making a shorter plant. There is an abundance of foliage held high because of the congestion of branches formed by the rapidly tapering culms. I have seen a mature plant growing alongside *P. aureosulcata* f. *aureocaulis* and it is quite different.

Phyllostachys aureosulcata 'Lama Tempel'.

Phyllostachys aureosulcata 'Harbin'

Hardiness: min. -26˚C (-15˚F), zone 5
Aspect: sun or light shade.
Height: 3–7.5 m (10–24.6 ft.), average 5 m (16.5 ft.)
Spread: 75 cm.–1.5 m (2.5–5 ft.) in 10 years,
usually clumping.
Habit: tight, tidy and vertical.
Culms: maximum diameter 4.5 cm. (1.75 in.),
evenly striped green and yellow.
Leaves: 17 x 1.5 cm. (6.5 x 0.6 in.), mid green.

The culms are distinct from other forms of *P. aureosulcata* in having longitudinal ridges as well as a grooved sulcus. The culm colour is confusing with irregular striping of yellow and green, with green often the dominant colour. For identification purposes the combined striping and ridging is unique among the temperate species.

This bamboo is quite rare in cultivation, particularly in Europe, as it is difficult to propagate either from open ground or from young nursery plants. It will grow strongly in warmer areas, but its reluctance to grow in the colder climate is no reflection on its hardiness.

Uses

Although a collector's item and difficult to obtain, it is worthy of good placement because of its unusual culm structure; close to the house would be ideal.

Others

Phyllostachys aureosulcata 'Harbin Inversa' is even more desirable than 'Harbin', and just as difficult and rare. The grooving is similar but less obvious because the culms are predominantly yellow with a multitude of thin green stripes. There are often orange and pink tints to the culms in full sun and these vivid colour combinations make it much sought-after. Leaves can sometimes have subtle streaks of cream and yellow.

Phyllostachys aureosulcata 'Harbin'.

Contrasting culm sheaths of *Phyllostachys aureosulcata* 'Harbin Inversa'.

Phyllostachys aureosulcata f. spectabilis

Hardiness: min. -26˚C (-15˚F), zone 5
Aspect: sun or light shade.
Height: 4–9 m (13–30 ft.), average 6 m (20 ft.)
Spread: 1–3 m (3.3–10 ft.) in 10 years, open, but clumping.
Habit: bold and tidy, vertical culms when mature.
Culms: maximum diameter 4.5 cm. (1.75 in.), bright golden yellow with dark green sulci.
Leaves: 17 x 1.5 cm. (6.5 x 0.6 in.), deep green, some with faint variegation.

The striping on the rare *Phyllostachys aureosulcata* 'Harbin Inversa'.

New culms of *Phyllostachys aureosulcata* f. *spectabilis* are often tinted red.

It is difficult to convey in words the beauty of this bamboo. Suffice to say that if I was limited to one bamboo I would not take the rare, the difficult or the most expensive, I would take the most rewarding, which this bamboo surely is.

The contrast between the vivid custard yellow culms and the dark green sulci is more pronounced than on any other temperate bamboo. New culms are paler,

bloomy below the nodes and frequently pink or copper tinged as they emerge from the pink-and-green-striped culm sheaths. Branches on young culms can also tint red or pink in the sun. Zigzag culms are frequent, adding to the ornamental value and, in keeping with the species, it is early to shoot and reliable in production. The dark and glossy leaves have occasional splashes of creamy variegation and they are glaucous on the undersides, offering a two-tone effect when fluttering in a breeze.

A young plant can be bushy and congested for a few years and then, during a season of its own choosing, it will produce vertical culms twice as thick and tall as maturity is reached. At this point it can spread to make a respectable open grove but without taking on monstrous proportions, after a few more years much of the older, bushy juvenile structure can be removed. The transformation of the plant in my garden from juvenile to adult was so speedy and dramatic that it leapt unchallenged to the top of my all-time best-bamboo list.

Phyllostachys aureosulcata f. *spectabilis* is widely planted and shows great variation in habit and height according to climate and aspect. It responds well to warmth and grows much more vigorously than in cold or exposed areas, where it takes longer to mature. It is always a good performer but I believe it shows better

The regular striping on *Phyllostachys aureosulcata* 'Argus'.

Phyllostachys aureosulcata f. *spectabilis* showing the brightness of its culms in the sunlight.

colour in an open quite harsh aspect. In an exposed situation on acid soil in a garden near to mine the wind has successfully restricted its height to no more than 3 m (10 ft.) and it has formed a dense colony, wider than high but still compact. The culm colour and gloss of the dark foliage belie its bleak location.

Uses

A versatile and essential bamboo, so do not hide it. I have it growing against a dark background with young culms of *Pleioblastus shibuyanus* 'Tsuboi' romping around it. After my initial reaction to remove a competitor, I decided the variegation of the *Pleioblastus* makes a pleasing contrast so for now it remains, but in a controlled manner.

Others

Phyllostachys aureosulcata 'Argus' is a new offering found as a rogue among a batch of imported *P. aureosulcata* f. *spectabilis* from China by Michael Brisbane. He was persuaded to part with this plant at a carefully calculated moment of weakness, when the pressure of daily nursery business was foremost in his mind. An empty wallet later (mine of course), it was in my sole possession with the promise made that he would be able to visit my newly adopted subject by appointment only.

The yellow culms are striped green with longitudinal striae and the sulcus remains green. It combines the robust qualities of the species with the desirable colouring of the frustrating *P. aureosulcata* 'Harbin Inversa', with similar striping and occasional pink colouring. Production is going well and plants should be available soon.

Phyllostachys bambusoides

Hardiness: min. -18°C (0°F), zone 6
Aspect: sun or light shade.
Height: 6–20 m (20–65 ft.), average 8 m (26 ft.)
Spread: 1–4 m (3.3–13 ft.) in 10 years, open grove but well behaved.
Habit: very bold with foliage arching the culm tips.
Culms: maximum diameter 15 cm. (6 in.), bright lustrous green.
Leaves: large for a Phyllostachys, particularly at branch tips and on immature plants, 19 x 3.5 cm. (7 x 1.4 in.), bright lustrous green.

This is the archetypal bamboo of ancient drawings, with stout vertical culms and long rigid branches supporting layers of leaves that angle perfectly on long stalks to catch the light. The giant timber bamboo, as it is known, covers a great swathe of China from Hebei in the north to

Guangdong in the south, from Yunnan in the west to Fujian in the east, and is used widely throughout. It has also been naturalized in Japan where it is equally revered and used in construction.

In southwest England, *Phyllostachys bambusoides* reaches over 14 m (46 ft.) but rarely exceeds 6 m (20 ft.) in the colder north and east. The culms are glossy green emerging from pale buff-red sheaths and the branches are long and rigid, holding the leaves evenly and with some grace. The life expectancy of an individual culm is said to be between twenty-five and thirty-five years, much longer than for any other hardy bamboo.

For those who garden in very cool areas with short summers plants will take time to reach their potential and may never mature into the giants of warmer regions. They are perfectly hardy, and show good colour and form, but are slow to develop in less favourable climates where they rarely produce the thick culms they are capable of. (If culm girth is your desire and forms of *Phyllostachys bambusoides* have proved frustrating, then try *P. vivax* and its cultivars, or *P. nigra* f. *henonis* or *P. iridescens*. For speed and equal ornamental value but never thick culms, the forms of *P. aureosulcata* will give reward.)

In my garden in the east of England I find most forms, once established, have good vigour and individuality but do not show their exuberant nature as they would further south or west. A few thick culms shoot late in the season and these just manage to leaf before the onset of winter. Culms that are not mature in leaf rarely survive the cold season unscathed. The older the plant, the more chance the culms have of maturing in the short growing season.

During a short humid summer, *Phyllostachys bambusoides* and some of its forms may suffer aphid attack, and the sticky secretions attract dust and dirt which make the leaves look unsightly. No harm is done to the plant and it is washed clean by the autumn rain. It is also common to see an army of ants marching along the culms to feed off the aphids. However, do protect newly acquired plants from infestation with an occasional high pressure blast of cold water or a spray of light oil or insecticidal soap, so the leaves do not blacken and prevent the intake of energy from the sunlight.

Uses

This all-green species offers much character to a garden structure such as a timber gazebo when planted close by or, more frivolously, through the struts of a pergola. You will need no other plant; just add some gravel, a rock or two, and a hammock in which to dream of another world.

Others

Phyllostachys bambusoides 'Slender Crookstem' and 'White Crookstem' are little known in Europe and rare in the United States. Both have geniculated culms on the lower internodes but they are gently curving, rather than the sharply angled *P. aureosulcata* forms. Both have narrower culms than the species but those of 'White Crookstem' have a persistent white powder which can provide ornamental value to the appearance of some culms.

Phyllostachys bambusoides 'Allgold' (syn. *'Holochrysa'*)

Hardiness: min. -15°C (5°F), zone 7
Aspect: sun or light shade.
Height: 4–9 m (13–39 ft.), average 6 m (20 ft.)
Spread: 1–3 m (3.3–10 ft.) in 10 years, open, but clumping.
Habit: V-shaped at first, more vertical with age.
Culms: maximum diameter 6 cm. (2.4 in.), deep orange-gold.
Leaves: 15 x 3.5 cm. (6 x 1.4 in.), rich green.

I admit to the correct name of *Phyllostachys bambusoides* 'Holochrysa' but am compelled to call it 'Allgold' as it is known in the United States. It is distinct from *P. aurea* 'Holochrysa' but similar in name, which is confusing to the uninitiated.

The almost translucent orange culm colouring acts like a homing beacon for visitors to the nursery. Compared to my plant in the garden that is in full sun, the nursery plants always appear deeper in colour. I believe this is because of the very light shade they are grown under and the bold colouring of the culms brightens the darker surroundings. My garden plant used to grow in some shade but the low lying area it inhabited flooded and it had to be moved to higher ground to recover. I might add that it had been standing in water, which covered the base of the culms, for nearly five months and was still alive; most other garden plants would have given up long before. The recovering plant has lost some of its sheen but is progressing well.

Occasional faint green striping appears as if it has been brushed on to the culms, and some of the leaves also exhibit a creamy streak. It has a very refined and clean appearance requiring little management apart from the removal of lower branches on very young plants. *Phyllostachys bambusoides* 'Allgold' is unequalled in colour and should certainly be sought after, regardless of your location.

Deep golden culms of *Phyllostachys bambusoides* 'Allgold'.

Phyllostachys bambusoides 'Allgold' shows the contrast between its culm and leaf colouring.

Uses

It will brighten up the dullest of areas, particularly in light woodland or against dense green backgrounds. Try planting a deep red *Clematis viticella* at distance, where it has its own moisture, and direct it annually to scramble through the culms and high branches. A late-flowering blue clematis or possibly some fast growing annual climbers would also work well.

Phyllostachys bambusoides 'Castillonis'

Hardiness: min. -18˚C (0˚F), zone 6
Aspect: sun or light shade.
Height: 4–10 m (13–22 ft.), average 6 m (20 ft.)
Spread: 75 cm.–2m in 10 years, usually clumping.
Habit: tidy and impressive, almost vertical.
Culms: maximum diameter 6.5 cm. (2.5 in.), bright golden with green sulci.
Leaves: 15 x 3.5cm. (6 x 1.4 in.), pale green with some faint creamy striping.

'Castillonis' was the first *bambusoides* cultivar in my once windswept garden. It took time to establish and now stands proud at 6 m (20 ft.) on the point of a border central to the garden, dominating its surroundings. New culms are very bright butter yellow, which darkens through hardening, and the green striping in the sulcus is very broad and obvious from some distance. Culms are well spaced but still form a compact, slightly V-shaped plant, with only one culm in its fifteen-year existence departing outwards and underground. Habits can vary from place to place, for I know of plants only slightly older than mine growing vertical with very well-spaced culms. Foliage is always pale on my plant and there may be a nutrient deficiency due to the dense *Hedera helix* 'Ivalace' growing through and around the base of the plant. The mat of ivy prevents old leaves and sheaths from filtering to the ground, to rot down and provide necessary food. However, the paleness contrasts well with many of the darker background bamboos.

Between one and three culms are produced on my specimen each year and I remove one or two for exhibition use, so it is well balanced. Compare this to *Phyllostachys. aureosulcata* f. *spectabilis*, of similar colouring and slightly younger, which produces between ten and twenty culms a year, and it is easy to relate to the differences between the two species and their native habitat. *Phyllostachys bambusoides* types come from further south in China than *P. aureosulcata*, are used to longer warmer summers than the average temperate garden can offer, so they shoot late and culm production is sparse. The more northerly *P. aureosulcata* forms have a shorter summer, in keeping with our temperate climate, and shoot earlier and are more productive in consequence.

I have seen some fine example of 'Castillonis' in Scotland, particularly in the mild southwest, and it grows successfully in continental Europe albeit shorter and compact in habit. The colour is good and mature plants are never a nuisance.

Uses

A feature plant that is particularly impressive against a wall or in front of dark greenery. Plants in pots starve quickly and are prone to aphid attack, so keep it in the ground. Apart from the dark green ivy around the base of my plant, there is a rambling honeysuckle (*Lonicera implexa*) close by. One or two shoots always manage to twine up the culms and the dark red and creamy white flowers accentuate the culm colour.

Others

Phyllostachys bambusoides 'Castillonis Variegata' (zones 8–9) is much weaker than 'Castillonis' but well variegated. I have never seen a particularly good

Phyllostachys bambusoides 'Castillonis' surrounded by a dense carpet of *Hedera helix* 'Ivalace'.

Colourful culm sheath blades on *Phyllostachys bambusoides* 'Castillonis'.

specimen apart from Peter Addington's at Stream Cottage. The small piece I inherited sadly died, and I have never tried it since. The leaves are finely striated silvery white, creating a pale spectral image.

Phyllostachys bambusoides 'Richard Haubrich' (zones 8–9) has been found recently in the United States and is a sport from 'Castillonis'. It is much slower growing than its parent, with bold green stripes on white leaves.

Phyllostachys bambusoides 'Castillonis Inversa'

Hardiness: min. -18˚C (0˚F), zone 6
Aspect: sun or light shade.
Height: 4–10 m (13–33 ft.), average 6 m (20 ft.)
Spread: 1–3 m (3.3–10 ft.) in 10 years, generally open, rarely invasive.
Habit: imposing and stately, almost vertical.
Culms: maximum diameter 6.5 cm. (2.5 in.), deep green with deep yellow sulci.
Leaves: 18 x 3.5 cm (7 x 1.4 in.), green.

The darkest of green culms emerge in midsummer with deep mustard yellow in the sulcus; the contrast is most vivid for bamboos of this coloration. The branches are long and distribute the bowing weight of the foliage evenly. Older culms pale to a soft green, providing contrast to the darker young ones.

Of all the *Phyllostachys bambusoides* forms this has provided the best results in the least time in my garden and I can recommend it as being the most tolerant of a cold, short-summer climate. Rather strangely this plant at Stream Cottage was very tight in comparison to a broad stand of 'Castillonis' which was close by. My two plants are in similar proximity to each other and they have done the opposite to those at Stream Cottage. My 'Castillonis Inversa' is two thirds the age of the 'Castillonis' and takes up far more room, with thicker and taller, well-spaced, vertical culms in comparison to any other *bambusoides* in the garden. Most surprising was the fact that it was a division from the tight plant at Stream Cottage, pruned back and nurtured lovingly in a pot for a few years before planting out, but sulking all the time. It looked sadder by the season and showed little growth until, like a bolt from the blue, it produced a culm of great size. It has continued to produce two or three such culms annually and is very healthy.

As good as it is in the garden, it is a frustrating nursery plant and never remains juvenile for long making propagation difficult and results few. It will always be in short supply.

Uses

It makes an excellent foil for bamboos with golden culms and green sulci. My plant shadows a fine specimen of *Viburnum plicatum* 'Nanum Semperflorens' (syn. 'Watanabe') which has white lacecap flowers all summer. The dark foliage of the bamboo and the flecks of white from the viburnum flowers, glimpsed through or against the culms, is a delight.

Others

Phyllostachys bambusoides 'Castillonis Inversa Variegata' (zones 8–9) is undoubtedly a plant to yearn for, but very difficult to grow and almost unobtainable. The original plant that came in from New Zealand was without doubt the best specimen of its kind: slow growing, very congested and quite short, with amazing orange-tinted white variegation, shown off beautifully by the dark culms. It is still on my wish list.

Phyllostachys bambusoides 'Kawadana'

Hardiness: min. -18˚C (0˚F), zone 6
Aspect: light shade.
Height: 4–9 m (13–30 ft.), average 6 m (20 ft.)
Spread: 1–2 m (2.2–6.5 ft.) in 10 years, mostly clumping.
Habit: tidy and upright, leafy top.
Culms: maximum diameter 6 cm. (2.4 in.), pale green streaked with yellow.
Leaves: 15 x 3.5 cm. (6 x 1.4 in.), subtle lime green variegations.

Often generalized with the other variegated forms, I believe this deserves special mention because it is more reliable and has the strength of the species and the stronger cultivars. 'Kawadana' appears to have a few variations in its form and potential origin. The clone most commonly grown was a sport from a regenerating plant of *Phyllostachys bambusoides* 'Castillonis' that flowered at Bicton College in Devon, southwest England, in approximately 1983. Although recorded in Oriental literature it was thought to be no longer in cultivation and was certainly not known in the West. The sport from the Bicton plant does not perfectly match the original description, and there may well be a better, more boldly variegated form still to be collected.

The potentially thick culms have irregular yellow striping, often on the higher internodes at eye level, which is very convenient. Leaves are evenly striped gold-green and plentiful, a colouring unique to this bamboo. Unfortunately this bamboo is finicky and needs to be placed correctly; too much sun and the culm colours will rarely develop, too much shade and the leaf variegation is lost. A place under permanent dappled shade without competition at the roots or in the shade of a large building, where it catches a glimmer of the early morning sun, is ideal.

I have seen a few good specimens of 'Kawadana' and when mature it is a wondrous sight. The plant in Mike Bell's garden in Cornwall, England will always remain in my mind and I know it is special to him. It rose uninhibitedly upwards to the overhang of the trees above, with perfect markings on the thick culms. The froth of pale greenery was alive with the flickering rays of sunlight which filtered through the protective broadleaf canopy high above.

Uses

Plant it in a light woodland glade as a surprise among dark surroundings. The dark needles and rusty bark of Scots pine (*Pinus sylvestris*), a timber bench for contemplation and the softness of the bamboo will provide for moments of ethereal experience.

Others

Phyllostachys bambusoides 'Subvariegata' (zone 6) is a very beautiful but slow cultivar with pale green culms and

A close view of the delicately striping on the leaves of *Phyllostachys bambusoides* 'Kawadana', which gives the foliage a distinct lime green hue from a distance.

Phyllostachys bambusoides 'Kawadana', showing a fine example of the potential culm striping.

dark leaves striped a paler green. It also needs careful positioning as too much sun or shade will affect this colouring.

Phyllostachys bambusoides 'Albovariegata' (zones 8–9) has more pronounced variegation and some orange colouring on the new leaves. There appear to be two forms of this cultivar; one from the United States has bolder colouring but much less vigour, and so it may be less hardy than the other which seems to be grown in Europe.

Phyllostachys bambusoides f. lacrima-deae (syn. *P. bambusoides* f. *tanakae*)

Hardiness: min. -18°C (0°F), zone 6
Aspect: sun or light shade.
Height: 4–9 m (13–30 ft.), average 6 m (20 ft.)
Spread: 1–2 m (3.3–6.5 ft.) in 10 years, open, but clumping.
Habit: vertical with slightly arching foliage canopy.
Culms: maximum diameter 5 cm. (2 in.), green paling to grey-green and mottled purple-brown
Leaves: 18 x 3.5 cm. (7 x 1.4 in.), plain green, like the species.

Known in China by the name above but it is more familiar as *Phyllostachys bambusoides* f. *tanakae*. Not rated very highly by some of my colleagues in the bamboo world, probably because there are very few specimens in gardens to note. I have recently imported young plants from China and they are stunning, with distinct markings on the culms.

A Compendium of Chinese Bamboo (China Forestry Publishing House) describes this simply as "a famous ornamental species", and after drooling over my recently acquired stock, I am inclined to agree. The older culms are pale grey-green with brownish purple spotting and stains that extend to the

A mottled culm of *Phyllostachys bambusoides* f. *lacrima-deae*.

branches. These markings are random but more pronounced on the lower internodes. New culms are green and start to show their markings at the end of the first season, colouring well in the second year. The closest comparisons are *Phyllostachys glauca* 'Yunzhu' and *P. nigra* 'Boryana' but as a *bambusoides*, it is a worthy competitor to these other two fine plants.

Uses
Undoubtedly a specimen to be admired; plant it so the fine culm markings can be appreciated.

Others

Phyllostachys bambusoides f. *mixta* has not to my knowledge been introduced in the West, but judging by its appearance should be worth a special pilgrimage to China to seek it out. Culms are mottled as for *P. bambusoides* f. *lacrima-deae* but the internodal grooves are stained yellow.

Phyllostachys bambusoides 'Marliacea'

Hardiness: min. -18°C (0°F), zone 6
Aspect: sun or light shade.
Height: 3–6 m (10–20 ft.), average 4 m (13 ft.)
Spread: 75 cm.–1.5 m (2.5–5 ft.) in 10 years, well-spaced culms but clumping.
Habit: Bold and stately, with long nodding branches.
Culms: maximum diameter 6 cm. (2.4 in.), pale olive green and wrinkled.
Leaves: slim and pointed in dense bunches, 13 x 1.8 cm. (5 x 0.7 in.), paler green than most Phyllostachys.

It was a plant of 'Marliacea' that led to my bamboo addiction; and I must have been blessed for this bamboo to present itself to me before any other. One day, as I sat in my office punching the laptop, a customer appeared from nowhere. The gentleman turned out to be a novice, starting a new garden, and so was guided through the bamboo collection with catalogue in hand. I left him to wander while I returned to work, keeping an eye on him through the loose culms of my 'Marliacea' planted outside of the window.

Phyllostachys bambusoides 'Marliacea' in the author's garden, growing in association with a pale-leaved *Phormium*.

Phyllostachys bissetii is one of the most cold-hardy and wind-tolerant bamboos, considering its potentially large size and stature.

After a lengthy amble around the garden he reappeared, studied the 'Marliacea' from all angles and turned to go, but stopped, returned his gaze to the bamboo and murmured "Wow!". Like me many years ago he was smitten by its beauty.

Known as *shibo-chiku*, or wrinkled bamboo, in Japan where it is more common and used for making flowerpots and items in the traditional tea ceremony. The culms are longitudinally wrinkled with grooves and ridges all round their circumference. Plants are generally slow-growing, quite short compared with the species, with culms narrowly tapering at the top but very thick lower down on mature plants. Long arching branches hold out graceful flattened fans of leaves.

It is very difficult to propagate; young plants do not stay juvenile for long and usually only one or two culms per plant are produced annually and very close together in pots, making them infuriating to divide. The plant in my garden is similar, with only one or two shoots a year, and they appear very late in summer.

Uses

Position it with care where its beauty can be appreciated. My specimen is accompanied by a variegated phormium, a bergenia and backed at a lower level by *Choisya ternata* Sundance ('Lich').

Others

Phyllostachys bambusoides 'Katashibo' is a plant of future legend; planted at the Hyogo Prefecture in Tatsuno City in Japan, it has been designated a natural monument. It is distinct from 'Marliacea' in that the wrinkles appear only in and just next to the sulcus on each internode.

Phyllostachys bissetii

Hardiness: min. -22°C (-8°F), zone 6
Aspect: sun or light shade.
Height: 5–12 m (16.5–30 ft.), average 7 m (23 ft.)
Spread: 1.5–4 m (5–13 ft.) in 10 years, evenly spreading.
Habit: tidy, dense and vigorous.
Culms: maximum diameter 5 cm. (2 in.), very dark when young ageing pale to olive yellow.
Leaves: stunted but plentiful,
9 x 1.5 cm.
(3.5 x 0.6 in.),
deep green.

A useful bamboo native to the Chinese provinces of Sichuan and Zhejiang, it was introduced to America in 1941 and England as late as 1987. It is now widely planted, with proven ability to remain unscathed even in the hardest of winters.

Like other plain green *Phyllostachys* it is often difficult to identify, so look for the pale yellow-green culm sheaths that are delicately stained ruby-red. The new culms emerge quite dark, paling slightly with age. The foliage is always dense and glossy, looking fresh throughout the seasons. The term green phyllostachys is almost an insult, this plant more than justifies itself among many others of similar stature and colouring.

It is particularly suitable for hedging and screening, providing shelter very quickly with the masses of culms it produces each year, but adequate room is needed as it grows wide. I have a well-established, well-behaved plant that performs the job for which it was intended in exemplary fashion. It was planted in a group of three to screen a large polythene tunnel from the house and garden. The bamboo is now twice the height of the 4 m (13 ft.) tunnel and is visible from a great distance. It catches the full force of the prevailing wind and almost relishes its exposed aspect.

Uses

For a hedge, screen, grove, or cane production, if you have plenty of space. This bamboo also makes a fine dark background for a brighter specimen plant.

Others

Phyllostachys bissetii 'Dwarf' is listed in the United States and distinguished by whitish patches on the culms.

Phyllostachys dulcis

Hardiness: min. -18°C (0°F), zone 6
Aspect: sun or light shade.
Height: 6–12 m (20–40 ft.), average 8 m (26 ft.)
Spread: 1.5–4 m (5–13 ft.) in 10 years, open grove.
Habit: mostly upright with some culms twisting and turning before becoming vertical.
Culms: maximum diameter 7 cm. (2.75 in.), matt green, emerging bloomy from the sheaths.
Leaves: typical Phyllostachys, 12 x 2 cm. (5 x 0.75 in.), matt green.

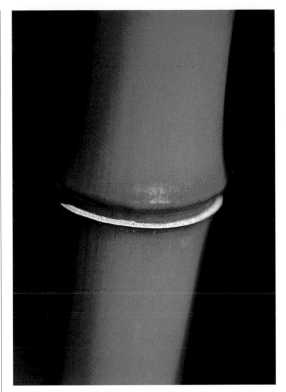

Fresh new culm of *Phyllostachys dulcis*.

The very edible sweetshoot bamboo has been grown in the United States since 1908 but only recently in Europe. It does well in both warm and cooler regions usually forming a grove of stately culms, however not as tall or thick in colder continental areas.

New culms often curve outwards towards the sun before reverting to the vertical and are often thick at the base, tapering dramatically towards the tips which provides a distinctive habit.

The emerging shoots are highlighted by the very pale creamy green sheaths, often striated with even paler stripes. New culms are powdery white as they emerge and the nodes become slightly swollen as they age. During hot summers *Phyllostachys dulcis* will develop rapidly and produce many new culms, which speeds the process of maturity. It does not respond well to very dry soils and a heavy organic mulch will provide nourishment and preserve soil moisture as an insurance against weak growth.

The leaf canopy is always held high and waves about in the breeze *en masse*, gently rocking the culms. It is a very architectural plant and always in demand because of the spectacular results it can provide. The plant in my garden is a division from a good form and has a few thick culms, but for five years, although healthy, put on no growth at all. There appeared to be no reason for this as the conditions are good. It is sometimes difficult to accept that not everything planted in the garden will be successful, but my hope that my plant will surprise me with a few huge culms has at last been realized with a dozen large new shoots appearing just before this book goes to press.

Uses

Plant as a specimen on its own. For an alternative long-term approach, try planting it with a *Phyllostachys vivax* f. *aureocaulis* of similar vigour. Eventually the two will merge and the mixture of green and yellow culms will make a remarkable feature.

Phyllostachys edulis

Hardiness: min. -20°C (-4°F), zone 6
Aspect: sun or light shade.
Height: 4–20 m (13–65 ft.), average 10 m (33 ft.)
Spread: 1–5 m (3.3–16.5 ft.) in 10 years, open grove.
Habit: ultimately forest-like.
Culms: maximum diameter 18 cm. (7 in.), pubescent, silvery grey turning yellow-green, with dark culm sheaths.
Leaves: small for the plant, 6 x 1.5 cm. (2.4 x 0.6 in.), pale green.

One of the bamboos most in demand, but it only reaches majestic proportions in favourable temperate regions that have warm summers, soils of reliable moisture and fertility, and good light. This is revered as the *moso* of the Orient, a plant of great eminence. In China it grows as a forest, covering vast swathes of land and is by far the most dominant bamboo. It is also widely cultivated in Japan.

Its growth character differs hugely according to region. For example in Cornwall, in southwest England, it takes time to mature – twenty-five to thirty years – but eventually grows tall with thick culms. Compare this with the more continental climate found 400 miles to the east where it hardly performs at all. In the moist and milder west and northwest of England there is the favour of oceanic influence with the Gulf Stream from the Atlantic Ocean. Here, *Phyllostachys edulis* tries very hard to match the proportions of the plants in Cornwall, but requires heavy feeding and a lifetime of patience. Unless you are blessed with a warm, mild climate or a desirable microclimate, or can duplicate the conditions of its native habitat; try something else. (*Phyllostachys vivax* would be a suitable alternative.)

During the late 1980s there was a crop of young

plants produced from seed, available from many sources, which are still juvenile in most gardens and show no culm structure. These seedling plants have large leaves with distinct bristles, or oral setae, and look nothing like a *Phyllostachys*. I am sure that one year they will surprise their owners and start to produce mature culms, the juvenile growth at this time will die out. Young plants divided from juvenile stock, not seed produced, can also remain juvenile for many years.

In all its mature glory *Phyllostachys edulis* is easy to identify. The grey-green, almost pale blue culms are covered with a dense white powder when newly emerged, and contrast well with the older, smooth pale green ones. The culms sheaths are a dark red-brown and heavily spotted. The leaves are small for the genus, held in plumes high on short branches. If you cannot grow *P. edulis*, it is worth a pilgrimage to the Bambouseraie, Prafrance in the south of France, or Hakone Gardens in Saratoga, California, and take it home as a memory.

Uses

A small forest if you have the room and excellent for construction if you are prepared to cut it down.

Others

The following three cultivars are listed here because of their affinity to the species, but do not share the same hardiness in cooler gardens, so beware.

Phyllostachys edulis 'Bicolor' (zones 8–9) has pale yellow culms with some green striping. *Phyllostachys edulis* 'Goldstripe' (zones 8–9) is an American cultivar from a seedling plant. The culms are randomly striped green and gold with some early white variegations on the leaves. Both these cultivars are more difficult than the species, even in a favoured location, but if you can give them full attention and the best growing conditions they will survive and show their best assets.

Phyllostachys edulis 'Heterocycla' (zones 8–9) is better known as the tortoise shell bamboo, with basal nodes that slant alternately in opposite directions. It is much in demand but almost impossible to grow in cold locations.

Phyllostachys flexuosa

Hardiness: min. -20°C (-4°F), zone 6
Aspect: sun or light shade.
Height: 4–9 m (13–30 ft.), average 5 m (16.5 ft.)
Spread: 1–2 m (3.3–6.5 ft.) in 10 years, rarely wanders.
Habit: tight clumps of arching culms and foliage.
Culms: maximum diameter 6 cm. (2.4 in.), deep green tint yellow with age and are often stained black.
Leaves: strappy, 13 x 2 cm. (5 x 0.8 in.), dark and glossy green.

Phyllostachys flexuosa displays its bright culm sheathing.

A variable plant according to location, it is usually vertical, forming a broad colony of culms in very warm areas. Mostly it lives up to its specific name and arches gracefully. It performs particularly well in the cooler areas of North America and the United Kingdom.

The culms are unusually sinuous with twisting and frequent zigzags similar to those of *Phyllostachys aureosulcata*. When young they are dark, glossy green and a pale olive-yellow when aged, often with sporadic dark brown or black patches as if left by a faint brush stroke. The culm sheaths are a dusky cinnamon red with darker spotting and are most vivid together with the bright emerging culms. The branching system and foliage is very loose and airy, not casting the heavy shade that could be a problem to surrounding plants in smaller gardens.

It is very tolerant of a broad spectrum of situations, growing well in salty alluvial soils, high alkalinity and sharply drained sandy soils where moisture is limited.

Phyllostachys flexuosa remains gloriously fresh even after the cold blast of winter storm.

This species has recently flowered, though some plants have yet to do so and it is possible there are two clones. Some dying plants produced seed and a new generation is already growing strongly to replace those now lost.

Uses

A useful species for a smaller garden placed as a central feature away from a path. Its light and airy habit makes it suitable for underplanting. The dark green shoots and reddish sheaths should not be hidden, so a low carpet of silver-variegated *Lamium* and some low spring bulbs and autumn crocuses will provide additional interest.

Others

Phyllostachys flexuosa 'Kimmei' is a new cultivar (1992) in the United States from seed generated by the recent flowering. The golden culms have green sulci and good variegation shows on the leaves.

Phyllostachys glauca

Hardiness: -20°C (-4°F), zone 6
Aspect: sun or light shade.
Height: 5–12 m (16.5–40 ft.), average 8 m (26 ft.)
Spread: 1–4 m (3.3–13 ft.) in 10 years, open grove.
Habit: mainly vertical with arching culm tips.
Culms: maximum diameter 6 cm. (2.4 in.), pale bloomy grey turning green.
Leaves: 12 x 1.5 cm. (4.75 x 0.6 in.), pale green.

A robust species that is capable of growing almost anywhere. Plants have proved adept at withstanding waterlogged soils when established and often inhabit alluvial plains in China, which are also alkaline and salty. In Norfolk, in eastern England, it spreads extravagantly in the driest areas in the dustiest, sandy soil. The coarse texture of the leaves and hard culms make it very wind and cold tolerant. It is keen to grow and reaches maturity very quickly.

The silvery blue bloom on the new culms lasts for some time and because of their number, makes a striking feature. The colourful culm sheaths are green and subtly washed with claret red stains.

Vivid spotting on *Phyllostachys glauca* f. *yunzhu*.

Although F. A. McClure introduced this bamboo to the United States in 1926 and it is now known in Europe, it is not widely grown. Its positive response to the harshest of climates is surely enough to recommend it, with the bonus of alternative colouring to the more widely used and also vigorous *Phyllostachys viridiglaucescens*.

Uses

A broad screen, hedge, windbreak or a large central feature in parkland. Culm production is so profuse that an established plant can be cropped for canes, or pathways cut through a grove to form a maze or bamboo tunnel.

Others

Phyllostachys glauca 'Notso' is known in the United States and is "not so" blue, hence the cultivar name. This may be the variety *P. glauca* var. *variabilis* in Chinese literature. Both are described as lacking the young pruinose bluish culms, but possibly more tolerant of lower temperatures than the species.

Phyllostachys glauca f. yunzhu

Hardiness: min. -18°C (0°F), zone 6
Aspect: prefers full sun.
Height: 4–9 m (13–30 ft.), average 6 m (20 ft.)
Spread: 75 cm.–1.5 m (2.5–5 ft.) in 10 years, usually clumping.
Habit: broad V-shape when young becoming upright.
Culms: maximum diameter 8 cm. (2.7 in.), pale green, spotted and blotched like a Dalmatian dog.
Leaves: as for P. glauca.

This form is of limited distribution in China, native only to the Henan and Shanxi Provinces. It has the ability to be as vigorous as *Phyllostachys glauca* but requires a warmer climate to do so, and often the distinctive culm colouring is lost.

Most of the plants I know are quite short and compact, with tight culms, even after two decades. This makes them difficult to propagate and therefore quite rare. I have to say that the best colouring and blotching occurs on plants grown in colder areas and, for ornamental purposes, this is the only reason to grow this bamboo.

New culms are always pale grey-green and disappointing, as the markings do not appear until the second season. However, because shooting is unreliable, there is always a dominance of older culms and so the blotching is more than obvious. Some lower branch pruning is necessary to expose the culms and the thinning of old culms is essential, as they quickly turn woody and brown. A well-kept plant is an awe-inspiring sight, and another example of how different bamboos can be.

Uses

Place close by the house, where it can be well tended and lovingly appreciated.

Phyllostachys heteroclada ('Straight Stem')

Hardiness: min. -21°C (-5°F), zone 6
Aspect: sun or part shade.
Height: 4–9 m (13–30 ft.), average 6 m (20 ft.)
Spread: 75 cm.–1.5 m (2.5–5 ft.) in 10 years, open, but clumping.
Habit: stiff and erect.
Culms: maximum diameter 3 cm. (1.2 in.), pale very bloomy, silvery grey when young.
Leaves: small and narrow, 7.5 x 1.3 cm. (2 x 0.5 in.), light green with glaucous underside.

Often known as the water bamboo because of its tolerance of waterlogged soils, due to the air channels present in the rhizomes. Its nomenclature is much confused and currently it is listed as *Phyllostachys purpurata* in many references. It is widely distributed in China with slight variation in form, making the identification of the true species problematic. The species is usually known with the cultivar name of 'Straight Stem' attached, which satisfactorily describes the characteristically vertical and rigid culms.

In general, this has proved to be one of the shorter species in the majority of gardens with a tidy habit, congested but mainly vertical at first and more open but still limited in spread when older. New culms are a bright, bloomy, emerald green and the culm sheaths are only slightly paler. As the new culms emerge into the heat of

Waxy bloom on a new culm of *Phyllostachys heteroclada*.

A culm of *Phyllostachys humilis*.

the summer they take on a silvery and waxy bloom and appear much paler than the older culms – a very distinct colouring which helps in identifying this bamboo.

Phyllostachys heteroclada rarely shows promise as a youngster and it requires regular thinning to encourage the thicker, truly vertical waxy culms, but time and patience will be well rewarded. I have seen it grown best in a narrow clearing of a woodland garden, where the ghostly new culms rocket skywards, holding their leaves high to the sunlight.

Uses

Offers an alternative colouring and habit to many bamboos. Try planting it with other species that will also light up partly shaded areas, such as *Phyllostachys aureosulcata* f. *aureocaulis* for golden culms and *Thamnocalamus crassinodus* 'Lang Tang' for blue.

Underplant with short, prickly *Ruscus* and *Carex morrowii* 'Variegata', which holds it colour even in deep shade.

Others

Phyllostachys heteroclada f. *purpurata* has distinct spear-shaped, purple culm sheath blades that break up the monotone colouring of the newly emerging culms. It is more slender in habit than the species, with arching culms and longer internodes.

Phyllostachys heteroclada f. *solida* has solid internodes on the lower half of the culms and adopts a loose habit. This form has many uses in China because of the long-lasting woody canes it produces.

Phyllostachys humilis

Hardiness: min. -25°C (-13°F), zone 5
Aspect: sun or light shade.
Height: 3–5 m (10–16.5 ft.), average 3.5m (11.5 ft.)
Spread: 1–3 m (3.3–10 ft.) in 10 years, open grove.
Habit: Usually a short but broad, forest-like stand.
Culms: maximum diameter 2.5 cm. (1 in.), emerging dark and then turn fresh green, old ones tint orange-yellow in sun.
Leaves: small, 7 x 1.2 cm. (2.75 x 0.5 in.), matt yellow–olive green with glaucous underside.

Thought originally to be of Chinese origin, from Sichuan, this bamboo is now more widely cultivated in Japan where it is used for the arts of bonsai and penjing. *Phyllostachys humilis* may be easily pruned and stunted but it must also be protected from frost and desiccation when treated in this way.

In relation to its vigour this is one of the shortest *Phyllostachys* but makes up for it with great character and a delicate appearance; a twenty-year-old colony in my locality is only 2.5 m (8 ft.) high. A copious amount of thin culms is produced annually on a mature grove, often filling in any open spaces as well as growing around the edge. At this stage the bamboo appreciates some judicious thinning unless it is grown for density, to provide a screen or noise barrier. The young culms are dark red-brown turning green; in subsequent years they age to a rich, burnished yellow-orange. The combination of the three different culm colours during the growing season is appealing, and enhanced by the profusion of small leaves that continually twist and flutter in the breeze, showing their glaucous undersides.

Uses

Because of its tolerance to pruning and good recovery, it is ideal as a trimmed hedge. It is also a useful plant for stabilising steep banks, or as a low grove or screen. Try planting it in a large tub and you will be able to prune and shape it at leisure.

Phyllostachys iridescens

Hardiness: min. -18°C (0°F), zone 6
Aspect: sun or light shade
Height: 6–12m (20–40 ft.), average 8 m (26 ft.)
Spread: 1–2.5 m (3.3–10 ft.) in 10 years, usually clumping
Habit: bold and mostly vertical.
Culms: maximum diameter 8 cm. (3 in.), emerging rich green with white nodal rings, mature culms striped violet and yellow.
Leaves: quite small, 10 x 1.5 cm. (4 x 0.6 in.), fresh sea green.

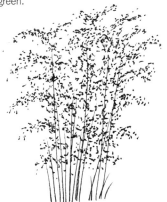

Little known, yet so beautiful, this plant can be likened to a refined form of *Phyllostachys violascens*, with similarly striped and coloured old culms. The natural distribution in the east of China is limited and it has been introduced into many other provinces because of its prized sweet shoots and use in construction. It has proved adaptable to various habitats during this migration in China and so is equally at home in the various climatic extremes of our temperate gardens.

Always short in supply because of its ability to mature quickly from a young plants, providing good height within a few years of planting. The new culms emerge tight to the main clump for a few years and plants have a slightly vase-shaped habit at this stage. Eventually the rhizomes will thicken and extend to produce some giant culms, thick for their height, a little distance from the main plant but not invasively so. The emerging shoots are clothed in rich crimson-red sheaths which fall after a week or two, and this colouring is quite spectacular when set against the fresh green new culms and a dark background. The red culm sheaths are made more attractive by the large pendulous culm sheath blades, which are rainbow coloured and wave in the wind, acting like beacons to signify the position of the newly emerging shoots. In dry weather, a ring of white bloom is evident below the nodes as they emerge from the sheaths.

Phyllostachys iridescens.

Old culms take time to develop their random stripes of pale yellow and violet in various thicknesses along the length of the internodes; these markings are normally on the lower sections of the culms. The culms colour well regardless of the amount of sunshine although they do benefit from a good polish with a damp cloth to remove algae after the winter. Rigid branches hold the leaves with nodding elegance and never mask the low culm colouring. It is altogether a very tidy and rewarding bamboo. In my garden this has been one of the best performers in recent years and has provided the thickest culms of any, and only from a ten-year-old plant.

I first knew this species as *Phyllostachys rubicunda*, which I believed was attributed to the reddish new shoots, but found later it was *P. iridescens* after consulting descriptions from China. I have since acquired a plant of *P. rubicunda* (a synonym for *P. concava*) and the only similarities are the purple striae on the culm sheaths.

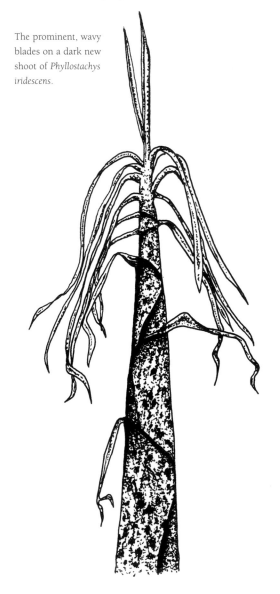

The prominent, wavy blades on a dark new shoot of *Phyllostachys iridescens*.

Two of the thick culms produced by *Phyllostachys iridescens* in the author's garden.

Uses

Plant this as a bold focal point in sun or light woodland, or as a central feature to an island bed surrounded by a patchwork of ground-hugging junipers.

Phyllostachys mannii 'Decora'

Hardiness: min. -22°C (-8°F), zone 6
Aspect: sun or light shade.
Height: 4–9 m (13–30 ft.), average 6 m (20 ft.)
Spread: 1–2 m (3.3–6.5 ft.) in 10 years, slow spreading but not invasive.
Habit: usually bolt upright with a tumbling mass of foliage.
Culms: maximum diameter 4 cm. (1.6 in.), pale green tinting orange-yellow in the sun. Striped culm sheaths.
Leaves: quite short for the genus, drooping, 8 x 1.5 cm. (3 x 0.6 in.), a matt mid green.

Long known as *Phyllostachys decora*, this has now been identified as a cultivar of the species *P. mannii*. A bamboo of some style, it is known as *mei-chu*, beautiful bamboo, in China and it fully deserves this epithet. It is distributed in the areas along the Yangtze and Yellow Rivers in China and is cultivated in Tibet, a fact that says something about its versatility and hardiness. It is tolerant of a wide pH range, dry sandy soils and extremes in temperature.

The vertical culms are generally a soft green and can be colourfully tinted orange-yellow in full sun. The luxuriant mass of cascading foliage is held high by the strong culms. The new shoots appear early and wrapped in culm sheaths that are striped cream and green and edged with rich plum purple. Most people would classify 'Decora' as just another green bamboo, but with all these attributes it is far from that.

Uses

It will grow in many situations including the most unlikely, such as on poor soils in exposed locations, yet is always well behaved. The beautiful habit is best appreciated from a distance, but inspect it closely during the shooting season to see it flaunt the stylishly colour-coordinated culm sheaths.

Phyllostachys mannii 'Mannii'

Hardiness: min. -21°C (-5°F), zone 6
Aspect: sun or light shade.
Height: 3–9 m (10–30 ft.), average 5 m (16.5 ft.)
Spread: 75 cm.–1.5m (2.5–5 ft.) in 10 years, usually clumping.
Habit: a tight V-shape at first, maturing to vertical.
Culms: maximum diameter 3 cm. (1.2 in.), bright fresh green.
Leaves: narrow and twisting, 10 x 1.5 cm. (4 x 0.6 in.), pale green.

Phyllostachys mannii 'Mannii' is usually stocky and compact in cool temperate gardens.

First discovered in northern India and later in the southern provinces of China, but as with many species of *Phyllostachys* has become widely distributed because of cultivation throughout the East. The culms are very durable, and most useful in Chinese culture for splitting and the production of mats and screens.

It does not have the dramatic new culm colours of 'Decora', but is very versatile and has proved one of the most drought-resistant bamboos in my garden. I have it planted close to the corner of a raised border, only a short distance from the retaining wall. In the driest and hottest summer in my experience the soil shrank and a gap appeared next to the brickwork. The bamboo was unperturbed and, instead of curling its leaves and crisping like the surrounding shrubs, it shed a small percentage to compensate for dryness at the roots. After a week of yellow leaf drop, it looked as good as new with no additional water to help it. In such a difficult aspect this green bamboo remains quite short and compact, with a "bubbling" habit, but it is capable of putting on a more generous show in warmer climates and richer soils.

The leaves twist and fold through 180 degrees along their length, as if being held at each end and turned in opposite directions.

Uses

Useful as a small garden plant in cold areas, or try it as a feature in a dry gravel garden.

Phyllostachys meyeri

Hardiness: min. -18˚C (0˚F), zone 6
Aspect: sun or light shade.
Height: 5–10 m (16.5–33ft.) average 6m (20 ft.)
Spread: 80 cm.–1.5 m (2.6–5 ft.) in 10 years, clumping.
Habit: tight and vertical.
Culms: maximum diameter 5 cm. (2 in.), mid green and pale sheaths.
Leaves: 13 x 2 cm. (5 x 0.75 in.), green.

In China this is an important bamboo commercially as it produces strong hard culms used for weaving, splitting and the manufacture of many goods for export. It is similar in habit to the stately *Phyllostachys aurea* but without the compressed internodes. It forms a vertical and tidy plant in most localities and can be relied upon to provide height quickly. The mid green culms emerge

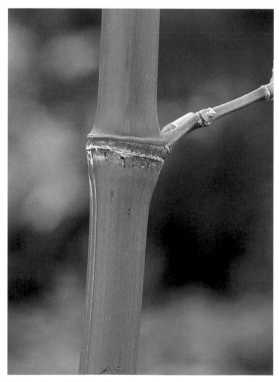

Phyllostachys nidularia with an irregular node.

from pale buff sheaths, with very long and narrow sheath blades that hang loosely after a few days. *Phyllostachys meyeri* prefers full sun and a reasonably rich soil with some moisture to gain its full height. Plants in very dry soils often look pale and chlorotic and are not very rewarding.

Uses

Performs well in the friable and nutrient-rich soil of an old walled garden or similar protected environment. Its narrow habit lends it to plant associations, for example in combination with the larger drooping leaves of *Viburnum rhytidophyllum* and a bold-leaved catalpa or paulownia, stooled annually, with low mounds of *Miscanthus sinensis* 'Yakushima Dwarf' around the base of the shrubs to complete the picture.

Phyllostachys nidularia

Hardiness: min. -18˚C (0˚F), zone 6
Aspect: sun or light shade.
Height: 5–10 m (16.5–33 ft.) average 6 m (20 ft.)
Spread: 1–2 m (3.3–6.5 ft.) in 10 years, open clumps.
Habit: generally tidy and upright.
Culms: maximum diameter 4 cm. (1.6 in.), pale green with colourful sheaths.
Leaves: taper bluntly at the tips, 9 x 1.8 cm. (3.5 x 0.7 in.), green.

A bamboo with many subtleties that makes it easy to identify. The culms are sinuous, gently twisted with occasional faint grooving, dark at first and paling with age. The nodes are markedly flared and on new culms are covered with a bead of dark hairs. The culm sheaths are deep olive green and vividly marked with white and claret striae. The sheath blades are particularly noticeable, with large dark red-brown auricles wrapped around the emerging culm. The auricles are further highlighted by the bloomy node above each sheath as the culm emerges.

The overall structure of the plant is one of strength and character, and it is mostly well behaved, although in dry soils I have seen it roam. In China it is grown for its sweet-tasting well-textured shoots, which are processed for dried food.

Uses

This bamboo is at its best grown as an isolated clump where the fine culm structure can be viewed; try lighting it from behind for a ghostly night-time silhouette. It will also make a fine loose screen or hedge.

Others

These three forms are collector's curiosities, and none is superior to the species.

Phyllostachys nidularia f. *farcta* has solid culms in the lower sections of the plant. The culms are very strong and durable, and are used whole in China in small construction projects.

Phyllostachys nidularia 'Smoothsheath', correctly named *P. nidularia* f. *glabrovagina*, is identical to the species only lacking the dark hairs on the culm sheaths and nodal sheath scar.

Phyllostachys nidularia 'June Barbara' is a new seedling cultivar in the United States, with pale slightly variegated leaves. It lacks the vigour and possibly the hardiness of the species.

Phyllostachys nigra

Hardiness: min. -18°C (0°F), zone 6
Aspect: full sun.
Height: 4–12 m (13–40 ft.), average 6 m (20 ft.)
Spread: 75 cm.–1.5 m (2.5–5m) in 10 years,
usually tight clumping.
Habit: rarely untidy, slightly V-shaped or vertical.
Culms: maximum diameter 5 cm. (2 in.), green when young ageing to jet black.
Leaves: on the small side for Phyllostachys, 8 x 1.3 cm. (3 x 0.5 In.) green.

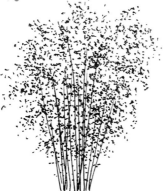

The black bamboo is probably the most popular ornamental bamboo in the world, with the demand in China and Japan equalling that in the West. It is now rare in the wild, but fortunately it is still planted widely in China for commercial purposes. The new shoots are edible, and the black glossy culms, when dried correctly, will maintain their colour and are used in fine craftwork for furniture making and framing.

It was the first temperate bamboo to be introduced to the West, acquired by Loddiges Nursery in Britain in

A jet-black culm of *Phyllostachys nigra* shows the rings of pale culm sheath scars below the nodes.

1823 and widely distributed by them. It was introduced to America in 1827. It was not until the latter half of the nineteenth century that other bamboos were introduced and by this time *Phyllostachys nigra* had proved its worth, so the interest in these new woody plants surged. *Phyllostachys nigra* is not the type form of the species however. This is attributed to the green-culmed *P. nigra* f. *henonis*.

The shoots emerge from the soil with sheaths of a very striking pale pink or sometimes cinnamon colour. When the new culms and branches emerge they are dark green and turn shiny black within a season or two. On very black culms the culm sheath scar appears almost white, as a narrow ring under the base of each node. Culm production is usually plentiful, although a young plant will take time to develop. The habit of the black

Right: Markings on a culm of *Phyllostachys nigra* f. *punctata*.

Left: A new shoot of *Phyllostachys nigra*.

bamboo is reliable, mostly clumping and tidy, only venturing in quest of new surroundings in very warm areas, and occasionally on very dry soil in cooler gardens. It is variable in height according to location and I know of many fine plants in the United Kingdom, some as tall as 9 m (30 ft.) and others only 3 m (10 ft.). Culm thickness varies according to plant height, the taller the culms usually the thicker they are. Good light is needed for the culms to blacken, but very high light levels can result in silvery patches on the old culms. It will be necessary to remove some lower branches to expose the culms, particularly on short congested plants.

The canopy of branches and foliage is always dense, and taller plants can have an arching habit, although this can be resolved as this species is easily pruned and can be used for hedging. The fine leaves bleach slightly at the tips. This is noticeable in the winter months and not unattractive.

Some of the original introductions flowered in the early part of the twentieth century and some seeded, others recovered. Young plants are usually true from seed and it is likely there are a few clones in cultivation, which is good insurance against any future gregarious flowering. However, there are some inferior forms available with poor black colouring so before purchasing a new plant, always look at the one-year-old culms at the end of the first growing season; if they are predominantly black, the young culms have coloured quickly from green, and it is likely you will have found a good form.

Uses

This is easy to recommend because it has many uses in the garden and for general landscaping. Good in pots and planted anywhere except in dense shade. The black culms, unique among temperate bamboos, show well with almost any plant or structure. It is useful for hedging, particularly when mixed with other bamboos of similar stature.

Others

There are various forms and cultivars, and it may be that they all are just notable selections of the true, very variable species, selected for their habit or colouring.

Phyllostachys nigra 'Hale', 'Othello' and 'Wisley' are compact cultivars, all very similar to each other, and grow well in colder gardens. Their culms turn black very early in the first season. It is reported that 'Hale' grows very vigorously in the mild winters of the Pacific northwest coast of America and exceeds the height of the species. The closely packed culm formation makes them difficult to propagate so they are still rare.

Phyllostachys nigra f. *nigra* is similar to the above but weaker in growth, although the colouring is outstanding.

Phyllostachys nigra 'Daikokuchiku' is a selection from California that is purportedly larger than the species and also has early culm colouring.

Phyllostachys nigra f. *muchisasa* is an old seedling form, now rarely seen, with less dense colouring than the species and may now have become mixed with the inferior forms of *P. nigra*.

Phyllostachys nigra f. *punctata* is the name usually given to *Phyllostachys nigra* in Europe, and plants imported to the United Kingdom as such are not always good forms. The correct identification of f. *punctata* is a plant of vigorous habit with culms that rarely turn completely black although are still attractive, being a mixture of green, brown, silver and black. Selections of f. *punctata* from various locations have been made; my plant originates from the famous Pitt White Garden in Devon, England, and is most impressive.

Phyllostachys nigra 'Boryana'

Hardiness: min. -18°C (0°F), zone 6
Aspect: sun or light shade.
Height: 5–15 m (16.5–50 ft.), average 7 m (23 ft.)
Spread: 1–4 m (3.3–13 ft.) in 10 years, clumps or runs.
Habit: variable from tight to grove forming.
Culms: maximum diameter 10 cm. (4 in.), green with dark brown blotching.
Leaves: 9 x 1.5 cm. (3.5 x 0.6 in.), green.

A cultivar that originates from Japan, can grow much larger than the species and it is one of the most variable plants I know in the United Kingdom. The plant in my garden is very slim, after twelve years I can circle my arms around it, whereas a plant in the more favourable climate of Cornwall, England, at Mike Bell's garden, is so huge and colonizing it is possible to walk between some of the tall, thick culms. It can grow to a favourable size in cool gardens but takes much longer to mature. Another plant in my locality has recently generated two or three very large culms from a dense congestion of thin ones, which now looks sad as the new thick culms take the water and nutrient in preference.

New culms emerge green and start to colour towards the end of the first season with brown or purplish black uneven spots. These markings become more pronounced as the culm ages and the green turns to an olive yellow. As with the species, and compared to the stature of 'Boryana', the leaves are quite small and enhance the appearance of this very ornamental cultivar.

Uses

Makes a magnificent isolated specimen as a mature plant, the unusual culm colouring showing well in good light. The culms retain their marking when dried so it proves useful for decorative purposes.

Others

Phyllostachys nigra 'Tosaensis' has a similar habit to 'Boryana', with the culms streaked dark brown in patches rather than spotted. The leaves are said to be occasionally variegated, although I have not noticed this yet.

Phyllostachys nigra 'Fulva'

Hardiness: min. -18°C (0°F), zone 6
Aspect: sun or light shade.
Culms: maximum diameter 3 cm. (1.2 in.)
Height: 3–7.5 m (10–24.6 ft.), average 5 m (16.5 ft.)
Spread: 75 cm.–1.5 m (2.5–5 ft.) in 10 years, clumping.
Habit: tight V-shape until mature.
Culms: maximum diameter 3 cm. (1.2 in.), tawny sometimes reddening.
Leaves: 9 x 1.5 cm. (3.5 x 0.6 in.), pale yellow-green.

This fine bamboo appears to have disappeared into oblivion during the past three decades; it has rarely been listed, and the form that was

Established culms of
Phyllostachys nigra 'Boryana'.

Phyllostachys nigra 'Tosaensis'.

grown by one or two enthusiasts flowered and never matched the correct description. In his authoritative work *Bamboos: A Gardener's Guide to their Cultivation in Temperate Climates*, A. H. Lawson describes this rare bamboo perfectly as *Phyllostachys fulva*.

Originating in Japan, it was introduced into England in 1898 and was said to have similar vigour to *Phyllostachys nigra* 'Boryana', although I have not seen it with this stature. Its distinguishing feature is the tawny culm colouring, which is uniform along the length of the culms but variable in tone according to each one's age. Very old culms may be darker on one side and darker patches often appear. The culm sheath scar forms a very obvious, narrow pale ring below each node, in keeping with the species. The leaves are very pale yellow-green and particularly attractive in combination with the lightly arching branches, which are coloured like the culms.

I was fortunate to be able to identify plants of *Phyllostachys nigra* 'Fulva' in the gardens of the late Maurice Mason in my home county of Norfolk. An avid collector, he imported a large collection of bamboos from Germany; the *P. nigra* 'Fulva' were incorrectly labelled *P. nigra* 'Megurochiku'.

Uses

Very slow growing so needs a special site where the light is good and it is not crowded by other plants; the pale foliage is best set against a dark background. It grows well in containers as long as winter shelter is offered – under glass, beneath trees or against a warm wall – in cold exposed gardens. The culm colours are more vivid when the plant is restricted.

Phyllostachys nigra f. henonis

Hardiness: min. -26°C (-15°F), zone 5
Aspect: sun or light shade.
Height: 6–20 m (20–65.5 ft.), average 8 m (26 ft.)
Spread: 1.5–3.5 m (5–11.5 ft.) in 10 years, open clumps.
Habit: tidily vertical.
Culms: maximum diameter 10 cm. (4 in.), fresh green turning pale yellow-green.
Leaves: small and massed, 9 x 1.5 cm. (3.5 x 0.6 in.), glossy green.

Undeniably the strongest form of the species and noted for its elegance and tolerance of climatic extremes. In strange botanical fashion this should be the true species, being the parent of all other nigra forms and cultivars, including *Phyllostachys nigra*. However the black bamboo was registered first and this green form has to tolerate a lower nomenclatural status. It was introduced into the United Kingdom in the 1890s and planted on large estates where, in some cases, it still exists.

This is one of few temperate bamboos capable of maturing to a great size and even in the wide open skies of eastern England there are plants of 12 m (40 ft.). In China and Japan it is an important timber bamboo and also used for ornamental purposes, being given the name *ha-chiku*, which means the light and volatile bamboo. The other two important timber bamboos are *P. bambusoides* and *P. edulis*, but *P. nigra* f. *henonis* is more tolerant of cold and so grown in areas where the other two species are not successful.

This *Phyllostachys nigra* f. *henonis* may look robust, but it is still at the juvenile stage.

The culms emerge fresh green and are dusted with a mealy bloom below the nodes, particularly in dry weather. Older culms attain a whitish yellow-green tinge and grow straight when thick, with very slim nodes. On young plants, branches can occur low down, hiding the culms, but mature plants hold them higher. The small leaves are a deep shiny green on the upper surface and a matt blue-green underneath, and the flattened sprays shimmer in the light on a breezy day. The huge foam of greenery overhead sometimes arches the weaker culms, but not to the point of nuisance. Some minor leaf-tip bleaching is common but offers character to the bamboo, breaking up the mass of green, giving perspective to the plant.

For its size this bamboo usually keeps within bounds, but bear in mind a plant of some age with tall, thick culms will fill a large area and cast shade for some distance, so think carefully about its position. Even in early life this bamboo has lush, architectural qualities; but when it does eventually mature and surprise you with something outrageously huge from below ground, you will wish you had planted it in more than one place.

Uses

This will form a stately specimen, screen or windbreak. The foliage and culms are also tolerant of trimming, which will help to keep the plant juvenile should you want to kerb its monstrous proportions. I have mine planted alongside *Phyllostachys bissetii* and together they form a dense screen. Even though both bamboos are essentially green, there are differences in foliage shade, style and habit and the effect is pleasing.

Others

Phyllostachys nigra 'Shimadake' is little known in Europe. It has occasional dark brown or black vertical striping along the length of the internodes and is similar in vigour to f. *henonis*.

Phyllostachys nigra 'Megurochiku'

Hardiness: min. -21°C (-5°F), zone 6
Aspect: sun or very light shade.
Height: 5–15 m (16.5–50 ft.), average 7 m (23 ft.)
Spread: 75 cm.–1.5 m (2.5–5 ft.) in 10 years,
openly clumping.
Habit: strong and vertical.
Culms: maximum diameter 3 cm. (1.2 in.), green ageing to
a pale olive green with almost black grooves.
Leaves: slim, 9 x 1.5 cm. (3.5 x 0.6 in.), light green.

A magical bamboo that we are fortunate to have in the Western world, as it is a protected plant only growing on the Japanese island of Awaji. There is little information as to how it emigrated from its homeland.

At one time this was only grown by a few enthusiasts because there were so few plants and propagation is difficult, but now with luck or patience it is available from a few nurseries. Some persuasion may be needed because if others are like myself, I find it difficult to part with a plant of such beauty, even if I have an abundance of them.

Disappointing at first as the plain green culms emerge, and they usually stay this colour for the first season, taking another year or two before the sulci develop their dark purple-black colour. A young plant will always have more green than coloured culms, and you must be patient for an increase in numbers. Older culms age to a pale olive green, almost yellow, more vivid than is possible to describe and intensified by the contrast with the black grooves. Careful thinning of a selection of branches will make the culms more visible and allow light in to ripen the wood, providing colour. The best plants I have seen are in cool, open aspects with full sun. Large plants in very warm areas or with some shade, offer little appeal; much of the character and colour seemingly is lost with the greater strength and thickness of the culms. It would be appropriate, therefore, to match the cold and exposed conditions of the island where it originated.

Uses

A prized possession, so bring it to the foreground on the sunny side of a sunny border. A few randomly placed jagged rocks is all you need in association; there should be nothing else close by to distract you.

Others

There is a bamboo of tale and mystery that has the reverse colouring of 'Megurochiku', with black culms and green grooving. The whispers "I've heard about it" and "I don't know what it's called" are most aggravating and I only hope that one day it will appear.

Phyllostachys nuda

Hardiness: min. -26°C (-15°F), zone 5
Aspect: sun or half shade.
Height: 4–10 m (13–33 ft.), average 5.5 m (18 ft.)
Spread: 1–2.5 m (3.3–8.2 ft.) in 10 years, open,
but clumping.
Habit: forms a respectable dense grove.
Culms: maximum diameter 4 cm. (1.6 in.), dark and
bloomy when new turning rich green.
Leaves: narrow, 10 x 1.3 cm. (4 x 0.5 in.),
dark matt olive green.

Old culms of *Phyllostachys nigra* 'Megurochiku' are distinguishable by their intensely black sulci.

A new culm *of Phyllostachys nuda* shows dark colouring and the white felted nodal ring.

This species is extensively cultivated in China for many uses and its sweet shoots, and it is widely agreed to be among the top few bamboos for tolerating climatic extremes. It is rewarding on account of its speed of development, quickly forming an exuberant mound of delicate greenery with the deep coloured culms only just visible at the base. New culms are very dark and graduate in tone on each internode from a blackish wine red to lush green, with white-felted nodal rings, which highlight the structure of the culms. Some lower branch pruning may be necessary before shooting time so the new culms can be admired. On older plants, a few culms will appear with zigzag shaping. The epithet *nuda* refers to the lack of oral setae and auricles on both the culm and leaf sheaths.

Plants in colder regions remain short and bubbly, whereas in warmer areas the culms are taller, and well spread, making the foliage canopy less dense.

Uses

A good species to use as a background plant, which if thinned regularly will provide strong garden canes. It is equally as effective as a dense screen and can be trimmed as a hedge. Quite dark in leaf, so a good foil for other ornamental plants. My *Phyllostachys nuda* grows between the glaucous and willowy *Yushania maculata* and a tall spruce, *Picea orientalis* 'Aurea'. In early summer this grouping creates a pleasing medley of form and foliage colour, particularly when the new shoots of the spruce emerge a glaring sunshine-yellow.

Others

Phyllostachys nuda f. *localis* is a rarely seen form with plentiful dark purple-brown spots, streaks and stains on the lower internodes. The colouring appears at the end of the first season and on old culms the markings may sometimes blend together for uniform colour.

A new culm of *Phyllostachys nuda* displays geniculation.

Phyllostachys parvifolia

Hardiness: min. -21°C (-5°F), zone 6
Aspect: sun or light shade.
Height: 4–12 m (13–40 ft.), average 7 m (23 ft.)
Spread: 75 cm.–1.5m (2.5–5 ft.) in 10 years. open,
but clumping.
Habit: truly vertical and stately.
Culms: maximum diameter 10 cm. (4 in.), dark green
paling with age.
Leaves: very small for Phyllostachys, to a maximum of
7 x 1.3 cm. (2.75 x 0.5 in.), deep green.

This is a potential giant in cooler areas and can exceed
the dimensions of even the best *Phyllostachys vivax*,
which has similar attributes. *Phyllostachys parvifolia* has
in the past been confused with *P. nuda* because it is
quite similar in leaf, especially on juvenile plants.

Very limited in its natural distribution, mainly
from Zheijang Province in China, and it has not
migrated through cultivation to many other areas. It is
not widely grown in the Western world either, which
is a great shame for this bamboo has much to offer
that is different from other species and I rate it highly.

The thick culms are tall for a species that grows in
a cold environment and rigidly vertical, tapering
quickly at their tips, ensuring the culms remain thick
most of the way up. Branches are quite short with
small leaves, opening late on young culms, and even
smaller on older ones. A mature plant will have evenly
spaced culms with distinct narrow columns of foliage.
It is this habit that is most individual, as the plant is
usually green in all its parts, although the culm
sheaths do offer some early summer colour with their
deep golden brown lustre and creamy yellow striping.
A young juvenile plant matures quickly so you will
not have to wait long for good results, however
availability is limited because propagation is difficult.

Uses

This makes a noble focal feature with a fastidiously
vertical habit, similar to *Semiarundinaria fastuosa* but

without the spread. The thick culms are visible at some
height within the bamboo so underplanting is a
possibility. For a contemporary Oriental ambience, plant
a bold *Trachycarpus wagnerianus* (dwarf chusan palm) in
the foreground, with a carpet of evergreen *Epimedium*.

Phyllostachys praecox

Hardiness: min. -18°C (0°F), zone 6
Aspect: sun or light shade.
Height: 4–11 m (13–36 ft.), average 6 m (20 ft.)
Spread: 75 cm.–1.5 m (2.5–5 ft.) in 10 years, open,
but clumping.
Habit: upright, well-spaced culms.
Culms: maximum diameter 7 cm. (2.75 in.), bloomy when
young with purplish nodes; some striped yellow-green.
Leaves: quite small, 10 x 1.3 cm. (4 x 0.5 in.)

Rarely grown but worth the effort for its culm form and
colouring, and also for the early shoots, which are a
spring delicacy in Shanghai and the surrounding

provinces where this bamboo grows. The pale brown
sheathed shoots emerge early in the spring and produce
the thick, rich green culms quickly. These are covered
initially in a thick white bloom and as this fades the
nodes are stained purple. On mature plants, some of the
thicker culms will age with faint yellow-green
longitudinal bands, which are visible as the branches
and leaves are held high. One of the most noticeable
features of this species are the short internodes, which
give the culms a most attractive silhouette when
showing against a pale background.

In the last decade, batches of imported *Phyllostachys
propinqua* from China have had *P. praecox* mixed in with
them, and I know of more instances where other species
have been supplied together. Unfortunately young plants
of many *Phyllostachys* look similar; it is not until
maturity that they show their true colours and character.
This mixing of batches creates problems for nurseries
and gardeners alike.

Uses

A plant would look gorgeous illuminated from behind to
highlight the short internodes.

Others

Three forms of this species exist, all rare in cultivation but worth looking out for.

Phyllostachys praecox f. *notata* has yellow striping, limited to the internodal grooves.

Phyllostachys praecox f. *prevernalis* has narrower internodes, smaller in diameter at the centre of their length, which makes the nodes appear more swollen.

Phyllostachys praecox f. *viridisulcata* is perhaps the most noteworthy. A very fine looking plant not yet cultivated in Europe or the United States to my knowledge, it has pale yellow culms randomly striped with faint green and broad, deep green sulci. This would be a welcome addition to the range of bamboos with golden culms.

Phyllostachys propinqua

Hardiness: min. -23°C (-10°F), zone 6
Aspect: sun or light shade.
Height: 4–9 m (13–30 ft.), average 6 m (20 ft.)
Spread: 75 cm.–1.5 m (2.5–5 ft.) in 10 years, moderate clumps.
Habit: usually vertical, rarely a nuisance.
Culms: maximum diameter 5 cm. (2 in.), deep green.
Leaves: dark and glossy, narrow, 12 x 1.3 cm. (4.75 x 0.5 in.), deep green.

Not well known until its hardiness was noted in continental Germany and, in consequence, it has recently become more common. It is a reliable bamboo that usually stays put and, if wandering, tends only to form a new clump a short distance from its mother plant.

It originates from many of the central and eastern provinces in China, which experience great climatic extremes. The hardiness listed above may be conservative as a few sources list it as being tolerant of -30°C (-22°F), which stretches into hardiness zone 4, placing it alongside the elite in terms of cold tolerance. It does come through all weathers unscathed, the deep gloss of the foliage shining with evergreen lustre and the thick culms remaining strong and unbending with their girth and strong nodes.

Similar in habit to *Phyllostachys meyeri* but *P. propinqua* has the edge in cooler gardens. There have

been recent flowerings on a few plants, so clonal variation is likely, or the mix-up of imported plants has created more confusion than was first thought.

Uses

Suitable for exposed and open aspects with a beefy stature and dark colouring that looks best against the light of a distant horizon or a paler background bamboo.

Others

Phyllostachys propinqua 'Bicolor' is a recent import to the United Kingdom from China and the few plants known have all flowered to my knowledge. A few are hanging on and it is to be hoped they will recover, for this is a fine bamboo. The soft golden culms are randomly striped green with bold green sulci, similar to the colouring of *P. praecox* f. *viridisulcata*, and rather unusually the leaves are slightly curled at the edges, making them appear long and narrow. In fact it is so similar in description to f. *viridisulcata* I wonder if it is the same plant; I can find no references to 'Bicolor' in literature or on the internet.

Phyllostachys propinqua 'Li Yu Gan' is a clone from Beijing that is reputedly the hardiest form and tougher than the species. It may be in existence widely already but not separated from the species, which has already proved its cold tolerance. I have a plant of 'Li Yu Gan', but it is still young and comparison is therefore difficult.

Phyllostachys rubromarginata

Hardiness: min. -21°C (-5°F), zone 6
Aspect: sun or light shade.
Height: 5–18 m (16.5–60 ft.), average 7 m (23 ft.)
Spread: 75 cm.–1.5 m (2.5–5 ft.) in 10 years, clumping when cool.
Habit: tall and vertical.
Culms: maximum diameter 7.5 cm. (3 in.), green ageing yellow-grey.
Leaves: 12 x 2.5 cm. (5 x 1 in.), green.

A tried and tested species in the United States, where in some locations it reaches giant proportions. In the cooler maritime climate of the United Kingdom it is somewhat more refined although puts on good height and solidity.

The most noticeable feature is the long internodes of the culms, which separate the branches creating layers of foliage. The plant does have to be well thinned, as there is usually a great congestion of culms at the base, especially in cooler gardens. The culms sheaths are vividly margined red, and relate to the species name of rubromarginata. The culms emerge from the sheaths fresh green and develop rapidly, ageing to a softer yellow-green with grey undertones.

I have seen wide variations between specimens, some majestic and individual in their appearance compared with surrounding bamboos; and others, usually growing on very dry soils, struggling to reach maturity, looking very poor and starved with pale culms and foliage. For success this species should be planted in fertile soil enriched with organic matter, but it is tolerant of a broad pH range.

Uses

In cooler gardens this species forms a narrow vertical column, so a large plot is not necessary. Because it tolerates both acid and alkaline soils it can be associated with an extensive range of other plants.

Phyllostachys sulphurea ('Robert Young')

Hardiness: min. -20°C (-4°F), zone 6
Aspect: sun or light shade.
Height: 7–18 m (23–60 ft.), average 8 m (26 ft.)
Spread: 1.5–4 m (5–13 ft.) In 10 years, open, slowly spreading.
Habit: bold and vertical.
Culms: maximum diameter 9 cm. (3.5 in.), soft green ageing to sulphur yellow with some green striping.
Leaves: 10 x 2 cm. (4 x 0.8 in.), mainly green, occasional cream stripes.

A beautifully coloured culm of *Phyllostachys sulphurea*.

This species is known as *Phyllostachys viridis* in the United States, and to American readers I apologize. With the confusion in naming I am adhering to the nomenclature of Chinese literature and how this bamboo is known in Britain. To allay misunderstandings synonyms are listed in Appendix 2.

The well-known cultivar 'Robert Young' is often confused with *Phyllostachys sulphurea* but is given a different description in Chinese literature, apparently having green colouring on the groove or flattened part of the branches. I have not noticed this minor attribute on any plants in the United Kingdom, although some striping does occur randomly as on the culms. I would imagine for the sake of argument and the fact that the species and cultivar are visibly alike they are better grouped as one.

Phyllostachys sulphurea is a bamboo of great beauty, but somewhat like *P. bambusoides* in its shy performance in cold eastern or northerly gardens. After much time and patience, however, it has started to produce tall, strong and colourful culms in my locality. New culms emerge pale green and colour quickly to soft yellow in the sun, irregular green striping appears dark at first and later becomes softer in tone as the culms ripen. The striping is completely random and can appear anywhere around the circumference of a culm. Branches hold the leaves very high, allowing the first-class culms to be

A snaking rhizome of *Phyllostachys sulphurea* also shows colouring, as well as the shape of the sulci.

viewed without interruption. In cooler areas with low light levels the oldest culms never develop the true sulphurous yellow of those plants grown in warmer areas. If the bright golden culms are required, I suggest growing *P. vivax* f. *aureocaulis* which is infinitely more rewarding in cool gardens.

As with many of the bamboos in my memory, the finest plant I have seen was at Peter Addington's Stream Cottage. It was positioned near the entrance to the garden to greet visitors, and therefore the last to be viewed on departure. The quality, stark form and cleanliness of this particular specimen was indicative of everything in the garden and the enthusiasm of its keeper.

Uses

In warm gardens this should be the dominant plant and be placed accordingly. In colder areas it is best used with other bamboos, where it can be compared and its fine culm detail more appreciated. I seem to remember Peter had a bold swathe of blue *Scilla* bulbs around the base of the golden culms to announce the arrival of spring.

Others

Phyllostachys sulphurea 'Houzeau' is, like the species, a wildly variable plant according to location and responds to warmth. (An alternative for a cold climate would be the recently introduced *P. vivax* f. *huanvenzhu*.) 'Houzeau' is not common in cultivation and difficult to obtain, I have not seen many specimens and it certainly does not

perform well with me. The pale green culms with their broad yellow sulci are most rewarding when they reach large proportions.

Phyllostachys sulphurea f. *viridis* has completely green culms of pigskin texture. It is impressive when mature in warm areas, but weak and unspectacular elsewhere.

Phyllostachys violascens

Hardiness: min. -18°C (0°F), zone 6
Aspect: sun or half shade.
Height: 6–15 m (20–50 ft.), average 8 m (26 ft.)
Spread: 2–4 m (6.5–13 ft.) in 10 years, open usually running.
Habit: impressively robust and with tall, thick culms.
Culms: maximum diameter 7.5 cm. (3 in.), dark violet and yellow striping, often dominant on the culm internodes.
Leaves: 13 x 2.5 cm. (5 x 1 in.), green.

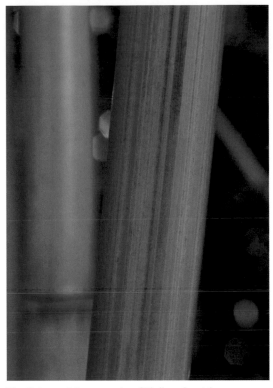

The distinct striping on a culm of *Phyllostachys violascens*.

A large grove of *Phyllostachys violascens* backlit by the late evening sun.

There are two forms of this bamboo. I have them both as very large specimens in my garden and they are very different. The species is not listed in many Chinese references and it is difficult to place this bamboo's origin. It does have Japanese names but none specific to China; it is also more widely cultivated in Japan. Professor Dieter Ohrnberger's valuable papers which collectively form the publication *Bamboos of the World* clearly classify the two forms: one likely to be the true species and the other a possible form of the species *Phyllostachys bambusoides*, although with some reservation. It has since been suggested that the second form of *P. violascens* could be a subspecies or form of *P. praecox*. This theory is more believable as *P. praecox* and *P. praecox* f. *notata* have yellow striping low on the culms or around the sulcus. Both forms of *P. violascens* have similar colouring with the addition of dark violet striping alongside the yellow, and one form could credibly be attributed to *P. praecox*.

The main differences between the two forms of *Phyllostachys violascens* are their stature and early coloration of the new shoots. The true *P. violascens* has very dark violet-purple, newly emerging culms; these remain dark in colour until, in subsequent years, the yellow-and-violet striping appears and the remaining dark brown pales. It is a very statuesque form but quite rampant, providing impressive growth from the youngest of plants. New culms emerge in the last weeks of late spring and have usually reached their full height within six or eight weeks; an impressive statistic that a bamboo novice will find difficult to believe unless experienced at first hand.

The supposedly inferior form lacks the height and impact of the true *P. violescens* and does not have the early, very dark culm tones. With me it shows its violet and yellow colouring more profusely, having a multitude of thinner stripes rather than the broad vertical banding of the true species. The inferior form is more even in its spread and is a better screening plant, having similarities in habit to *P. bissetii*. In my garden, this so-called inferior bamboo has recently produced a thick culm with yellow sulci in the lawn adjacent to the main plant, and this exciting offering is carefully guarded.

Both forms have ornamental value and are very cold tolerant, but grow so vigorously that occasional culms can be loosened in the wind. Regular thinning and general tidying is necessary to keep up their appearance. You will also need a large garden, or if you choose this and have a small plot, limit yourself to this bamboo alone or it will appear where least expected and can penetrate the clump of the most compact *Fargesia*.

Uses
Let it form a large grove and thin it at leisure to create a walkway through, or a hidden area for contemplation or sulking.

Phyllostachys viridiglaucescens

Hardiness: min. -21˚C (-5˚F), zone 6
Aspect: sun or light shade.
Height: 5–12 m (16.5–40 ft.), average 7 m (23 ft.)
Spread: 1–3 m (3.3–10 ft.) in 10 years, open, evenly spreading.
Habit: mostly vertical, curving culms sometimes at the perimeter of a grove.
Culms: maximum diameter 6 cm. (2.4 in.), emerge fresh green turning buff-yellow.
Leaves: narrow, 12 x 1.5 cm. (4.75 x 0.6 in.), pale green with glaucous undersides.

One of the earliest bamboo introductions to Europe – it arrived in France in 1846 – and it is common in many older gardens with Victorian plant collections. It is still widely grown and popular with landscape designers who desire a quick and reliable bamboo for impact.

In warmer areas it is quite rampant and tall, but it can be equally impressive in a cool climate with more colourful culms and a billowing yet graceful structure. The fresh green culms emerge from pale buff sheaths, which are streaked green and spotted with brown or dark violet. The colour of this sheathing is important for identification as the culm structure is similar to other green bamboos. The main attribute is the substantial number of culms that can be produced annually, even in cold locations. The leaves are pubescent, or faintly hairy, and are markedly blue-green on the underside; this explains the botanical name of *viridiglaucescens*.

If there is one drawback with this bamboo, it is how quickly it shows its discontent with poor, malnourished soil by producing very pale, sometimes yellow-orange culms and yellow-green leaves. It can display this colouring in containers and I have often seen it labelled incorrectly as *Phyllostachys aurea*.

Uses

It is useful for garden cane production, as a fast screen or windbreak. Feed it well and it will reward you quickly.

Phyllostachys vivax

Hardiness: min. -23˚C (-10˚F), zone 5–6
Aspect: full sun.
Height: 6–20 m (20–65.5 ft.), average 8 m (26 ft.)
Spread: 75 cm.–2 m (2.5–6.5 ft.) in 10 years, varies in spread.
Habit: bolt upright.
Culms: maximum diameter 13 cm. (5 in.), deep green turning paler with age.
Leaves: average 13 x 2.5 cm. (5 x 1 in.) sometimes larger, green.

The most cold hardy of the timber bamboos and has proved very reliable in cold gardens. In a warm location it can take on monstrous proportions with very tall, thick and rigidly vertical culms. Although more refined in a cold climate, forming tighter clumps, it can still be tall and produce massive culms. The thickest culm of any bamboo I know of in my locality was produced from this species inhabiting the driest and most inhospitable of sites.

Phyllostachys vivax shoots early in the summer. Dark lustrous green culms with obvious pale nodes emerge from very colourful sheaths, which are pale cream-buff but impressively splattered with many brown spots giving them a dark appearance. They are the most colourful and interesting culm sheaths in the genus and it is a pity they are not more persistent. Older culms pale with age and contrast well with the new shoots, and the very faint vertical ribbing on the internodes also becomes visible. The foliage and branches are well spaced and layered, elegantly arching in great curves from the culms; it is this architectural quality, best appreciated from a distance, that gives *P. vivax* its distinction.

Uses

Grow this bamboo for its great architectural quality. Although best seen in isolation, it could also be grown

Phyllostachys vivax displays its thick, dark new culms in contrast to the older, paler ones from previous years.

with carpets of creeping *Cotoneaster horizontalis* or *Mahonia repens*, in which case make sure the bamboo is well nourished, as the old leaves and sheaths will not be able to filter through the ground cover to provide nutrients.

Phyllostachys vivax f. aureocaulis

Hardiness: min. -21°C (-5°F), zone 6
Aspect: sun.
Height: 6–20 m (20–65.6 ft.), average 8m (26 ft.)
Spread: 1–3 m (3.3–10 ft.) in 10 years, usually open but can clump.
Habit: usually more vigorous than the species.
Culms: maximum diameter 13 cm. (5 in.), bright yellow with random green stripes around the circumference.
Leaves: as for the species.

I have described this as the eighth wonder of the world in my nursery catalogue and still hold it in equal high regard, for it is one of the most ornamental and rewarding of hardy bamboos. It is at least equivalent in stature to the species, and has the capacity to exceed it in height, culm girth and spread, even in a cold garden.

The beautiful golden culms emerge skywards from their dark, spotted culm sheaths with great energy, almost visibly during peak growth in June (midsummer). The green striping is random and on some culms non-existent, on others similar to bar coding, with groups of stripes of varying thickness. The best colouring is low down on the culms and always in view. The curving branches are held high with the fresh greenery casting flickering shadows.

Striping on a culm of *Phyllostachys vivax* f. *aureocaulis*.

Although easy to recommend for its many fine qualities, this form can surprise with its unpredictable spread, or lack of it. Usually a plant of substance, it can move outwards quickly and evenly with a multitude of strong, vertical culms, but is rarely so invasive that it appears in the neighbouring garden. It does take up room, and you must be prepared for a large grove of reasonably close culms, for this is its natural habit. I have come across some specimens of a good age that have generated only very tight clumps of culms, more like the habit of the species in a very cool garden. These have always been well tended and in favourable situations, with no excuse to be found for their lack of outward development. Whatever the habit, this bamboo always adds an alluring quality to its surroundings, and it matures quickly from a nursery plant.

Uses

The vivid colouring, stature and elegance will give life to any area except deep woodland. If you have a large natural pond allow this bamboo to naturalize where you can see its reflection in the water framed by the sky.

Phyllostachys vivax f. huanvenzhu

Hardiness: min. -21°C (-5°F), zone 6
Aspect: sun or light shade.
Height: 6–20 m (20–65.6 ft.), average 8 m (26 ft.)
Spread: 1–3 m (3.3–10 ft.) in 10 years, usually open but can clump.
Habit: similar to the species.
Culms: maximum diameter 13 cm. (5 in.), pale green with yellow sulci.
Leaves: as for the species.

A recent introduction to the West and assured of success because it is a form of the wonderfully reliable *Pyllostachys vivax*. Suffice to say it is equally refreshing as the species and its golden offspring, but this time with culms of green and yellow sulci. I have also seen f. *huanvenzhu* growing well in shade, the yellow sulci showing better in a dull light.

If you are unfortunate, you may acquire a plant of

Phyllostachys vivax f. *aureocaulis* shows its impressive structure and colouring.

Plyllostachys vivax f. *huanvenzhu* that remains consistent in colouring throughout its life, with the thick green culms flaunting their pale yellow sulci. However, if you are favoured, you may get a plant that occasionally reverts to the golden f. *aureocaulis*. In fact this is quite common, and the two culm colours growing together is most attractive in my opinion. On the subject of reversion I have also seen the golden form revert to f. *huanvenzhu* as well as the mother species, *P. vivax*.

Uses
As for *Phyllostachys vivax*. Two bamboos for the price of one – what more do you want?

Lesser-known Phyllostachys species
Many of the following are either recent introductions or currently being assessed for garden use. They are all green species, of which there are many more in their native China, where they have numerous uses in day-to-day life. Unless otherwise stated the species fall into hardiness zone 6, withstanding minimum temperature of between -18° to -23°C (0° to -10°F).

Phyllostachys concava
This is probably the correct name for any young plants labelled *Phyllostachys rubicunda* that have ventured into the West from China. The species is native to the far-eastern provinces and the culms are used whole for rods, poles and general construction.

Phyllostachys elegans
A species with good stature, erect with tapering culms, and shows similarities to *Phyllostachys viridiglaucescens* in a warm climate. Culms are dull green with small brown spots and the leaves are small and lance shaped, giving credibility to the epithet *elegans*. There may be more than one clone, as some plants have flowered regularly but with no ill effect to their growth.

Phyllostachys lithophila
A native of Taiwan where it is widely used as construction material, the culms being hard with good elasticity. There are very few plants in the West that are sufficiently established to judge it further.

Green culms with yellow sulci grow strongly alongside the golden culms of *Phyllostachys vivax* f. *aureocaulis*. In fact, this is a single plant of *P. vivax* f. *huanvenzhu* showing reversion to f. *aureocaulis*.

Phyllostachys lofushanensis

Reputedly quite short in its native environment, the Luofushan Mountains of Guangdong Province in China, where it grows in forests at 800 m (2,620 ft.). A very recent introduction that has yet to prove itself, but its maximum height in temperate gardens may also be very short making it potentially valuable as a landscape plant.

Phyllostachys makinoi

This is reasonably well known and similar to Phyllostachys sulphurea f. viridis in habit, and also in the pigskin texture of the culms. The new culms are impressively vertical, and emerge from the falling sheaths covered in a dense white bloom and turn pale green with some faint brown spotting. It pulps well and is used in papermaking. This species is native to the island of Taiwan and Fujian Province and, though hardy, is rarely impressive in cold areas.

Phyllostachys nigella

Well used in China for eating and timber, which are good enough reasons to try it in the West. I grow this plant and it does indeed produce plenty of new culms annually which, because of their durability, make excellent garden canes.

Phyllostachys platyglossa

This is known in the United States and has recently been introduced to Europe. It shows good qualities for landscape use and has delicious sweet shoots. The culms are dark, rich green with white bloom below the nodes, ageing to a matt grey-green. The internodes are long. Culm sheaths are reddish buff, sometimes darker in good light, and appear more persistent than in other Phyllostachys species.

Phyllostachys robustiramea (zone 7)

A short species that rarely exceeds 7 m (23 ft.) even in the wild, and grows much shorter in temperate gardens. It has reasonable culm thickness and short ribbed internodes, which become pale and blotched with age. It is grown for its edible qualities but would seem to show ornamental promise on account of its short stature.

Phyllostachys stimulosa

This is a recent introduction to Europe and the United States. The only distinguishing feature at present is the prominent culm nodes and with little information available, even in Chinese literature, it will need to be assessed further.

Phyllostachys virella

From Zhejiang Province in China and very hardy, this grows to a maximum height of 6 m (20 ft.), with a good annual crop of heavily felted, young green culms. It may be a form of Phyllostachys atrovaginata as it has a similar incense scent when the culms are rubbed.

Pleioblastus

Originally classified within Arundinaria, this large genus presents a great variety of forms and colours for use in the landscape. The species range from the shortest in the group of temperate bamboos to some fine, very architectural arborescent forms. All complement other bamboo genera, the generally thin or small leaves of Pleioblastus contrasting particularly well with large-leaved Sasa or Indocalamus and the stout culm structure of Phyllostachys.

There is some confusion with nomenclature and some species and cultivar names have been altered recently. Many of the species that exist today are in fact hybrids, as flowering within the genus is not infrequent, and plants often recover quickly or produce seed. Parentage of these hybrids is unknown and so they have been allocated species status; as knowledge of the genus improves there is no doubt new names will be assigned.

The genus is mostly native to Japan with a few, mainly taller shrubby species, originating in China. There are a few key features of Pleioblastus species that makes them simple to identify. The leptomorph rhizomes can be strongly invasive especially on the very short species, but less so on the taller forms. The rounded culms, often quite thin, have persistent sheaths and multiple branches (from three to seven per node), which produce dense foliage often held in bunches at the branch tips. Many of the shorter species are grassy in appearance and can be sheared to the ground during late winter. Fresh growth appears quickly and with much vigour the following spring. In exposed areas the leaves of these short species can bleach and burn in winter, so this ability to be pruned is useful in the landscape.

Pleioblastus are often overlooked because of their association with the few short and rampant species. There is however a plethora of fine coloured forms and the genus, in general, is of merit, as long as each species is properly managed. A little work for great reward is, in my view, a good arrangement.

Pleioblastus amarus

Hardiness: min. -18°C (0°F), zone 6
Aspect: light shade.
Height: 3–5 m (10–16.5 ft.), average 4 m (13 ft.)
Spread: 1–3 m (3.3–10 ft.) in 10 years, open but tidy.
Habit: vertical with dense arching foliage.
Culms: maximum diameter 2 cm. (0.75 in.), deep green with thick white bloom.
Leaves: long and narrow, 20 x 2 cm. (8 x 0.75 in.), green.

Little known as yet in Europe, this is one of the more woody Chinese species and fairly cold tolerant. However, the leaves naturally bleach at the tips, looking unsightly on very young plants. On more mature specimens old growth can be regularly removed leaving the fresher young culms. The main features of this species are the white powdery bloom enveloping the new culms, and the heavy branch system that carries the fingered greenery in stoic manner. In China this species is used for various crafts, including umbrella struts and small novelty items.

Uses

This makes a short, dense, leafy screen and is good for cut cane production. Culms are quite pliable when cured correctly and ideal for making bamboo sculptures.

Pleioblastus argenteostriatus 'Akebono'

Hardiness: min. -20°C (-4°F), zone 6
Aspect: partial shade.
Height: 30 cm.–1 m (1–3.3 ft.), average 50 cm. (1.6 ft.)
Spread: 50 cm.–1 m (1.6–3.3 ft.) in 10 years, nearly always clumping.
Habit: low with a compact array of foliage.
Culms: maximum diameter 0.6 cm. (0.25 in.), green.
Leaves: pointed, 6 x 1 cm. (2.5 x 0.4 in.), pale and silvery.

This was formerly listed as *Pleioblastus akebono* and has now been given cultivar status within the new species *argenteostriatus*.

A truly beautiful dwarf bamboo, which shows great reluctance to spread and is therefore quite rare in cultivation. The slim pointed leaves with their pale silvery hue show a most desirable effect: they unfold pale green and rapidly develop to a darker green at the base paling quickly to snow white towards the tips. The colour lasts longer and shines more brightly in a partially shaded area, away from the potentially scorching effect of full sun.

Sadly I have tried this fine bamboo on a few occasions and it dies every time. It appears to have a grievance with me because there are fine examples growing in my locality and it is perfectly hardy. Gardening is very much a challenge; there is always something, no matter how beautiful, that shows great reluctance to perform for you. I now pay homage to this bamboo in other people's gardens.

Uses

It hates competition, so give it the best location you can find close at hand, so you can view it regularly. Goes

well with blue or purple plants; the rounded leaves of an established purple *Cotinus* and short blue spruce, such as *Picea pungens* 'Globosa', will provide enough shade for this little beauty to flaunt itself.

Pleioblastus argenteostriatus 'Okinadake'

Hardiness: min. -15°C (5°F), zone 7
Aspect: sun or part shade.
Height: 50 cm.–1 m (1.6–3.3 ft.), average 75 cm. (2.5 ft.)
Spread: 1–2 m (3.3–6.5 ft.) in 10 years, open, but clumping.
Habit: usually low forming dense mounds.
Culms: maximum diameter 0.6 cm. (0.25 in.), green, purple tinted.
Leaves: 12 x 1.5 cm. (4.75 x 0.6 in.), irregular creamy yellow striping.

This was originally the type species and listed as *Pleioblastus argenteostriatus*, but now has been given a cultivar name as there are other forms. It is a typical lush Japanese *Pleioblastus*, with short culms and a mass of foliage forming broad grass-like mounds.

The leaves have random longitudinal pale cream or white stripes, some leaves are essentially green and others more cream than green. The new flush of spring growth is always the most attractive, especially after a plant has been mown down a month or two beforehand. In bright winter conditions the tips of the branches that are not covered in sheaths turn a velvety purple, which is common to many *Pleioblastus* species.

Uses

Forms good ground cover for taller arborescent bamboos or in light woodland, among trees and shrubs. Very suitable for growing in a pot or large shallow pan, when it must be trimmed annually but can last for a few years without supplementary food; the colour often looks better when a plant is slightly starved. Pots will be filled quickly with the vigorous rhizome producing rapid and fresh growth.

Others

Pleioblastus argenteostriatus f. *pumilus* is a confusing name for a plant formerly listed as *P. humilis* var. *pumilus* and often associated with either *P. humilis* or *P.* 'Gauntlettii'. It is more like 'Gauntlettii' (see p182) and may in fact be the same plant.

Pleioblastus argenteostriatus 'Okinadake'.

Pleioblastus chino

Hardiness: min. -25°C (-13°F), zone 5
Aspect: half shade.
Height: 2–4 m (6.5–13 ft.), average 2.5 m (8.2 ft.)
Spread: 1–3 m (3.3–10 ft.) in 10 years, open,
but can clump.
Habit: very variable; can be aggressive and short or narrow
and arching.
Culms: maximum diameter 2 cm. (0.75 in.), green.
Leaves: narrow and lanceolate, 20 x 2 cm. (8 x 0.75 cm.),
intensely green.

Usually a wildly aggressive bamboo with the ability to
cover great tracts in woodland areas, however I know of
specimens that take on large shrubby proportions, tight
in habit and certainly pleasing. It must be said that these
specimens have been rigorously kept in check by
mowing, digging or frequent applications of contact
herbicide, forcing new culms to generate close to the
main plant.

Pleioblastus chino is a tough Japanese species now
cultivated in areas on the east coast of China, probably
as winter bedding for livestock. Plants are very leafy and
after cutting would also provide good insulation around
tender crops.

There are some pleasing forms that have developed
from this very cold-tolerant species showing very
different habits and colouring.

Uses

This would make excellent game cover in large wooded
areas or planted to stabilize steep banks.

Others

Pleioblastus chino f. *angustifolius* and *P. chino*
'Murakamianus' have both flowered in the past fifteen
years and may be on the point of extinction in the
United Kingdom; I have not found either for sale, unless
they are hidden away, recovering. The former had very
narrow leaves with a touch of variegation and the latter
was very beautiful with almost white leaves but required
partial shade. Both are still listed in the United States so
recovery may be possible.

Pleioblastus chino f. *aureostriatus* has white to creamy
yellow leaf variegation and is smaller than the species. It
often stays compact but arches outward in a loose dome
and prefers light shade.

Pleioblastus chino 'Kimmei' is striped yellow in leaf,
compact, and also offers some culm colouring with
narrow yellow and green striping.

Pleioblastus chino 'Vaginatus Variegatus' is delicately
variegated and listed in the United States. It would
appear to be similar to the little known *P. chino* f.
argenteostriatus sometimes grown in the United Kingdom.

Pleioblastus chino f. elegantissimus

Hardiness: min. -18°C (0°F), zone 6
Aspect: sun or part shade.
Height: 1–2 m (3.3–6.5 ft.), average 1.5 m (5 ft.)
Spread: 75 cm.–1.5 m (2.5–5 ft.) in 10 years, usually clumping.
Habit: dense domes of hanging leaves.
Culms: maximum diameter 1.25 cm. (0.5 in.), colouring very pale in overall effect.
Leaves: very narrow, 9 x 0.5 cm. (3.5 x 0.2 in.), green with fine white variegation.

This has been afforded the honour of its own place in this listing because it is superior in all its qualities to the other variegated forms of the species. Given its unique silvery white hue from the masses of thin, variegated leaves and mostly globular shape, it is a useful contrast to just about any bamboo.

Young nursery plants stay short until a suitable rhizome system has been produced, at which time taller culms will emerge and start to form the bamboo's true shape. It has the ability to spread, but usually forms a tight dome or flat-topped bush of equal proportions in width and height before moving on to new territory. Any "runners" are simply checked with a sharp downward chop from a spade, ensuring the rhizome is severed, not just newly emerging culms, and then removed from the soil.

Many years ago I borrowed a substantial specimen of f. *elegantissimus* from Tony Churly, a good friend and local bamboo enthusiast. It was in a large container and ripe for exhibition with beautiful colour and a fine shape. It continued to look the same for another eight years and the plant has not yet been returned. In fact it is now two plants, divided in the ninth year, but remained top class for the previous eight, with only a little thinning and winter protection, and no extra food. It was divided and potted only because the container had disintegrated; the bamboo was still in perfect order. I am not suggesting the plant should be starved to provide good appearance, merely stating that bamboos never cease to amaze me and continue to reward with little or no attention.

Uses

As stated, this is a fine container plant, but offer it some protection in the winter by plunging it in the soil or moving it in to a cold glasshouse or similar unheated structure. If the roots are prevented from freezing in the pot, above ground the foliage will not desiccate.

Above: Pleioblastus chino f. *elegantissimus* showing good colour and compact habit in light woodland.

Right: Close up of a leaf of *Pleioblastus chino* f. *elegantissimus.*

Pleioblastus chino var. hisauchii

Hardiness: min. -25°C (-13°F), zone 5
Aspect: sun or light shade.
Height: 2.5–5 m (8.2–16.5 ft.), average 3.5 m (11.5 ft.)
Spread: 75 cm.–1.5 m (2.5–1.5 ft.) in 10 years, open, but clumping.
Habit: vertical with arching foliage.
Culms: maximum diameter 2.5 cm. (1 in.), mid green with pale persistent sheaths.
Leaves: long and narrow, 23 x 1.25 cm. (9 x 0.5 in.), green.

A distinct and quite woody variety that often exceeds the height and culm girth given in Chinese references, particularly in sheltered or warm aspects. Small juvenile plants can sprout tall culms very quickly and hold narrow leaves on the many branches that develop from the nodes, creating a fountain-like effect. More often than not this bamboo will form a tight clump, having a tendency to spread only in dry soils where it will also stay short and juvenile.

It is used as an ornamental plant in China, which is indeed high acclaim considering how widespread the bamboo family is throughout the country. Not well known in the West, but young plants are now being produced and should be more widely planted.

Uses

As a solitary specimen or against a high wall where its architectural qualities can be appreciated.

Pleioblastus fortunei (syn. *P. variegatus*)

Hardiness: min. -25°C (-13°F), zone 5
Aspect: sun or part shade.
Height: 60 cm.–1.5 m (2–5 ft.), average 90 cm. (3 ft.)
Spread: 1–1.5 m (3.3–5 ft.) in 10 years, usually clumps.
Habit: low and leafy in broad mounds.
Culms: maximum diameter 0.6 cm. (0.25 in.), green.
Leaves: 12 x 1.25 cm. (5 x 0.5 in.), brightly variegated, with creamy striping on leaves.

An early introduction from Japan by Robert Fortune and as popular now as it ever was. It is of uncertain origin, having been found only in cultivation.

This dwarf bamboo shows great virtue in its many garden uses and is equally at home in a shallow container as it is ambling among other plants in an open border or light woodland. The pointed, slightly curving leaves are dramatically striped white or cream, The leaf coloration can vary according to the soil pH and nutrient levels, and the degree of exposure, but plants always appear clean and refreshing in their vigour during the growing season, the foliage massing together in spiky tufts. It is rarely a nuisance and easy to uproot when it does wander sideways.

Some colour will be lost in dense shade so keep it in good light, not necessarily full sun where, if it is dry, the leaves may scorch. Established plants are best sheared to the ground before spring growth begins, especially after a freezing winter which can result in seared and shredded foliage. Plants left unclipped often look gaunt and leggy, particularly in shade.

Uses

A well-grown plant will be one of the brightest in the garden and *Pleioblastus fortunei* is adept at bringing to life the dullest and most inhospitable areas. In terms of colour association, the possibilities are endless and this should be a first choice when creating a bright tapestry of plants. It is excellent in the foreground of a perennial border, with reds or other brazen colours erupting from behind. It is also good in pots.

Pleioblastus 'Gauntlettii'

Hardiness: min. -18°C (0°F), zone 6
Aspect: sun or part shade.
Height: 40–80 cm. (1.3–2.6 ft.) , average 50 cm. (1.6 ft.)
Spread: 75 cm.–1.5 m (2.5–5 ft.) in 10 years, runs slightly.
Habit: Low spreading mounds.
Culms: maximum diameter 0.6 cm. (0.25 in.), green.
Leaves: pointed, 9 x 1.5 cm. (3.5 x 0.6 in.), fresh green.

I have an old plant catalogue *circa* 1910 from the Japanese Nurseries of V. N. Gauntlett and Co. Ltd, from Chiddingfold, Surrey, England, who were responsible for propagating and distributing many of the new plants being brought into the country at that time. *Pleioblastus* 'Gauntlettii' was first described, and obviously named by them, but as a species of greater height than described above. This bamboo can reach 2 m (6.5 ft.) if grown without annual clipping and this was the height listed in the catalogue; perhaps because in the early years, before the First World War, bamboos were viewed as potentially woody plants and gardeners may have shown restraint in limiting their growth.

Pleioblastus humilis, with which 'Gauntlettii' is associated, was listed separately in Gauntlett's catalogue as a "Japanese Dwarf" with a height of 75 cm. (2.5 ft.). This is more in keeping with the height of 'Gauntlettii' as we know it now rather than *P. humilis*, which grows taller. It may be that during the twentieth century these two plants have inadvertently swapped names. Confused? Well to exacerbate the situation 'Gauntlettii' is often thought to be synonymous with *Pleioblastus humilis* var. *pumilus*, now renamed *P. argenteostriatus* f. *pumilus*.

Having said all this, to most gardeners it is not the name that is important, but more the character and appearance of the plant and whether it appeals. *Pleioblastus* 'Gauntlettii' is a good choice; and although it offers no more than its fresh tufted greenery, it is easy to maintain, of robust quality, provides quick effect and associates well with a myriad of other plants.

Uses
Versatile in sun, shade and pots. Plant it with bright foliage or flowers or use it to edge a path.

Others

Pleioblastus humilis cannot be given equal merit, as it is particularly invasive and suitable only for areas of wilderness or large woodland. The elongated culms, meandering at all angles through anything in their path, each hold a sparse array of drooping, mid green leaves.

Pleioblastus gramineus

Hardiness: min. -20°C (-4°F), zone 6
Aspect: sun or shade.
Height: 2–5 m (6.5–16.5 ft.), average 3 m (10 ft.)
Spread: 1–2 m (3.3–6.5 ft.) in 10 years, usually clumping.
Habit: willowy and elegant with arching foliage.
Culms: maximum diameter 2 cm. (0.8 in.), mid green.
Leaves: long and narrow, 23 x 1.25 cm. (9 x 0.5 in.), mid green.

Almost identical in appearance to *Pleioblastus linearis* apart from having smooth culm sheaths with attached oral setae and leaves that twist at the tips. It can develop a different habit to *P. linearis*, which is perhaps less invasive in an open aspect. Both plants are ideal in fairly dense shade or woodland where they are less likely to invade.

Pleioblastus gramineus has become better known in recent years due to the sudden flowering of *P. linearis*. The latter was well known for producing the very desirable tall and arching habit much sought after in landscaping, and *P. gramineus* has been a suitable replacement.

The long, slender, grass-like leaves arch from the branches in a fountain-like manner from the usually dense and rigid mass of culms. The persistent culm sheaths can become ragged but add to the unusual primordial appearance of this bamboo. It is native to the Japanese Ryukyu Islands and tolerates salt-laden winds. The foliage is quite tough and comes through most winters unscathed.

Uses
Plant it so it will arch over a path or pond edge, or place at the centre of an open woodland grove.

Others

Pleioblastus gramineus f. *monstrispiralis* is known in Japan by the cultivar name of 'Rasetu-chiku', and is endemic to the remote Japanese Islands of the Kagoshima Prefecture. It is still rare in the the United Kingdom and the United States, and almost unheard of in Europe. It produces some tillering culms with a pronounced spiral effect from sympodial sections of the rhizome, and normal culms from monopodial sections. It is classed as an amphipodial bamboo, which is very rare.

Pleioblastus hindsii

Hardiness: min. -20°C (-4°F), zone 6
Aspect: sun or shade.
Height: 3–5.5 m (10–18 ft.), average 4 m (13 ft.)
Spread: 1–2 m (3.3–6.5 ft.) in 10 years, generally clumping.
Habit: bold and vertical, with upward pointing branches.
Culms: maximum diameter 3 cm. (1.2 in.), grey-green.
Leaves: narrow, often pointing upwards, 18 x 1.5 cm. (7 x 0.6 in.), matt olive green.

A native of China but widely grown in Japan, this is a robust woody species that can spread but is usually refined, particularly in woodland areas. The culms have persistent

sheaths which become ragged or torn at their tips and lend the plant an informal appearance rather than the well-manicured look. The many branches on the upper nodes are upward pointing and carry the pointed leaves in a similar upright stance, creating a discernible brush-like effect.

The robust, vertical culms vary in colour from a matt grey-green to richer olive tones depending on their age. The leaves are equally non-reflecting and dark in tone, slender and narrowing sharply to a pronounced tip. The leaf texture is leathery and this bamboo will tolerate much exposure and salty air. Shoots appear regularly throughout the growing season and are a delicacy in Japan providing a long season of culinary delight.

Uses

As stately as it is, its dark and severe appearance suits a background role or, for larger group plantings, as screening or windbreaks. An ideal accompaniment to Gothic follies and gloomy woodland should you wish to reach out to your dark side.

Others

Pleioblastus oleosus is of similar habit and equal hardiness to *P. hindsii* but a fresher green in all its parts, older culms often ageing to yellow. It would be a fine partner for *P. hindsii*, combining their light and dark colouring.

Pleioblastus kongosanensis 'Aureostriatus'

Hardiness: min. -20˚C (-4˚F), zone 6
Aspect: sun or light shade.
Height: 1–1.8 m (3.3–6 ft.), average 1.2 m (4 ft.)
Spread: 75 cm.–1.5 m (2.5–5 ft.) in 10 years, open, running slightly.
Habit: short and upright with hanging leaves.
Culms: maximum diameter 1 cm. (0.4 in.), green.
Leaves: long, and thin, 20 x 2 cm. (8 x 0.8 in.), green with sporadic yellow striping.

A variable cultivar in habit and colouring, depending on its placement in the garden. The thin culms hold the leaves high on the plant with little branching low down and give 'Aureostiatus' a different appearance to many of the other short *Pleioblastus*. The leaves are normally pale green with the lighter, yellow striping more visible in slight shade and fertile soil. The best foliage is always on plants that have been hard pruned in the dormant season, and pruning will help to reduce the height so

the foliage is in better view. Allow this bamboo to establish for a few seasons before you start to prune, so it can develop the strong rhizome system necessary to generate vigorous growth.

Uses

Essentially a collector's item but it does offer pleasing contrast to other plants. Try it waving about in the open border with robust deciduous shrubs, or on the high bank of a pond. The framework of the leaves is similar to that of a *Phragmites* reed and equally effective when blowing horizontally in the wind.

Pleioblastus linearis

Hardiness: min. -20˚C (-4˚F), zone 6
Aspect: sun or some shade.
Height: 2–5 m (6.5–16.5 ft.), average 4 m (13 ft.)
Spread: 1–2 m (3.3–6.5 ft.) in 10 years, mostly clumping.
Habit: elegant, bold and tidy, quite vertical.
Culms: maximum diameter 2 cm. (0.8 in.), pale green. The persistent sheaths are green when young, paling to buff.
Leaves: long and narrow, 20 x 1.25 cm. (8 x 0.5 in.), fresh green.

This species forms brilliant arches of plumed foliage from a central, usually dense column of culms and has great architectural value. It looks very similar to *Pleioblastus gramineus* but is perhaps more versatile, and I have found it does as well in full sun as in shade. The leaves are rich green, flat, very narrow and long, almost grass-like in quality. New culms emerge in a stark manner, much paler in colour than the foliage, before the green culm sheaths lose their colour and turn to buff.

Very hardy and tolerant of extremes in climate, it was planted widely until recent flowering occurred. A new seedling generation has already been produced, showing strength and early maturity, so this species should once again become popular.

Uses

A fine landscape plant, useful to break up the monotony of metropolitan architecture. In a more rural setting, view it from a distance amid large areas of open parkland or a woodland clearing. For association try it with ferns and vast swathes of spring bulbs or simple low ground cover plants, such as ivies or *Lonicera pileata*.

Long leaves of *Pleioblastus linearis* touched by the frost.

Pleioblastus longifimbriatus

Hardiness: min. -20°C (-4°F), zone 6
Aspect: sun or shade.
Height: 2–4 m (6.5–13 ft.), average 2.5 m (8.2 ft.)
Spread: 75 cm.–1.5 m (2.5–5 ft.) in 10 years, bold clumps.
Habit: upright, dense
forming colonies.
Culms: maximum diameter
1.5 cm. (0.6 in.),
light green, yellowing
with age.
Leaves: thin and narrow,
14 x 2 cm. (5.5 x 0.8 in.),
pale green.

A little known species erroneously listed as *Sinobambusa intermedia* by at least one source in the United Kingdom, which is a completely different Chinese bamboo. Native to Guangdong Province and grown elsewhere in China this bamboo provides a multitude of thin durable culms used for fencing and screening.

    Pleioblastus longifimbriatus produces dense foliage on the plentiful culms and matures fast, filling a space quickly. It is best thinned regularly so some of the character of its culm structure is visible. The culms emerge light green with a pale bloom and develop quickly, sprouting the abundant leaves. Older culms pale to a yellow-green and on close inspection minute purple speckling is often visible. Branching is short and tight to the culms, holding the curving leaves outward like the fingers on an open hand.

    Although quite shrubby and seemingly hardy the leaves are sometimes damaged in the winter and should selective pruning be a chore, it can be cut to the ground. The resulting growth may not be as strong but it will be much fresher. It can form large dense patches where left uncontrolled and forgotten, but is not aggressive to the point of nuisance.

Uses

Good for woodland ground cover or, if thinned frequently, will provide plenty of thin support canes for herbaceous plants.

Pleioblastus pygmaeus

Hardiness: min. -29°C (-20°F), zone 4
Aspect: sun or light shade.
Height: 20–60 cm. (0.6–2 ft.), average 30 cm. (1 ft.)
Spread: 1–4 m (3.3–13 ft.) in 10 years, nearly always invasive.
Habit: short, squat and spiky.
Culms: maximum diameter 0.3 cm. (0.15 in.), green.
Leaves: small, in rows, 5 x 0.5 cm. (2 x 0.2 in.), deep green, with some winter bleaching.

There is enormous variation within this species and some superior forms are available. The plants that usually have the tiniest of leaves are nearly always the ones that have the shortest and most pleasing habit. The problem with this quality specification is that chemical dwarfing agents are often used in wholesale plant production, and as this is a very pretty plant that appeals to impulse buyers, what you see is not necessarily what you get. The true species is the smallest of all the temperate bamboos, rarely exceeding 30 cm. (1 ft.). It is vigorous but not as pernicious as some of the larger clones.

The tiny leaves have a fern-like form, held rigidly on the wispy culms. Some winter bleaching can occur, but against the dark greenery this effect is uniform and attractive. The whole plant is easily sheared to the ground late in the winter, which keeps growth fresh and short. Larger clones will colonize areas to the point of complete domination, particularly in shady woodland where plants are best mown continually, which may eventually give control. Better to select a good cultivar and keep a close eye on it, rather than regret you ever planted it.

Uses

A widely used amenity plant for parks and urban planting. It looks stunning in swathes across raised beds with the white bark of birch trees piercing the greenery. If you have a small garden it grows successfully in large, shallow pans and troughs.

Others

Pleioblastus pygmaeus 'Distichus' is most similar to the species in appearance except it is taller with a broader fan of leaves at the top of each culm, growing to 60 cm. (2 ft.) high. As with the species it relishes being pruned hard before new growth sprouts in spring but can also be clipped during the growing season to keep it stunted. Two other cultivars, 'Ramosissimus' and 'Mirrezuzume' are similar, but both are more vigorous than the species.

The distinct leaf arrangement of *Pleioblastus pygmaeus* 'Distichus'.

Pleioblastus shibuyanus 'Tsuboi'

Hardiness: min. -25°C (-13°F), zone 5
Aspect: sun or light shade.
Height: 1–2.5 m (3.3–8.2 ft.), average 2 m (6.5 ft.)
Spread: 1 cm.–4 m (3.3–14 ft.) in 10 years, usually invades.
Culms: maximum diameter 1.25 cm. (0.5 in.), green.
Habit: mounds of stiff culms with dense foliage.
Leaves: narrow, 15 x 2 cm. (6 x 0.8 in.), bright green with broad creamy variegation.

This is undoubtedly one of the boldest and brightest bamboos in my garden, covering at least 15 sq. m (160 sq. ft.) in as many years. It is very dense in appearance and creates a huge plume of colourful foliage in a half-shaded area, central to the garden, where it is surrounded by taller, more arborescent forms such as *Thamnocalamus spathiflorus, Phyllostachys aureosulcata* f. *spectabilis, Phyllostachys violascens* and *Fargesia robusta*, all of which have different shapes, colouring and texture. The tallest culms on my specimen are now 3 m (10 ft.) rising through the centre of the colony, which never fail to surprise me as plants I see in other gardens are considerably shorter. The leaves, the brightest for the species, are artistically streaked and suffused with white and pale cream, and the young growth is especially bright with more white than green. Whether in the garden or a pot it is not abashed by the vagaries of winter weather and the leaves nearly always remain fresh.

Although vigorous, this cultivar at least spreads evenly and predictably. If you need to control it, then do a little work annually on one side, and on other sides in rotation in the years that follow, allowing it some room and time for recovery. It is easily clipped to make a dwarf dense colony or can be cut through to create narrow tunnels and pathways.

This cultivar is maddening when it comes to propagation time. New, accessible culms can take a year or two before they put on feeding roots suitable for establishing in a container, but the new culms of 'Tsuboi' rely on the mother plant to support them so they can concentrate their energy into development of leaves and further shoot production. The most successful method is to bury long pieces of cut rhizome in trays and forget about them for a year or two. The result is a grassy crop of young juvenile shoots ideal for division and growing on.

The brightly variegated foliage of *Pleioblastus shibuyanus* 'Tsuboi'.

Uses

'Tsuboi' makes a fine backdrop to other genera that have tall and thick culms, the darkness of the taller bamboos will be accented by the bright foliage behind. For all its vigour this cultivar also makes a rewarding container plant and rarely looks starved.

Pleioblastus simonii

Hardiness: min. -25°C (-13°F), zone 5
Aspect: sun or part shade.
Height: 3–6 m (10–20 ft.), average 4 m (13 ft.)
Spread: 75 cm.–1.5 m (2.5–5 ft.) in 10 years, open, but clumping.
Habit: always stout and vertical.
Culms: maximum diameter 3 cm. (1.2 in.), green with pale sheaths.
Leaves: narrow, 20 x 2 cm. (8 x 0.8 in.), green.

This has always been a well-used plant, introduced very early into Western gardens and widely used in China and Japan as an ornamental and for various crafts. It produces large amounts of fresh green, vertical culms annually, some very late in the season. The narrow, willowy leaves are borne on a congested cluster of branches which, like the culms, have persistent parchment-coloured sheaths.

I have seen this bamboo in many gardens, well kept and with good shape due to frequent thinning of older culms, which can become ragged. Some of the later shoots come too late in the year to develop fully and they may die back during the advance of winter, so are also best removed. It is rarely aggressive and clumps well, particularly in a harsh aspect, rich soil and a sheltered situation will encourage it to be more adventurous.

This species has flowered on a few occasions in the past century and a half, but either plants regenerate quickly or produce viable seed.

Uses

This is one of the best bamboos for screens and windbreaks. Regular thinning will generate a steady supply of strong, very straight culms for use elsewhere in the garden.

Others

Pleioblastus simonii 'Variegatus' was formerly known as *P. simonii* var. *heterophyllus*, which is a better descriptive name. The leaves are shyly variegated and only become bright when the bamboo is under stress (which makes it good for growing in pots) or has been reduced in stature by thinning and topping. *Heterophyllus* refers to the uneven sizes of the leaves: some are like the species, others are of shoelace thickness and produced in clusters. The thinner leaves are usually the most variegated and should you have the time, some of the thicker leaves can be removed, which will help to stunt the plant as well as improve its appearance. This cultivar usually produces flowers in association with the finer leaves as part of its natural growth pattern, but seed is rarely produced and the plant continues to grow.

Pleioblastus viridistriatus

Hardiness: min. -25°C (-13°F), zone 5
Aspect: sun or half shade.
Height: 1–1.8 m (3.3–6 ft.), average 1.2 m (4 ft.)
Spread: 1–2 m (3.3–6.5 ft.) in 10 years, open but clumping.
Habit: short colonies of leafy culms.
Culms: maximum diameter 1 cm. (0.4 in.), green, purple tints in sun.
Leaves: 18 x 2.5 cm. (7 x 1 in.), variegated golden yellow with green striping.

A charismatic species widely planted in landscapes and gardens for its foliage colouring, unique among bamboos. It was an early introduction to Europe from Japan in the 1870s and the brightest yellow-variegated garden plant available at the time.

Unfolding leaves quickly absorb the light and turn to an opaque banana yellow with random dark green striping, and in full sun there are some brief pink tints to accompany this. Culms are often purple-tinted in strong sunlight.

This bamboo can be a little choosy where it grows best. In a very hot location, especially when dry, it is liable to scorch and should be afforded some light shade. In very deep shade however the bright golden colouring is diminished and it looks washed out, turning a dull lime colour. In moist, cool gardens it is less fussy, and except in heavy shade the colour will always be bright and the plant performs well. As with some of the other *Pleioblastus*, annual shearing is the best way to generate fresh colour and will also prevent the bamboo from becoming woody or too leggy.

Pleioblastus viridistriatus.

Uses

Offers colour contrast to any planting scheme. I have seen it used effectively planted in vast colonies around ponds and backed by taller shrubs and trees, which cast changing shadows over the bright foliage below.

The vivid golden foliage of *Pleioblastus viridistriatus* var. *chrysophyllus*.

Others

Pleioblastus viridistriatus var. *chrysophyllus* is a variety with no green striping on the leaves and is my favourite form. It is generally shorter and more compact than the species, with dense plumes of rich amber-yellow leaves. Plant against a dark background where it will glow.

    Pleioblastus viridistriatus 'Bracken Hill' and 'Feesey's Form' are taller and shorter cultivars respectively, with identical colouring to the species. As all forms of this bamboo should be pruned annually neither of these is especially noteworthy.

Pseudosasa

This is a robust genus with many more species than the few we grow in Western gardens, most of them woody and arborescent in form and medium or tall in height. *Pseudosasa* has a leptomorph rhizome system that is rarely any trouble in temperate gardens, but does generate quantities of closely spaced culms forming solid groves. They originate from China and Japan.

    The main botanical characteristics are the single branch from the upper nodes, which can later be accompanied by two smaller branches. The culm sheaths are very persistent and in most cases remain tidy, giving the plant its well-known feature of alternating sheath and visible sections of internode on each culm. The leaves are quite large, arranged in palmate fashion at the ends of the long branches, but are not as substantial as the other genera that have single branches from the nodes, namely *Indocalamus*, *Sasa* and *Sasaella*.

Apart from the very short *Pseudosasa owatarii* the various species all make effective screens, hedges and windbreaks. Some are also valued as fine ornamental specimens.

Pseudosasa amabilis

Hardiness: min. -12°C (10°F), zone 8
Aspect: sun or light shade.
Height: 5–15 m (16.5–50 ft.), average 7 m (23 ft.)
Spread: 75 cm.–1.5 m (2.5–5 ft.) in 10 years, vigorously clumping.
Habit: impressively vertical.
Culms: maximum diameter 6 cm. (2.4 in.), green with pale sheaths.
Leaves: quite large 30 x 3 cm. (12 x 1.2 in.), green.

The Tonkin cane, or tea stick bamboo, is on the borderline for inclusion in this section as it needs a warm garden to perform to the best of its ability. It will survive in colder areas remaining juvenile, but a leafy plant with some character nevertheless. When grown in a warm temperate environment it will generate tall and evenly thick culms with little tapering. The branches are formed only on the top half of the culms and hold the large leaves with much flair, creating the archetypal image of bamboo. The other distinguishing feature is the new culms and sheaths, all of which are densely covered in bristly chestnut hairs, contrasting well with the older culms.

The culms are a valuable export commodity in southern China, where huge stands are cultivated for garden cane production, and also used exclusively to produce the best split-cane fly-fishing rods. Larger culms are more valuable and used for furniture or sports equipment, especially traditional poles for skiing and vaulting.

Uses
Save money and grow your own garden canes, but plant it in a warm, sheltered spot.

Pseudosasa japonica

Hardiness: min. -23°C (-10°F), zone 5–6
Aspect: sun or part shade.
Height: 3–5 m (10–16.5 ft.), average 4 m (13 ft.)
Spread: 1–3 m (3.3–10 ft.) in 10 years, speedily clumping.
Habit: upright and architectural.
Culms: maximum diameter 2 cm. (0.8 in.), pale sheathed.
Leaves: long and drooping, 30 x 3 cm. (12 x 1.2 in.), rich dusky green.

After the demise of *Fargesia murielae* due to flowering this probably became the most common bamboo in cultivation. It is common because it is a thing of beauty, with character, good stature, speed of development and an enviable ability to adapt to almost any location. I recommend it highly as a beginner's bamboo; its success is almost guaranteed and this should encourage the gardener to try more difficult types.

The species was introduced to Europe in 1850 and to the United States of America a decade later, one of the first bamboo introductions to both continents. Its origins are in Japan, in the north of the country, and South Korea, but it has migrated through cultivation to many other Asian countries. It remains one of the bamboos most in demand and is used extensively in landscaping, for specimen or windbreak use. The fact that it is regarded in China and Japan as a fine ornamental plant is surely proof that it will offer the imagery required to create an oriental or semi-tropical feel to the garden.

The pointed leaves are the largest on offer among the group of taller, woodier bamboos, and droop elegantly from branches, which are angled close to the culms. The culm and branch sheaths are persistent and at their best on younger culms; older growth should be removed as the sheaths shred rather untidily. It is very tolerant of wind and salt air, so particularly useful to give shelter in coastal areas, as well as adapting to positions of full sun or some shade. It is not too fussy about soil type, tolerating a wide range in pH, but will spoil in constantly waterlogged conditions, and run amok in the driest of sandy soils, where it can be used to stabilize steep banking. In most temperate gardens it forms a large compact grove and a ready supply of useable culms. I remember playing in old woodland stands of

Pseudosasa japonica as a child, cutting hideaways in the dense colonies of culms and making spears from the resulting debris. The common name for this plant is arrow bamboo because the uniform roundness of the culms, including the nodal sections, makes them suitable for arrows.

Uses

This always looks architectural against straight lines of brickwork or robust timber railed fencing. Well tried and tested as screening, security barriers, hedging and windbreaks, as well as a specimen plant.

Others

Pseudosasa japonica var. *pleioblastoides* is almost identical to the species except for being darker green, and more rigid and vertical. The slightly shorter and narrower leaves are two toned on the undersides. The leaves are held on a slightly different branch system to *P. japonica*, with the single branches quickly developing other secondary ones. New culms are often tinted dusky purple in full sun, which adds to the colour contrast of the pale persistent sheaths. I believe this variety to be much more cold and wind tolerant than the species; it exemplifies itself in my garden taking the full force of the north-easterly winter gales. It is also in the wettest part of the garden, which can flood in the winter, but never shows signs of regression for its ill treatment. Aside from this it has grown on either side of a lawn path and formed a natural tunnel. Any culms appearing in the grass are mown immediately to keep the pathway open.

Pseudosasa japonica var. *pleioblastoides* growing either side of a path forms a tunnel, opening into a grassy glade.

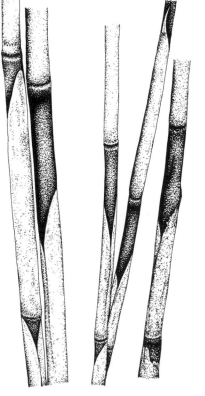

Persistent pale sheaths of *Pseudosasa japonica* var. *pleioblastoides*.

Pseudosasa japonica 'Akebonosuji' is identical in stature to the type form of *P. japonica*, and is a true beauty. The leaves are longitudinally striped with creamy yellow variegation, which varies considerably between each leaf. Reversion to green can occur, so occasional division must take place to keep the better variegated parts; it is well worth the effort. Sometimes a culm will produce leaves shading from green at the base to white at the tip, similar in effect to the tiny *Pleioblastus argenteostriatus* 'Akebono'. These culms can be separated, resulting in a plant of the recognised cultivar *Pseudosasa japonica* 'Akebono', the cultivar name describing the leaf colouring. Unfortunately 'Akebono' is more likely to revert to green than 'Akebonosuji'. When purchasing either of these cultivars, ensure you obtain a plant that is already showing good variegation with few, or preferably no, green leaves.

Plants labelled as *Pseudosasa japonica* 'Variegata' are nearly always 'Akebonosuji'.

Pseudosasa japonica 'Tsutsumiana'

Hardiness: min. -23°C (-10°F), zone 5–6
Aspect: sun or part shade.
Height: 2–5 m (6.5–16.5 ft.), average 3 m (10 ft.)
Spread: 1–13 m (3.3–11.5 ft.) in 10 years, slowly spreading.
Habit: stocky, lines of culms radiating from the central plant.
Culms: maximum diameter 2.5 cm. (1 in.), fresh green.
Leaves: slightly smaller than the species, fresh green.

A very distinct cultivar known as the green onion bamboo in the United States because some of the culms on mature plants swell in a bulbous manner above each node and this thickens the internode considerably, making it broader than the node. The swelling narrows sharply towards the node above and when this is very pronounced, the individual culm takes on spiralling or slight zigzag formation. To appreciate these generous swellings it is necessary to thin the plain culms regularly and also to remove the culm sheaths. If this is a chore, plant it in the background and remove some of the older more swollen culms for indoor decoration; they dry well and last for many years.

'Tsutsumiana' is normally shorter than *Pseudosasa japonica*, particularly in cool gardens, but in warm areas the height difference is hardly noticeable. It is as easy to grow and rarely fussy; however, it is inclined to wander with a profusion of juvenile, unshapely culms. Regular control will help force stronger culms close to the main clump and keep it easily within bounds.

Uses
Excellent for cutting and using in indoor arrangements, and you can impress the neighbours with your correct pronunciation of 'Tsutsumiana'.

Pseudosasa owatarii

Hardiness: min. -23°C (-10°F), zone 5–6
Aspect: sun or part shade.
Height: 10 cm.–1 m (0.3–3.3 ft.), average 50 cm. (1.6 ft.)
Spread: 75 cm.–1.5 m (2.5–5 ft.) in 10 years,
slow spreading.
Habit: varies from very squat to low and arching.
Culms: maximum diameter 1.5 cm. (0.6 in.), green.
Leaves: small and pointed, 8 x 1.25 cm. (3.2 x 0.5 in.),
dark green with faint tip bleaching.

The distinctive pointed leaves of *Pseudosasa japonica*.

Bulbous swellings on culms taken from a mature *Pseudosasa japonica* 'Tsutsumiana'.

A dwarf species from the Japanese island of Yakushima that may have two forms: one short and very compact from high altitudes, and the other more rampant from the forest floors. Both forms are suitable for clipping to keep them low and colourful. *Pseudosasa owatarii* is often mistaken for *P. pygmaeus*, but they are easy to tell apart as the latter has five or more short leaves in clusters whereas *P. owatarii* has fewer, longer and more pointed leaves with a glossier sheen. The short form is named *P. owatarii* 'Pygmaea', which adds to the confusion.

Uses

The short form, *Pseudosasa owatarii* 'Pygmaea', does not like crowding and prefers an open aspect. Keep it at the edge of a border and let it associate with dwarf shrubs or conifers; it is usually well behaved.

Pseudosasa usawai

Hardiness: min. -15°C (5°F), zone 7
Aspect: sun or part shade.
Height: 3–5 m (10–16.5 ft.), average 4 m (8.2 ft.)
Spread: 75 cm.–1.5 m (2.5–5 ft.) in 10 years, dense thickets.
Habit: vertical culms arching above.
Culms: maximum diameter 3 cm. (1.2 in.), deep green with bright culm sheaths.
Leaves: narrow, 30 x 2 cm. (12 x 0.8 in.), deep green.

A native of Taiwan and, although one of the less hardy species of *Pseudosasa*, it is well worth taking a risk with because of its beautiful habit. The new culms emerge dark green with white bloom below the nodes, and vivid sheath colouring of pale buff-orange and cream. Two or three branches develop at each node high up in the culms and carry a multitude of long, narrow leaves, which are displayed with fan-like grace.

It is best suited to a warm or sheltered area in the garden where it can perform impressively putting on culms strong enough to hold the weight of the foliage. Immature plants are weak, and arch from low down and become a nuisance.

Uses

Try it against a wall where, if it does decide to arch unnecessarily, it can easily be tied up.

Sasa

The word *sasa* is Japanese, *sa* meaning thin, and therefore *sasa* means even thinner. The reference is to the slender culms, which are usually less than the thickness of a pencil. *Sasa* could also have been derived from the Chinese *hsai-chu*, which translates as small bamboo, another general characteristic of this genus.

Aside from their mostly short stature and thin culms, the other main attribute of *Sasa* is an aggressive rhizome system, which in some species is the paramount quality and results in total garden domination. So choose wisely; not all species are wildly aggressive, some are reasonably controlled, but all can be restricted with a little effort and time. Some forms have quite large leaves, which makes them valuable for an authentic Japanese touch, or used *en masse* for a

Bright sheathing on a new culm of *Pseudosasa usawai*.

jungle-like effect; others have leaves that bleach dramatically in the winter months, appearing variegated. But beware of the two sides to these plants: they start their life in the garden slowly, storing their energy in readiness for mass invasion.

In small gardens they will have to be controlled. Barriers or pots plunged into the soil do not work. The rhizomes can travel through any opening, or romp up and over the sides of anything in their way. Digging or trenching is the only way to control them. In large gardens they can all too often be forgotten, but after many years they can cover large areas and dominate other planting. All this may sound extreme and is, in fact, the worse that can happen. With good planning, careful selection of species and regular maintenance, *Sasa* are valuable assets and full of character. I have four species planted. One is the very invasive *S. palmata* f. *nebulosa* which has only just shown signs of advancing outwards after eight or nine years. It now has the effect of a proudly marching army. In contrast *S. tsuboiana* has stayed incredibly tight in dry shade, and *S. kurilensis* 'Shimofuri' is a delight, with finely striped leaves held high on culms that spread evenly and sensibly. The fourth, *S. veitchii*, never fails to impress with its brightly bleached leaf margins, which glow in the dim light of a winters day.

I would not be without any of theses four plants as they offer a combination of features not found in other bamboos. The foliage is generally broad and large, held on the ends of the single branches produced from the nodes. The thin culms are flexible, and the taller species arch in the wind with the large leaves rustling like no other sound. Being extremely cold hardy they know of no boundaries; their natural habitat extends further north than any other bamboo, to the Kuril and Sakhalin Islands and at altitudes up to 2,700 m (8,900 ft.).

After a hard winter the foliage on some species can be torn, shredded and scorched. It is possible to raze them to the ground and they should recover over two years. However, secondary branching can occur from dormant buds on the culms which provides new leaves, and when these emerge you can remove the old foliage. It is a lengthy job but worth the effort on many of the taller species if you wish to retain the woody framework.

Taxonomically the genus is confusing and has recently been divided into *Sasa*, *Sasaella* and *Sasamorpha*, and many species within these genera are not grown in Western gardens. In the *Compendium of Chinese Bamboo* (China Forestry Publishing House) many of the short *Pleioblastus* that are already well known in gardens are still listed under *Sasa*. It would not be surprising to learn of further name changes as botanists publish their research findings.

I have described in detail only the plants I consider to be of exceptional quality and useful in the garden. Other forms are summarized at the end of the section according to their height.

Sasa kurilensis

Hardiness: min. -30° C (-22°F), zone 4
Aspect: sun or shade.
Height: 2–3 m (6.5–10 ft.), average 2.5 m (8.2 ft.)
Spread: 1–4 m (3.3–13 ft.) in 10 years, evenly spreading.
Habit: culms curving upwards.
Culms: maximum diameter 2 cm. (0.8 in.), pale green.
Leaves: medium to large, 20 x 5 cm. (8 x 2 in.), glossy mid green leaves.

The most northerly bamboo, from the harsh climates of the Kuril Isles and the Russian island of Sakhalin. The slender culms curve out of the ground turning sharply vertical and emerge green, quickly turning to a pale olive yellow. The leaves are dark and glossy, held in palmate formation at the tops of the culms and branches. This is a vigorous species and needs much effort to keep it both looking good and under control. It has produced two very useable garden forms which are much more rewarding and of equal hardiness.

Uses

Very effective on wide open heaths and moorland as a substitute for bracken. If you insist on planting it, put it next to a fence or wall but bear in mind that it will most likely grow through to the neighbouring garden. The new shoots are a delicacy in Japan, collected from the wild and pickled in salt.

Others

The species has produced two very refined forms, which make wonderful garden plants in comparison.

Sasa kurilensis 'Shimofuri' reaches 3 m (10 ft.) in my garden but usually grows to two thirds of that height. The culms emerge from very early in the season and grow quickly, this being one of the first bamboos to shoot. The colours on these new shoots are outstanding: pale yellow culms emerging from lime green sheaths that are lavishly edged deep purple. The nodes are also purple and dramatically enhanced by the white bloomy rings below. The colour lasts for a month or so before paling to a soft green with pale papery sheaths. Held high on the culms are the long broad leaves, delicately coloured with countless creamy white stripes. This variegation is unique in temperate bamboos and from a distance gives plants a silvery effect.

The low habit and large leaves of *Sasa kurilensis* short, contrast with the larger weeping *Fargesia utilis* (top left) and vertical *Chusquea andina* (top right).

My plant grows happily in full sun but you will find this cultivar often recommended for use in shade. There is very little winter bleaching, but when it does occur it is easily tidied by removing leaves, branches or entire culms. Although profuse in its generation of new culms it is a safe choice for most gardens, not anything like as rampant as the species. I was once visited by a lady who travelled from Finland with the sole purpose of collecting this plant for her garden. She arrived by plane to London, caught a train and then a taxi to the nursery. The taxi waited while we dug pieces of the plant from the garden, then she duly paid and left, returning home to Finland in the same day.

Sasa kurilensis short deserves a cultivar name. It is much shorter and darker than the species, possibly evolving in a very exposed location at higher altitude. The low mounds of large leaves are finger-like in formation and the foliage overlaps, creating an impenetrable colony rarely exceeding 1 m (3 ft.), but usually much lower. It is a fine specimen for container culture, but place it on hard standing such as concrete or mortared slabs so that escaping roots do not invade your garden. Although not as invasive as the species it can form dense swathes, but with great character.

Superb colouring on the early shoots of *Sasa kurilensis* 'Shimofuri'.

The finely striped leaves of *Sasa kurilensis* 'Shimofuri'.

Sasa nipponica

Hardiness: min. -25°C (-13°F), zone 5
Aspect: sun or shade.
Height: 20–40 cm. (0.6–1.3 ft.), average 30 cm. (1 ft.)
Spread: 1–3 m (3.3–10 ft.) in 10 years, slowly running.
Habit: low ground cover.
Culms: maximum diameter 0.5 cm. (0.2 in.), dark green.
Leaves: narrow and thin, 15 x 2 cm. (6 x 0.8 in.), leaf bleaching gives a variegated appearance.

One of the short species suitable for ground cover with uniformly bleached foliage in the winter months. It is essential to mow this down before new growth commences in spring, providing fresh deep greenery that will clothe the ground before bleaching again later in the year. In harsh, dry winter weather, and also in dry summers, the leaves often roll up as protection making the withered edges less obvious.

Uses

For covering areas between taller woody plants, or edging paths.

Others

Sasa nipponica 'Nippon-Kisuji' has some yellow striping on the leaves, which provides summer colour that is lacking in the species.

Sasa palmata f. nebulosa

Hardiness: min. -30° C (-22°F), zone 4
Aspect: sun or shade.
Height: 1.5–3 m (5–10 ft.), average 2 m (6.5 ft.)
Spread: 1.5–6 m (5–20 ft.) in 10 years, eventually invasive.
Habit: forms an upright marching grove.
Culms: maximum diameter 1.25 cm. (0.5 in.), green mottled brown-black.
Leaves: very large, 30 x 10 cm. (12 x 4 in.), fresh green.

Regardless of its pernicious tendencies to dominate its surrounding this *Sasa* is still desirable and creates a tropical appearance like no other temperate bamboo. It is widely planted but not very often well kept; regular thinning will enhance the vision this bamboo is supposed to offer, but beware of its aggression as a result.

The large leaves are thick and leathery and suffer only minimal withering during the winter. The pea green leaves are heavily veined and tessellated, and this is particularly obvious when sunlight shines through the leaves. The huge leaves are held high on the culms and upper branches, hanging slightly below the horizontal so

Fresh large leaves on *Sasa palmata* f. *nebulosa*.

Blotches and swirls on an old culm of *Sasa palmata* f. *nebulosa*.

their surface is teasingly in view. The culms, although thin, are very strong and can bend completely to the ground during heavy snow, springing back to vertical during the thaw. New culms are green with bloomy patches but eventually are covered with dense black-brown markings that blotch the culms to give a psychedelic effect, enhanced by the contrasting pale, persistent sheaths.

This species covers enormous areas in the mountainous regions in Japan, growing almost as far north as *Sasa kurilensis,* and so it is reliably cold hardy. In fact, it prefers colder gardens, reaching its full height and strength even in high exposed areas. In warm temperate zones it needs to be offered some shade. As this is a botanical form, there should be a type species, *S. palmata*, that has plain green culms, but it is not known in cultivation and I can find no record of it.

Uses

Absolutely essential for a tropical look and, if you do not have room in the garden, grow it in a large pot and thin old culms regularly; it can last for years even when congested and starved, but check very frequently for escaping rhizomes. For the best container gardening experience, associate it with other bamboos that are well able to survive in pots, such as *Pleioblastus chino* f. *elegantissimus*, which will complement with its lacy variegated foliage. Yuccas, ferns, phormiums, restios, grasses and a few carefully placed beach pebbles will make visitors believe you are a practised designer.

Others

Sasa palmata 'Warley Place' has yellow variegation but so far has proved unreliable.

A new culm of *Sasa palmata* f. *nebulosa* will eventually develop dark blotching after it has been exposed to light for some time.

Sasa tsuboiana

Hardiness: min. -25°C (-13°F), zone 5
Aspect: sun or shade.
Height: 1–2 m (3.3–6.5 ft.), average 1.5 m (5 ft.)
Spread: 1–2 m (3.3–6.5 ft.) in 10 years, reasonably clumping.
Habit: erect and usually compact.
Culms: maximum diameter 0.6 cm. (0.25 in.), pale green.
Leaves: 25 x 5 cm. (10 x 2 in.), dark green and glossy.

In my garden this bamboo grows in a dry position in light shade and has not spread at all. The erect habit and dark greenery is a foil to the more robust and woody plants around it, and good background to short colourful shrubs. In Japan it grows at quite high altitude and the leaves mostly remain undamaged in the winter, so in the garden maintenance is minimal. The leaves can grow larger than the measurement stated above but only when the plant is offered some shelter.

Uses

A superb foliage plant and, because of its usually refined manner, it can be used more widely than most *Sasa*.

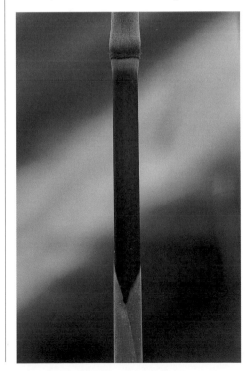

Sasa veitchii

Hardiness: min. -25°C (-13°F), zone 5
Aspect: sun or shade.
Height: 1–1.5 m (3.3–5 ft.), average 1.2 m (4 ft.).
Spread: 1–4 m (3.3–13 ft.) in 10 years, slowly spreading.
Habit: low and carpeting.
Culms: maximum diameter 0.6 cm. (0.25 in.), purple when visible.
Leaves: 25 x 6 cm. (10 x 0.25 in.), dark green uniformly bleached parchment.

A highly ornamental species, prized for its attractive winter colour produced by the uniform bleaching on the margins of the leaves. The thin culms when visible, mostly on taller plants, are deep purple in full sunlight.

Sasa veitchii forms dense carpets that vary in height, according to location or whether it has been annually sheared. The greater the size of the colony, the better the effect, and it should always be planted in an area large enough for it to grow unhindered. It is an adaptable species to moist or dry soils with varying pH, and will tolerate sun or shade. The form in my garden is outstanding and came from the Beth Chatto Gardens, near Colchester in southeast England, where it grows on cold unyielding clay, but admirably covers the bank on one side of a large reservoir and provides a stunning background to the other fine plants. It is short because of the soil conditions and degree of exposure, and far preferable to some of the taller, very gaunt plants seen growing in woodland at many other gardens.

Uses

Sasa veitchii has an inquisitive rhizome system, which is useful for stabilizing banks or eroded areas. Attractive in very large pots, troughs or barrels, where the foliage will be massed tightly together, bubbling softly over the hard edges of its containment. Also very attractive on a large scale when combined with trees such as *Fagus sylvatica* 'Dawyck Gold' or *Ulmus ×hollandica* 'Dampieri Aurea' (syn. 'Wredei'), and red poppies to give traffic-light colouring for contemporary landscaping.

Others

Sasa veitchii f. *minor* (syn. *S. veitchii* 'Nana') is the most rewarding form and is now probably mixed with the species. You will need to select carefully, preferably by seeing an established plant before purchase, as the short forms are far superior. My plant from Beth Chatto rarely exceeds 90 cm. (3 ft.), even if left unsheared, so it may be the short form.

There are tales of a form that hugs the contours of the ground like polythene vacuum packing, but I have yet to see it.

Other Sasa species of medium height

Sasa kagamiana
Leaves to 30 cm. (1 ft.) long on a plant with a shrubby appearance, which grows to 1.8 m (6 ft.) in height. This is available in the United States but not yet in Europe.

Sasa megalophylla
Grows with *Sasa kurilensis* and *S. palmata* f. *nebulosa* in the wild and is especially cold tolerant, attaining a height of 1.8 m (6 ft.) with large leaves to 30 cm. (1 ft.) in length. *Sasa megalophylla* 'Nobilis' is likely to be the same as the species.

Sasa oshidensis
Similar in height and stature to the previous two species, but with a greater tolerance of heat extremes. On the occasions I have seen this in gardens it has been clean and impressive and well worth a try.

Sasa senanensis
Normally grows to over 2 m (7 ft.) and is similar to *Sasa palmata* f. *nebulosa* in habit, but with fine hairs on the undersides of the more slender leaves. Plants in England are often very short and may be incorrectly named.

Sasa shimidzuana
Synonymous with *Sasa asahinae* and another shrubby species available in the United States but not yet in Europe, with large leaves covered with soft hairs on the underside.

Other short Sasa species

Sasa kagamiana subsp. yoshinoi
A rare subspecies from southwestern Honshu in Japan, growing to only 0.6 m (2 ft.) with smaller leaves than *Sasa kagamiana*.

Sasa nagimontana
Found growing on Mount Nagi in Japan, this dwarf species has large dark green leaves in relation to its height of 0.6 m (2 ft.).

Sasa quelpaertensis
A pretty little ground cover bamboo with good winter leaf bleaching, slightly broader leaves than *Sasa nipponica* but similar in appearance and often shorter, almost hugging the ground.

The leaves of *Sasa veitchii* take on a variegated effect with their marginal winter bleaching.

Sasaella

Plants in this genus are very much like *Sasa* in appearance but have smaller leaves, more upright culms and between one and three branches per node. They are shorter than many *Sasa* species and normally used for ground covering.

Sasaella are native mainly to Honshu in Japan and do not inhabit the northern extremes that *Sasa* is capable of, but are still very cold hardy, tolerating very low winter temperatures. Slight leaf withering or bleaching can occur in the cold season but is less pronounced than in *Sasa,* and like the smaller sasas and some *Pleioblastus,* Sasaella can be pruned hard to the ground before the flush of new spring growth.

Sasaella masamuneana

Hardiness: min. -23˚C (-10˚F), zone 5–6
Aspect: sun or shade.
Height: 1–2 m (3.3–6.5 ft.), average 1.2 m (4 ft.)
Spread: 1–5 m (3.3–16.5 ft.) in 10 years, mostly spreading.
Habit: broad drifts.
Culms: maximum diameter 0.6 cm. (0.25 in.), dark purple-black.
Leaves: narrow, 18 x 5 cm. (7 x 2 in.), mid green.

Formerly known as *Arundinaria atropurpurea* because of the dark purple culms, which develops boldly in good light. It is a plant for sun or shade and evenly covers the ground, forming undulating hummocks of stiff greenery. The species has uses in a large garden or landscaping scheme, but is usually overlooked in favour of its two variegated cultivars.

Uses

Forms an excellent short grove in open parkland where it can be mowed annually, although the purple culm colouring is stronger on old culms.

Others

The two variegated cultivars are similar in height to the species and will take some shade. They are also tidier in appearance and, if they become too widespread, are more easily controlled.

Sasaella masamuneana 'Albostriata' is a popular choice and brightly variegated in the summer months. The new growth is very colourful with the deep green leaves faintly edged and irregularly striped bright creamy yellow. The colours can also blend to form patches of pale silvery green and a well-kept plant is a worthy addition to any collection. The leaves can droop slightly during the winter and some of their colour is lost, so plants can be selectively thinned or sheared before the emergence of spring growth. I keep some specimens in containers for display and these are relieved of the old culms as the new emerge each year; they survive like this for many years, often without supplementary food.

Sasaella masamuneana 'Aureostriata' is rarely

Above: A large and meandering colony of *Sasaella masamuneana.*

Right: Fresh growth of *Sasaella masamuneana* 'Albostriata'.

grown, which is a pity because it is less spreading than its two relatives. It sometimes grows a little taller and needs careful positioning to see its subtle colouring. The leaves are slightly wider and striped mustard yellow, the colour being pronounced in light shade and poor soil conditions. The stripes are usually few in number and often quite broad, reminiscent of the yellow lines marked on roads. Use it as an edge to the driveway and it will prevent visitors from parking where they should not.

Sasaella ramosa

Hardiness: min. -30°C (-22°F), zone 4
Aspect: sun or shade.
Height: 60 cm.–2 m (2–6.5 ft.), average 1 m (3.3 ft.)
Spread: 2–6 m (6.5–20 ft.) in 10 years, wildly invasive.
Habit: huge flat colonies.
Culms: maximum diameter 0.6 cm. (0.25 in.), matt green.
Leaves: palmate formation, 15 x 2 cm. (6 x 0.8 in.), dark green with winter bleaching.

A very aggressive bamboo that forms large patches of low foliage, often shorter than the height given above. The leaves have a palmate arrangement and are a dark grey-green with winter bleaching, which is attractive in massed plantings in the cold light of winter. Unfortunately plants are often sold as *Pleioblastus pygmaeus*, which is completely different in appearance, and on occasions under the name *Sasa pygmaea,* which is invalid. *Sasaella ramosa* can be distinguished from the shorter sasas by its smaller and much narrower leaves.

Uses

For all its rampant behaviour I have seen it grown widely and effectively. In one large garden in my East Anglian region it successfully edges a tarred roadway through part of a large woodland garden with evenly spaced culms poking through the carpets of deciduous leaf litter.

Lesser-known Sasaella species

There are more *Sasaella* species on offer in the United States than in Europe and although none are of top-class ornamental value, they introduce variety of form in large landscape plantings or broadleaf woodland. All are hardy in zone 6 and likely to tolerate zone 5.

Sasaella bitchuensis
A species that can reach 1.8 m (6 ft.) and noted for its densely hairy culm sheaths. It prefers shade.

Sasaella hidaensis var. muraii
A short, green ground-covering bamboo that has smaller

leaves than other species. It can grow to 1.8 m (6 ft.) but is often much shorter.

Sasaella sasakiana
The most robust of the genus and can reach 3 m (10 ft.) with specifically three branches from each node. It has a shrubby habit and many leaves.

Sasaella shiobarensis
A useful green bamboo for ground cover, with hairless culm sheaths that grows to 1.8 m (6 ft.) or less.

Sasamorpha

Plants in this genus are sometimes listed as *Sasa* but have been separated taxonomically into this very small genus of which there is only one species currently grown in the West. The slight differences from *Sasa* are the more erect culms without any obvious swelling at the nodes. The genus occurs in China, Japan and Korea and there are only a handful of other species yet to be tried, but they do grow at northerly latitudes or high altitude in these countries.

Sasamorpha borealis

Hardiness: min. -23°C (-10°F), zone 6
Aspect: sun or shade.
Height: 1–3 m (3.3–10 ft.), average 2 m (6.5 ft.)
Spread: 1–2 m (3.3–6.5 ft.) in 10 years, evenly spreading.
Habit: similar to Pseudosasa japonica but more invasive.
Culms: maximum diameter 0.6 cm. (0.25 in.), green.
Leaves: variable size to 20 x 3 cm. (8 x 1.2 in.), deep green and glaucous beneath.

The lower part of the culm remains unbranched, and the leaves are held high and in congested fashion. It can be confused with *Pseudosasa japonica* in appearance but is usually shorter and with noticeable leaf bleaching. It is an extremely hardy species that is less invasive than *Sasa* but with similar qualities and tropical effect. Is natural habitat extends to Hokkaido, in the north of Japan, and it is tolerant of wind and salt air, as well as cold.

Uses

More widely grown in the United States than in Europe, it would prove useful in gardens as an alternative to some of the *Sasa* species.

Semiarundinaria

Native mainly to Japan but present in China, Korea and Taiwan, either as natives or naturalized long ago, the species mostly fall into the lowland and island categories. The genus has qualities of both *Phyllostachys* and *Pleioblastus*, and its origin may possibly be a hybrid between the two. Flowering has occurred in the past with little or no effect to the plants, and no seed has been produced, which would have told us something of its history. The few species from China have been allocated *Oligostachyum*, but this may not be valid until any previous hybridization has been identified and at the moment is only a reference to country of origin. The genus *Brachystachyum* is also closely linked to *Semiarundinaria*, but has a slightly different flower structure and is not as good for ornamental purposes.

In terms of structure, some species within *Semiarundinaria* are equivalent in their size, upright habit and culm thickness to *Phyllostachys*, but are easily distinguished by other features. There are usually three branches on the culm nodes of *Semiarundinaria*, sometimes increasing to seven on older culms; *Phyllostachys* have only two. The culms of *Semiarundinaria* are rounded and do not have an obvious sulcus running the length of each internode, as is seen on *Phyllostachys*. However, a partial, very shallow flattening can be present just above the nodes, a feature which may be attributed to its possible *Phyllostachys* parentage. This faint sulcus usually occurs on the upper internodes of the thickest culms and is rarely confusing for identification purposes.

The very obvious culm sheaths of *Semiarundinaria* adhere to the new, emerging culms, a little longer than on *Phyllostachys*. As the sheaths loosen, and just before falling, they are only joined at the centre of the base of each sheath – on *Phyllostachys* they are attached by the edge of the sheath. A minor distinction but very noticeable.

The rhizome structure is leptomorph and some species can be invasive, although not to extremes. With their upright habit and woody structure they make useful specimens, as well as being robust enough for windbreaks and hedging.

Semiarundinaria fastuosa

Hardiness: min. -25˚C (-13˚F), zone 5
Aspect: full sun.
Height: 6–10 m (20–33 ft.), average 7 m (23 ft.)
Spread: 1–3 m (3.3–10 ft.) in 10 years, large groves.
Habit: tall and stately.
Culms: maximum diameter 4 cm. (1.6 in.), mid green, can fade to purple with age, pale cream sheaths.
Leaves: narrow, 15 x 4 cm. (6 x 1.6 in.), mid green.

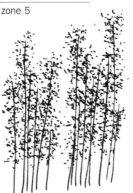

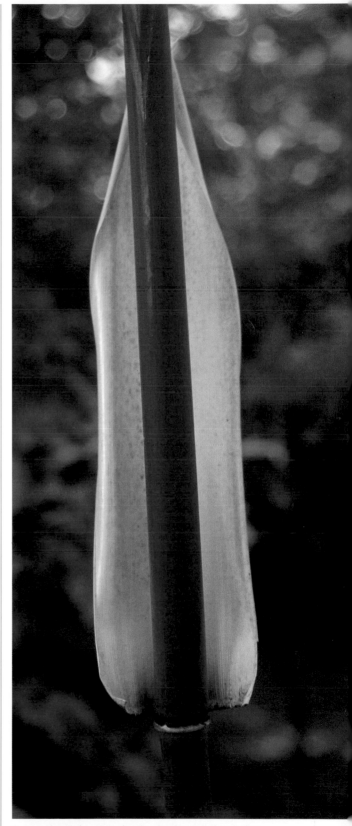

Semiarundinaria fastuosa with culm sheath attached at the base.

Semiarundinaria fastuosa has a vertical habit.

A fine ornamental species and by far the most impressive in the genus, it is quick to mature from a young plant and produces very tall, completely vertical culms, proving useful in confined space. I have often heard it called the noble bamboo on account of its steadfast manner, and the name is entirely appropriate as it does have an air of distinction.

Lush green new culms emerge quickly and are covered with iridescent creamy white culm sheaths, which also having pale wine colouring on their shiny inner surface. As the culms expand, the sheaths separate and start to swing outwards from the culms, but still attached at the base. Eventually they hang precariously by a seemingly invisible thread and point

Falling culm sheaths of
Semiarundinaria fastuosa.

downwards, parallel to the culms, until the first breeze frees them from their anchorage. This process can take a few days and is most entertaining. Once you are truly addicted you will no doubt mark it in your diary as a memorable annual event.

Older culms often fade with a patchwork of blotches and stains, having subtle tints of red, buff and purple. The fresh greenery is held closely to the culms on a rigid branch structure and a specimen with well-spaced culms has the effect of narrow vertical columns.

It is generally refined in habit only tending to spread in very warm gardens, although some plants (including mine) occasionally produce a straight line of culms away from the mother plant. Very hardy and suitable for cold and exposed gardens, it is also tolerant of salt-laden and polluted air, as well as dry or poorly draining soils. In any of these adverse condition it still grows respectably tall; what more could you want?

Uses
Extremely architectural and emphasizes anything vertical in its surroundings. Use it in municipal plantings or open areas where its stature will be valued and greatly admired.

A new branch develops on *Semiarundinaria fastuosa* var. *viridis* and loosens the pale culm sheath.

Others

Semiarundinaria fastuosa var. *viridis* is by its very name a variety with viridian colouring. The culms are a dark glaucous green, maintaining this colour with age; and the leaves are slightly smaller, also a deeper green. It is said to grow taller, and with more thickness than the species, although I have not noticed this on mine. My plant is well established, growing in two straight lines at a right angle from each other, away from the original clump. This unusual habit always provides interest for visitors to the garden and has occurred because the bamboo was planted close to the searching roots of a large pine tree. The bamboo has decided to grow away from the tree in search of open space, light and moisture at the root. Some visitors have asked how they can duplicate this effect and I suggest placing two large concrete slabs vertically in the ground adjacent to and on opposite sides of a newly planted specimen. This should force any developing rhizomes towards the openings and to travel in the direction you want. If you have success and the rhizome does develop lines of culms, the terminal bud on the end of the underground rhizome must never be stopped or damaged, as new growth will then develop at a different angle.

Semiarundinaria fortis

Hardiness: min. -25°C (-13°F), zone 5
Aspect: sun or light shade.
Height: 5–8 m (16.5–26 ft.), average 6 m (20 ft.)
Spread: 1–2 m (3.3–6.5 ft.) in 10 years, open but clumping.
Habit: vertical columns with tight branching.
Culms: maximum diameter 4 cm. (1.6 in.), dark green.
Leaves: 15 x 3 cm. (6 x 1.2 in.), dark green.

Not widely grown, but it is of ornamental value and similar to *Semiarundinaria fastuosa* in habit, although generally smaller, and very hardy. The culms and leaves are a lustrous dark green and hold their colour in all climates and light levels; new culms and their sheaths are covered in fine hairs and have a felted appearance. The tough leaves are sharply tapered at their base, and prove resilient in extremes of weather. The branches are sharply angled to the culms and produce tufts of foliage, creating narrow columns of greenery.

Uses

As this bamboo keeps its dark green colouring it is an admirable companion to many of the *Phyllostachys* with golden culms. It also makes a fine background plant for boldly variegated bamboos or shrubs.

Semiarundinaria kagamiana

Hardiness: min. -18°C (0°F), zone 6
Aspect: full sun.
Height: 5–10 m (16.5–33 ft.), average 6.5 m (21.3 ft.)
Spread: 1–3 m (3.3–10 ft.) in 10 years, open grove.
Habit: rigid colonies of stout culms.
Culms: maximum diameter 4 cm. (1.6 in.), turn red-purple with age.
Leaves: 15 x 3 cm. (6 x 1.2 in.), green.

This is the classic Japanese bamboo for figurative illustration. The plentiful culms are clothed with short branches that hold the fingered leaves like the spread of a practised hand dancing over the keys of a piano. The stout culms turn a pale shade of red or purple in full sun and, although tolerant of shade, is better grown where this colouring can be seen.

The height is always variable according to location and I have found it to be taller and more vigorous in warm gardens, but more colourful, stockier and less invasive in a cold aspect. It is perfectly hardy, but occasional leaf scorch can occur during a vicious winter. Older culms tend to deteriorate quickly and become depleted in leaf, sometimes dying back. Regular thinning is necessary on mature stands to prevent it from becoming congested, as it is capable of producing many culms annually.

Uses

This species could be used in a large Japanese garden with careful selection of the desired culms. Individual culms can also be pruned just above a node to shorten their height, and the new sprouting of leaves will create a topiary effect.

Semiarundinaria lubrica
(syn. *Oligostachyum lubricum*)

Hardiness: min. -22˚C (-8˚F), zone 6
Aspect: sun or light shade.
Height: 5–8 m 16.5–26 ft.), average 6 m (20 ft.)
Spread: 1–2 m (3.3–6.5 ft.) in 10 years. usually slow spreading.
Habit: compact, with dense foliage.
Culms: maximum diameter 3.5 cm. (1.4 in.), deep green.
Leaves: narrow, 13 x 1.5 cm. (5 x 0.6 in.), deep green.

Recently introduced to North America and it is almost as rare in cultivation in Europe. This Chinese species forms a natural, well-kempt stand of dark greenery held aloft on a compact base of culms. The leaves are thick and rarely seared by cutting winds, held high on the multi-branched culms. The new culms are smooth, and have the slight flattening on one side of the internode and two, quite widely spaced nodal rings, that suggest some affinity with *Phyllostachys*. The culms are open to view as the lower buds are dormant and do not produce branches.

This species is native to Fujian, Jiangxi and Fujian Provinces of southeastern China, the home of many *Phyllostachys*, and easily justifies its position alongside these with equivalent hardiness and character.

Uses
Use it as a complement to some of the taller *Phyllostachys* with well-spaced thick culms.

Semiarundinaria makinoi

Hardiness: min. -22˚C (-8˚F), zone 6
Aspect: sun or light shade.
Height: 2–5 m (6.5–16.5 ft.), average 3 m (10 ft.)
Spread: 1–3 m (3.3–10 ft.) in 10 years, very open, usually running.
Habit: thin, vertical culms in an open grove.
Culms: maximum diameter 2 cm. (0.8 in.), old culms redden in sunlight.
Leaves: small for the genus, 9 x 2 cm. (3.5 x 0.8 in.), olive green.

One if the smallest species in the genus and often confused with *Semiarundinaria kagamiana*, and may possibly be a subspecies. The thicker culms produced on a mature plant have a narrow raised swelling just below the nodes which helps distinguish it from *S. kagamiana*, and *S. makinoi* is also much shorter and more open in habit.

The culms are well spaced and emerge green, soon turning a rusty red-brown tint in good light. The leaves and branches are evenly distributed and do not block out the culms as can be the case on other *Semiarundinaria* species.

Uses
In dry soils it has a more searching rhizome system with suitably spaced culms, and is not too demanding of food and water. This enables it to be planted in borders of perennials and grasses where it can sprout at leisure, lending some woody, evergreen structure to an otherwise deciduous planting, and without causing too much annoyance.

Semiarundinaria okuboi (syn. *S. villosa*)

Hardiness: min. -18˚C (0˚F), zone 6
Aspect: full sun.
Height: 4–7.5 m (13–24.6 ft.), average 5 m (16.5 ft.)
Spread: 1–3 m (3.3–10 ft.) in 10 years, open, usually spreading.
Habit: large upright colonies of fresh foliage.
Culms: maximum diameter 3 cm. (1.2 in.), age to pale yellow-green.
Leaves: large for the species, 15 x 2.5 cm. (6 x 1 in.), green.

A useful species for the warmer garden, having large leaves that are resistant to the glare and heat of strong sunlight, without withering or folding. It proves equally robust in a cooler climate where it will be shorter and less invasive, unless on very dry soils where it can wander aimlessly.

The woody culms hold the leaves in dense clusters on the ends of the branches with a noticeably larger terminal leaf, which is often as large as on some *Sasa* species. This creates a lush, almost tropical effect, apart from when this species is grown at high altitude or subject to extreme exposure, when the leaves will be somewhat reduced in size. It is a fine landscape plant, but still rare in cultivation and should be more widely used for its bold impact and speedy establishment.

Uses

Needs control in a small garden but grows reliably in containers. Excellent in association with many smaller-leaved bamboos such as *Fargesia* or *Thamnocalmus* in the cool temperate garden, and *Phyllostachys* in warmer areas.

Semiarundinaria yashadake

Hardiness: min. -22°C (-8°F), zone 6
Aspect: sun or part shade.
Height: 3–7.5 m (10–24.6 ft.), average 4 m (13 ft.)
Spread: 1–2.5 m (3.3–8.2 ft.) in 10 years, mostly clumping.
Habit: usually vertical but bushy.
Culms: maximum diameter 4 cm. (1.6 in.), deep green.
Leaves: 14 x 1.25 cm. (5.5 x 0.5 in.), dark green.

A variable species formerly listed as a variety of *Semiarundinaria fastuosa*, and in some references it is classified as being equivalent in height and stature. In most gardens, however, it is considerably shorter and as

a young plant can have thin culms that arch slightly; in maturity it will be more rigid in appearance. It is more leafy than *Semiarundinaria fastuosa* and has distinctly hairy culm sheaths, lacking the colour on their inner surface which most members of this genus display.

It is a very reliable garden plant, tolerant of a broad range of aspects, and at home in moist or dry soils, although it is much more wide spreading in sandy soils. The leaves are tolerant of scorching sun and wind and have a glossy appearance, catching the dim light in shady areas.

Uses

As a compact, leafy grove in the centre of a woodland clearing, or as a background plant for more colourful planting. I have it growing successfully in large containers where it remains steadfastly upright. It is also a suitable candidate for shortening and selective pruning, to create tufts of foliage along the lengths of the culms in topiary fashion.

Others

Here we have a real motley crew of associated bamboos, though all have something valuable to offer in the garden.

Semiarundinaria yashadake f. *kimmei* is a delightful form that rarely exceeds 3.5 m (11.5 ft.) and is sometimes much shorter. The many thin golden culms have a single internodal green stripe above each branch bud, often tinting pink or dusky red in strong sunlight,

The bright golden culms of *Semiarundinaria yashadake* f. *kimmei* are enhanced by the foliage of *Indocalamus tessellatus*.

particularly on newer growth. Leaves are generally smaller than the species, on short branches held close to the culms, and can be sporadically striped creamy yellow against the very dark green undertone. I have seen it growing in many places, in sun and shade, never failing to impress and proving itself as one of the most rewarding and outstanding temperate bamboos.

Semiarundinaria sp. Korea has not been properly identified but is known in Europe and the United States. It has rich green winter colouring and is often the freshest looking plant around at that time. The oldest specimen I know in this country is 3 m (10 ft.) high, upright, with quite large leaves for the genus and forms a broad but compact colony on dry soil. The new culms have sheathing similar in effect to *Semiarundinaria fastuosa* and foliage in keeping with *Semiarundinaria okuboi*. It is a popular purchase from the nursery because of its appealing freshness.

Semiarundinaria yamadorii appears not to be recognized in the United States. It has been classified in the past as synonymous with *Semiarundinaria yashadake*, but plants currently grown in Europe are noticeably different. *Semiarundinaria yamadorii* may tolerate broader climatic extremes but has a more invasive root system, longer leaves, and culms that can arch with the weight of foliage and, as such, it demands more room in the garden. The whole plant has a greenish yellow hue, which contrasts well with other bamboos.

The single fine cultivar of this questionable species is *Semiarundinaria yamadorii* 'Brimscombe', which has soft new leaves of butter yellow lavishly displayed at the ends of the branches at the start of the growing season. On closer inspection there is some faint green striping and this is also apparent when the leaves are silhouetted against the light. Unfortunately the colouring is lost as the season progresses, but it is well worth reserving a sunny place in the garden for the early summer display in case you manage to acquire a plant, for it is still very rare.

Shibataea

A genus of the highest repute and allied to *Phyllostachys*, although horticulturally they have no resemblance. Of the eleven species and forms, which are mainly distributed in lowland regions of eastern China, with one also occurring in Japan, there are only two that are commonly grown in European and North American gardens, namely *Shibataea kumasasa* and *S. lancifolia*. They are native to open woodland areas and prefer cool, moisture-retentive, preferably acid soils. Usually they stay very compact and short in stature, a welcome change from some of the smaller invading bamboos of other genera.

The leptomorph rhizome structure rarely shows its true habit and *Shibataea* can be considered as clumping, producing dense tufts of short culms. The branches are also short and normally carry a single leaf at the end, sometimes two. The leaves are short on most species, but broad in relation to their length, and in some species have noticeable veining. Culms emerge flattened, later developing a solid D-shaped cross section, and are often display zigzag formation.

Shibataea kumasasa

Hardiness: min. -25°C (-13°F), zone 5
Aspect: light or half shade.
Height: 75 cm.–2 m (2.5–6.5 ft.), average 1 m (3.3 ft.)
Spread: 75 cm.–1.2 m (2.5–5 ft.) in 10 years, clumping.
Habit: short domes of pointed greenery.
Culms: maximum diameter 0.6 cm. (0.25 in.), pale green.
Leaves: 7 x 2 cm. (2.75 x 0.8 in.), dark green paling with age, some tip bleaching in winter.

The ruscus-like leaves of *Shibataea kumasasa*.

Shibataea kumasasa is suitable for container culture. Here it is backed by the golden culms of *Phyllostachys bambusoides* 'Castillonis', with *Carex morrowii* 'Evergold' at its base.

In Western references the specific epithet is invariably spelt *kumasaca*, which is arguable as it is listed as *Shibataea kumasasa* in many Chinese works. Spelling aside, it was an early introduction to the United Kingdom (in 1861) and America (in 1902) and is now the most widely grown of the species, and also used extensively as an ornamental in China and Japan. It is the only species of *Shibataea* native to Japan.

Overall the appearance is distinct with the squat leaves on short branches almost obscuring the thin supporting culms. It has often been likened to *Ruscus aculeatus* in habit, with its spiky and dense formation, hence its former misnomers of *Phyllostachys ruscifolia* and *Shibataea ruscifolia*. The tips of the pointed leaves will bleach uniformly in the slightest cold, and on an established plant this is quite appealing. It is possible to shear previous year's growth to the ground before the new spring flush emerges but I have found it better to selectively remove some of the old culms annually to prevent congestion. If required very vigorous plants can be clipped once the early season's growth has developed. Specimens are capable of growing to nearly 2 m (6.5 ft.), but half this height is more common.

This bamboo's only limitation is its preference for acid soils and reliable summer moisture. Leaves quickly become chlorotic on alkaline soils, turning yellow with their veining visibly darker – although some would say this is quite attractive.

Uses

Plant at the edge of a shady border, or in the dappled light of an open woodland. If you do not have the right soil conditions it can be easily grown in pots, using acid, or ericaceous, compost, and rainwater for irrigation. It also associates well with short woodland plants and bulbs, although prefers not to be crowded.

Others

Included here are two species rarely offered for sale, but worth seeking as they are both fine garden plants requiring similar conditions to *Shibataea kumasasa*.

Shibataea chiangshanensis is very dwarf with culms rarely exceeding 50 cm. (1.6 ft.). It is of delicate appearance, with small ovate leaves at the ends of stunted branches.

Shibataea chinensis is more akin to *Shibataea kumasasa* but usually shorter. It is tolerant of more alkaline conditions and, because of this attribute, should be more widely propagated by nurseries. There is a variegated form of *S. chinensis* listed in China.

There are also two reported variegated forms of *Shibataea kumasasa* but I only know the one with yellow stripes on the leaves, *Shibataea kumasasa* f. *aureostriata*, which is an unstable plant that needs much attention to prevent it reverting. The other form is *Shibataea kumasasa* f. *albostriata* with white-striped leaves that was collected in Japan in 1967.

Shibataea lancifolia

Hardiness: min. -21°C (-5°F), zone 6
Aspect: sun or light shade.
Height: 1–2 m (3.3–6.5 ft.), average 1.2 m (4 ft.)
Spread: 75 cm.–1.5 m (2.5–5 ft.) in 10 years, clumping.
Habit: tidy domes, often wider than high.
Culms: maximum diameter 0.6 cm. (0.25 in.), light green with pale sheaths.
Leaves: narrow, 10 x 1.25 cm. (4 x 0.5 in.), grey-green and darker in shade.

Now becoming more widely available as its hardiness appears to have been tested and plants are proving more reliable than was first thought. The long and narrow leaves make it easy to identify from the other *Shibataea* species, and give it an air of distinction. The thin, pale culm sheaths are often quite persistent; they curl as they dry but remain attached to the nodes on the newly developed culms, and wave in the breeze like straggly white hairs. A young plant is often very sparse until the rhizomes develop more strongly. When it is young it is most vulnerable to adverse weather conditions but as soon as the plant becomes visibly stronger it will reward with many new culms each year, eventually developing into a broad dome of fresh foliage. For speedy results in cold exposed gardens give *S. lancifolia* a sheltered position, otherwise it takes time to mature. A cool, neutral to acid soil is preferred and good light, for it can become languid and pale in heavy shade.

Uses

The rounded vision of formality presented by mature plants is useful for softening the edges of hard paving or brickwork, and could be used as a path edging instead of box (*Buxus*).

Thamnocalamus

This is a rewarding genus containing some very individual and special temperate bamboos. The majority are from the Himalayas, inhabiting the broadleaf and coniferous forests of high altitudes, and are well suited to cool temperate gardens. In warmer climates there is concern with heat tolerance and these bamboos may require cool shade and shelter to prevent the desiccation of the fine foliage by sun and wind. There is a single African species to mention, which is visually distinct

A mature plant of *Shibataea lancifolia* has a tidy shape.

from the Himalayan species and very tolerant of heat and cold.

There are many botanical differences that set *Thamnocalmus* apart from other genera which, should you become practised in the art of bamboo identification, are useful to know. *Thamnocalmus* differs from *Yushania* in having fewer but more robust branches and, more importantly, a pachymorph, or clumping, rhizome formation. There is perhaps greater confusion with some of the other pachymorph bamboos: *Drepanostachyum* and *Himalayacalamus* have a larger mass of branches and are without the tessellation on the leaves that is evident on *Thamnocalamus* species; *Fargesia* also has more branches, much shorter in length, but this is the genus most likened to *Thamnocalamus*.

The characteristics unique to *Thamnocalamus* that are the most obvious contribute to its stately appearance. There are usually five branches per node, which emerge parallel to the culms before turning sharply outwards and branching again. Culms are often waxy with a pale coloured bloom; this is a distinct blue on the species *T. crassinodus*, and an outstanding feature. The internodes of the culms also have faint swellings, invisible to the naked eye – you will have to run your fingers lightly along the internodal sections to feel them. Culms are generally thicker than those of *Fargesia* and the nodes are more pronounced. The culm sheaths, which can remain attached for much of the growing season, are usually hairy. Culm sheath blades are erect and pointed, not curved backward as with other genera.

Most species take time to establish from young plants, which is the best way to plant them; open-ground specimens with their dense rhizome and culm structure do not lend themselves to division. Although perfectly hardy, young juvenile plants benefit from being given some protection from scathing winds and beating sun, and they will mature quickly as a reward for this little extra care.

Thamnocalamus crassinodus and its cultivars

To me this species and its forms and cultivars are the epitome of all things bamboo, giving the garden something very special that no other plant is capable of.

Thamnocalamus crassinodus and its variations are from Tibet and occur at different altitudes, among the spruce and pine forests at elevations above 2,500 m (8,200 ft.), so hardiness may differ slightly between them. I have found, however, that they all acclimatize well to new surroundings, given time. When they were first introduced in the last quarter of the twentieth century, the few obsessive collectors who planted them were dubious about their hardiness because young juvenile plants and their new growth was easily damaged in the first few winters. After three or four years the new culms emerged much thicker, taller and stronger, and the plants showed less signs of suffering as they matured. The main attribute at this development stage was the bloomy, pale blue culms, which retain their colour well into the second growing season. The nodes are pronounced, often colouring

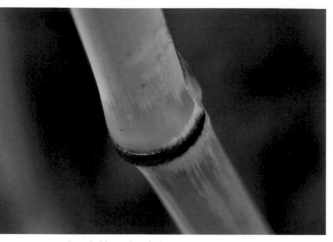

The pale blue culm of *Thamnocalamus crassinodus* 'Lang Tang' is also typical of other cultivars belonging to this species.

red-purple on young culms, and the branch buds are large and pale. Previously the only bamboo with similar colouring was *Himalayacalamus hookerianus,* also known as the blue bamboo, which, unfortunately, is not very hardy and only suitable for a large temperate glasshouse or a very mild location. As the *Thamnocalamus crassinodus* forms developed, it became obvious they were special and they rose quickly to the top of any bamboo collectors "must have" list.

In their native habitat, in the face of a bitter winter,

plants can defoliate and I have no doubt they would do the same in some temperate regions. However, the strong culms, mass of branches and healthy, productive rhizome system will ensure quick regeneration. Aside from this, the gardener should always start with a young juvenile specimen, and allow it to develop and mature at its own pace, put up with the early suffering but not miss out on those first blue culms. If you have any doubt about this waiting period, just try to slice a piece from an old plant (if someone will let you), and it will almost certainly sit and sulk before reverting to shorter juvenile growth.

All forms and cultivars are clumping and I grow them in light shade where the leaves are protected from the high summer sun and dappled light filters to the ground. High heat, extreme cold, particularly when dry and windy, will see the leaves close lengthways into a needle shape, a natural protection against moisture loss and also characteristic of some *Fargesia*, a genus of close affinity. *Thamnocalamus crassinodus* is often found listed as *Fargesia crassinoda* or *Thamnocalamus spathiflorus* var. *crassinodus,* and has also been confused with another recent introduction, *Borinda albocera.*

Uses for all cultivars and forms

Plants must be given prominence in the garden. Whichever form you select, ensure the blue culm colouring is visible, and try not to miss out on the hairy, pink-tinted sheaths on the new shoots. My specimens

Above: Thamnocalamus crassinodus 'Kew Beauty' has fine greenery that creates an airy effect around a hidden seating area.

Right: Dappled light shines through the culm sheaths of *Thamnocalamus crassinodus* 'Merlyn'.

A hairy new shoot of *Thamnocalamus crassinodus* 'Kew Beauty'.

The rarest of the forms with few examples to compare, but plants in the east of England have performed as well as those in warmer counties. Although short in stature it cannot be classed as a dwarf, and "short form" would be a better name. The V-shaped habit is formed by the tightest clump, with culms vying for position, but when the branches open, instead of becoming a cluttered mess, each culm bends away from the next, creating an open, airy plant. It has thinner culms than other *Thamnocalamus crassinodus* but they are equally blue, although not as profuse in their annual production. The overall effect is of a silvery green fountain and, to the innocent newcomer, not obviously bamboo-like.

Two mature plants I know of in England grow in different situations: one on a warm sunny wall in the south, and the other by the edge of a sheltered driveway in the rich soil of a border, in the north of East Anglia. The latter has outperformed the wall plant despite being less than half its age. I would suggest the richer soil and shady shelter has encouraged the plant to develop quickly. However, too much of a good thing can change the appearance, and not necessarily for the better; I believe the plant grown against the wall, with its poor soil and restricted area, looks far better.

are planted close to a path, where they are well spaced apart and I can compare their different habits. The culms look stunning when backed by a large spring forsythia, the yellow flowers intensifying the colour of the blue culms when they need it most.

Thamnocalmus crassinodus dwarf

Hardiness: min. -15˚C (5˚F), zone 7
Aspect: light shade.
Height: 2–3.5 m (6.5–11.5 ft.), average 2.5 m (8.2 ft.)
Spread: 75 cm.–1 m (2.5–3.3 ft.) in 10 years, clumping.
Habit: arching, V-shaped.
Culms: maximum diameter 1.5 cm. (0.6 in.), pale blue when new.
Leaves: very small, 6 x 0.5 cm. (2.4 x 0.2 in.), light green.

The low habit of *Thamnocalamus crassinodus* dwarf shows off the pale and delicate foliage.

Thamnocalamus crassinodus 'Gosainkund'

Hardiness: min. -15°C (5°F), zone 7
Aspect: light shade.
Height: 3–6 m (10–20 ft.), average 4 m (13 ft.)
Spread: 75 cm.–1.2 m (2.5–4 ft.) in 10 years, clumping.
Habit: upright culms with arching branches.
Culms: maximum diameter 2 cm. (0.8 in.), pale blue-grey.
Leaves: small, 9 x 0.75 cm. (3.5 x 0.3 in.), light green.

A form of distinction has finally been given the cultivar name of 'Gosainkund', attributed to the sacred lake close to its natural habitat. Formerly it was known as the true *Thamnocalamus crassinodus* and often by the epithet 'Glauca' (meaning blue), as a descriptive to separate it from other known forms.

Compared to the others 'Gosainkund' is slightly more open in habit with slightly larger leaves, forming a graceful plant of delicate appearance. The culms are a paler blue-grey, often silvery, and the branches can take on rich purple tones in the light. Its hardiness is disputed and it is thought not to be as robust as the

Thamnocalamus crassinodus 'Kew Beauty' may display red tints on the older culms and branches.

other forms of this species. However in the blows of our East Anglian winter, plants have performed well, sometimes in pots kept outside; they lose some of their leaves but recover quickly in the spring with little or no dieback. This is still very rare in cultivation and slow to propagate, but is the most special *crassinodus* and should be much sought after.

Thamnocalamus crassinodus 'Kew Beauty'

Hardiness: min. -15°C (5°F), zone 7
Aspect: light shade.
Height: 3.5–5.5 m (11.5–18 ft.), average 4 m (13 ft.)
Spread: 75 cm.–1.5 m (2.5–5 ft.) in 10 years, clumping.
Habit: upright, slightly arching at tips.
Culms: maximum diameter 2 cm. (0.8 in.), pale blue when new, red branches.
Leaves: very small, 6 x 0.5 cm. (2.4 x 0.2 in.), green.

Of the five forms listed here, this is the most colourful, with the bonus of a deep red hue to the older culms and branches. The new culms are a bright, pale sky blue, emerging from the tightly packed hairy sheaths at ground level in early to midsummer. As the new culms expand, the powder blue internodes become visible and the culm sheaths can briefly be tinted pale purple, before turning a raw parchment colour. Some of the sheaths can persist into the winter months, especially if they are protecting culms that emerged late, otherwise they hang loosely for a short while by a corner at their base. A culm on a mature plant will only take five or six weeks to reach its final height, and then produce branches and leaves.

I have 'Kew Beauty' growing under a tall canopy of a silver willow, *Salix alba* var. *sericea*, the purple birch, *Betula pendula* 'Purpurea', and the golden *Robinia pseudoacacia* 'Frisia'. The small leaves of all these trees offer just the right protection from the summer heat and cast changing shadows on the colourful culms of the *Thamnocalamus*. Like most good plant associations it was not planned. My plant now reaches 4.5 m (14.8 ft.) after ten years and has many culms, but not so densely packed as to block out the light from behind. The leaves and branches are held in the upper two thirds of the plant, allowing light, moisture and warmth to filter through to the rhizomes, which enables their maturity and, in turn, good sized culms. Even in light shade, there is an appealing combination of the subtle red older culms and the new blue ones.

As a contrast to my relatively cold and arid garden, a plant growing close to the Cumbrian coast, in the northwest of England, my mother's garden to be precise, had exceeded my own specimen in half the time. This plant faced a vicious north wind, swooping across the often snow-clad hills. Despite all this, it put on unbelievable growth in just five years; the extra moisture and more maritime climate perhaps giving it the perfect growing conditions. I use the past tense in describing this particular specimen as it was soon seconded by me for use an exhibition plant. This cultivar and the others in the species *crassinodus* perform particularly well on the western side of Scotland, all with speedy maturity.

Another tale of a plant in a different locality began when our local potter planted a 'Kew Beauty' in the middle of a paved area by removing a 90 cm. (3 ft.) slab. Six or seven years later the plant had also reached greater proportions than my own. Eventually it had to be removed as it was beginning to block access to a doorway. This specimen grew in full sun surrounded by reflective and heat-shimmering concrete It was necessary to feed and water it occasionally but it performed brilliantly in its open aspect; so although light shade is recommended, it is not absolutely essential.

New culms of *Thamnocalamus crassinodus* 'Kew Beauty'.

Thamnocalmus crassinodus 'Lang Tang'

Hardiness: min. -15°C (5°F), zone 7
Aspect: light shade.
Height: 2.5–4.5 m (8.2–14.8 ft.), average 3.5 m (11.5 ft.)
Spread: 75 cm.–1 m (2.5–3.3 ft.) in 10 years, clumping.
Habit: squat open V-shape, sometimes wider than high.
Culms: maximum diameter 2 cm. (0.8 in.), pale blue when new, becoming brighter with age.
Leaves: very small, 6 x 0.5 cm. (2.4 x 0.2 in.), light green.

The elegant hanging branches of *Thamnocalamus crassinodus* 'Lang Tang' (left), its tiny leaves in contrast to those large and yellow of *Cornus alba* 'Spaethii' and silvery striped of x *Hibanobambusa tranquillans* 'Shiroshima' (top right), which frames a gravel path in the author's garden.

A plant I drooled over on frequent visits to Peter Addington's Stream Cottage had bubbles of fresh filigree foliage erupting with great density from the tops of the culms. When he departed from his garden he allowed me to lift this bamboo as a whole, and after careful handling it has now established in its new home, my garden.

Close up the new pale blue culms are stunning; the plant is shorter than 'Kew Beauty' and 'Merlyn' but the culms are of equal thickness, looking bolder with their stumpiness and shorter internodes. From a distance the mass of leaves, which are usually the smallest of the species, create a froth of tumbling, pale greenery from the vigorous rebranching habit at the extremities of the culms. It would be wise to plant a pair some distance apart so you can study the subtleties without moving – one close by for the culms, the other further off for the habit.

Thamnocalamus crassinodus 'Merlyn'

Hardiness: min. -15°C (5°F), zone 7
Aspect: light shade.
Height: 4–6 m (13–20 ft.), average 4.5 m (14.8 ft.)
Spread: 75 cm.–1.5 m (2.5–5 ft.) in 10 years, clumping.
Habit: the most vertical in the species.
Culms: maximum diameter 2 cm. (0.8 in.), pale blue ageing yellow-green.
Leaves: very small, 6 x 0.5 cm. (2.4 x 0.2 in.), green.

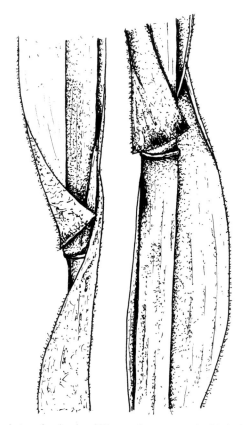

The hairy culm sheaths of *Thamnocalamus crassinodus* 'Merlyn'.

The tallest, most vertical of the *crassinodus* forms, and 'Merlyn' is also the quickest to mature. Plenty of culms are produced annually and make a dense clump, rarely deviating from their upright stance. It does not have the red tints of 'Kew Beauty' and the old culms turn pale yellow-green. Out of the five forms described this appears to be the most robust and always looks the freshest. This bamboo is named after Merlyn Edwards, who introduced the *crassinodus* forms into cultivation.

Thamnocalamus spathiflorus (syn. *T. aristatus*)

Hardiness: min. -18°C (0°F), zone 6
Aspect: sun or half shade.
Height: 4–8 m (13–26 ft.), average 6 m (20 ft.)
Spread: 75 cm.–1.5 m (2.5–5 ft.) in 10 years, clumping.
Habit: gracefully arching culms.
Culms: maximum diameter 2 cm. (0.8 in.), green ageing soft yellow, with pink tints in good light.
Leaves: 15 x 1.25 cm. (6 x 0.5 in.), soft green.

Due to recent reclassification this species now includes bamboos previously labelled as *Thamnocalamus aristatus*, although some would still argue that *aristatus* is at least a form of *T. spathiflorus*. In the United States, some plants of *T. crassinodus* may also erroneously be named *aristatus*. Native to Bhutan, Nepal, Tibet and northwest India at elevations up to 2,500 m (8,200 ft.), it is obviously widespread and no doubt there are small differences between plants of different provenance.

As a garden plant *Thamnocalamus spathiflorus* is very beautiful, if a little slow to establish. The fresh blue-green and bloomy culms emerge with swollen nodes from pale pink or red-tinted sheaths. These protective sheaths detach themselves slowly and become spathe-like, similar to those that surround the spadix of an *Arum*. (I prefer to liken this notable occurrence to many cobra heads with hood-like necks dilated.)

Old culms can pale with outstanding colouring – sometimes having pink, red or brown staining on the yellow-green culms – in vivid contrast to the darker new ones. The foliage is soft green and arches in layers from the long branches. The arching habit is more pronounced on immature plants than older ones, which are more vertical. Newly developing plants often produce late culms that never mature during the first winter and always die back, often making the plant slow to establish.

Uses

With its lush greenery, this is a fine bamboo for association, brightening up the darkest of backgrounds and always looking impressive against a wall, where its curves will soften hard materials. Create additional light in the foreground by planting hellebores and early spring bulbs as a promise of summer.

Others

Thamnocalamus spathiflorus subsp. *nepalensis* is indigenous to Nepal and more beautiful than the many Indian plants of *T. spathiflorus* in cultivation. Generally more upright than the species, with larger leaves that arch the branches in a layered formation. New culms are distinctly bloomy, often with white rings below the nodes, and the culm sheaths deliciously tinted a pale cherry red.

A new culm of *Thamnocalamus spathiflorus* subsp. *nepalensis*.

Thamnocalamus tessellatus

Hardiness: min. -23°C (-10°F), zone 5–6)
Aspect: full sun.
Height: 4–8 m (13–26 ft.), average 5.5 m (18 ft.)
Spread: 1–2 m (3.3–6.5 ft.) in 10 years, mostly tight clumping.
Habit: flat topped, dense V-shape.
Culms: maximum diameter 2.5 cm. (1 in.), pale green, new culms have white sheaths.
Leaves: 8 x 1 cm. (3.2 x 0.4 in.), grey-green.

The bergbamboes of South Africa have given their name to the mountain Bamboesberg because they grow in vast tracts over its slopes. In days gone by the culms were used by the Zulus for shields and making shafts for arrows and spears. This mountain bamboo is of more rugged character than the Himalayan species with their delicate finery.

Very upright in habit it performs well in an open aspect but hates being crowded. I have found this out to my cost when my established plant of *Thamnocalamus tessellatus* was rapidly overrun by the giant *Phyllostachys violascens*; it is now completely dead, succumbing to the shade and the competition. Its love of the open makes it a very wind-tolerant bamboo and one of the most resilient in times of drought. It also grows much taller in warm gardens than in cool and the culms are better spaced.

When it is well grown, it is outstandingly beautiful, but I have seen so many unkempt and dishevelled plants that they give the species a bad reputation. It looks better if many of the older culms are removed regularly, as the sheathing is quite persistent and becomes tattered with age. The new culms, however, emerge clothed in the brightest of sheaths, maroon tinted at first and turning almost pure white. It is for this feature alone that *Thamnocalamus tessellatus* should be grown. The branches are always high up, allowing the culms to be seen, and these hold dense tufts of leaves in a similar way to *Chusquea culeou*. Instead of removing too much of the old growth, you could if you have the time strip off the old sheathing; the pale green culms will tint purple in full sun.

Left: The new sheathing on culms of *Thamnocalamus tessellatus* is almost pure white.

Above: Fresh, arching greenery of *Yushania anceps.*

Uses

An effective and refined windbreak or, if well kept, it makes a very bright summer feature plant. In my experience it hates growing in pots, which is surprising considering its hardiness and drought tolerance.

Yushania

Yushania is a large genus of mountain bamboos mainly from China, but extending to Taiwan and India, with a single species known in Africa which is not hardy. The genus is distinct on account of its pachymorph but long-necked rhizome structure. These extended necks are often over 30 cm. (1 ft.) long, devoid of buds and roots and have no nodal structure; in optimum conditions they may extend further. The bamboo relies on the buds from the shorter rhizome lengths at the base of the culms to generate new top growth, and lower buds to produce more elongated rhizome. This has the effect of producing small colonies of culms well spaced from each other, particularly on mature plants.

The culm structure is usually quite strong, with vertical branches that point upwards tight to the culm, before arching under the weight of a normally luxuriant mass of foliage. Because of the rhizome structure, *Yushania* are classed as moderately invasive bamboos. However, their habit does depend on climate, location, soil type and drainage, and they appear to prefer a cool maritime climate rather than the high summer temperatures of a continental interior.

Yushania anceps

Hardiness: min. -18°C (0° F), zone 6
Aspect: sun or light shade.
Height: 3–5 m (10–16.5 ft.), average 4 m (13 ft.)
Spread: 1–3 m (3.3–10 ft.) in 10 years, open, reasonably clumping.
Habit: vertical culms with plumes of weeping foliage.
Culms: maximum diameter 2 cm. (0.8 in.), fresh green.
Leaves: long and narrow, 13 x 1.25 cm. (5 x 0.5 in.), fresh green.

The best known *Yushania* species in the Western world and it is still often referred to by its older names of *Arundinaria anceps* or *Arundinaria jaunsarensis.* This was one of the first bamboos to be introduced to England, in 1865, and was widely planted and revered for its delicate-looking habit and speedy growth. The species itself varies tremendously in height and habit; some specimens can be found that make a mockery of the average height of 4 m (13 ft.), exceeding this by up to twice as much. The different habits may be a result of clonal or geographical variation or, as with many other genera, because of the garden location, climate and conditions.

The vertical culms can arch dramatically at the top of the bamboo, being pulled over by the mass of small leaves, creating a layered, plume like effect that is very beautiful. Culms rarely flop to the ground and this bamboo can be considered as a very fresh, tidy and elegant garden plant.

Uses

A species of renowned architectural value, and is especially beautiful when viewed from a distance so that the foliage effect can be admired.

Others

Yushania anceps 'Pitt White' is an outstanding clone originating from the famous gardens of that name in England. It is unusually tall at 9 m (30 ft.) with a wonderful character, having many frothy layers of tiny leaves. Plants often sold of this clone are from seed collected from the mother plant when it succumbed to flowering. However, the original plant re-grew and plants can also be obtained labelled as *Yushania anceps* 'Pitt White Rejuvenated'. There is no doubt that stock of both origins have become mixed; but I have found the latter is preferable, often having darker culms of a rich, rusty brown when mature.

Yushania brevipaniculata (syn. *Y. chungii*)

Hardiness: min. -20°C (-4°F), zone 6
Aspect: sun or light shade.
Height: 1.5–3 m (5–10 ft.), average 2.5 m (8.2 ft.)
Spread: 1–2 m (3.3–6.5 ft.) in 10 years, open but clumping.
Habit: congested and leafy, arching culm.
Culms: maximum diameter 1.25 cm. (0.5 in.), dark sheaths on green culms, very dark, hairy new shoots.
Leaves: narrow, 9 x 1 cm. (3.2 x 0.4 in.), green.

A particularly fine and very hardy recent introduction but it may be confused in name. In Chinese literature *Yushania chungii* is synonymous with *Y. brevipaniculata* and fits the

A new shoot of *Yushania brevipaniculata* in close up.

description of this bamboo, particularly in relation to the very beautiful and distinct new culm shoots. To confuse matters further is the existence of the species *Y. chingii* from a different area of China. *Yushania exilis* is another species somewhat similar to *Y. brevipaniculta* in appearance and from the same mountainous regions in Sichuan, but at lower elevations. All very confusing, but evidence that there are other fine species of this useful genus yet to come to our shores from China.

Distributed at elevations between 1,800–3,800 m (5,900–11,500 ft.) and growing in different environments, this species shows its versatility by tolerating soils with a wide range of pH and moisture content, as well as coping with sun, part shade and extreme exposure. This all helps to makes it a very useful, reliable and easy garden plant.

The species has also some stunning visual qualities, starting with the new shoots that are dark and unusually hairy. The emerging culms have dark sheathing similar to *Yushania maculata* and the foliage is elegantly distributed in finger-like fans above the short culms. It is quite short in stature and a mature plant will be much wider than high, with a slowly spreading rhizome structure.

Uses

Exceptionally wind tolerant so use it by a helicopter landing pad. I would also imagine that, because of its tough constitution, containerised specimens will prove rewarding.

Yushania maculata

Hardiness: min. -18°C (0° F), zone 6
Aspect: sun or light shade.
Height: 3–5 m (10–16.5 ft.), average 3.5 m (11.5 ft.)
Spread: 1–2.5 m (3.3–8.2 ft.) in 10 years, open, spreading slowly.
Habit: strong and vertical with arching foliage.
Culms: maximum diameter 1.5 cm. (0.6 in.), olive green, bloomy when young with dark purplish sheaths.
Leaves: narrow and willowy, 13 x 1.25 cm. (5 x 0.5 in.), green.

I believe this species is possibly hardier than the minimum temperature listed above suggests. It inhabits pine forests at elevations of between 1,800–3,500 m (5,900–11,500 ft.) in the Chinese provinces of Sichuan and Yunnan and is much suited to windy gardens, staying completely fresh throughout the seasons.

The new culms are a bloomy blue-grey with the darkest of culm sheaths, varying in colour from a rich red-purple to a dusky dark brown. In the second year the culms lose their bloom and turn a dark olive green while the culm sheaths pale to the colour of old parchment, and at this stage the colour contrast is the reverse of the newer culms. The delicate-looking but exceptionally hardy foliage hangs teasingly from the branches high in the culms and, combined with the colour effects of the culms, makes this one of the finest bamboos I know. Regardless of its spread, which is

The elegant leaf formation of *Yushania maculata*.

broad but not invasive, *Yushania maculata* is one of the most popular choices for purchase in my experience.

The rhizome system is quite deep and would add some credibility to the fact that I have also found this bamboo to be very drought tolerant. The shoots emerge quite late in the growing season but usually mature before the cold of winter can damage them.

Uses

A good species to plant in association with other bamboos and its unusual culm colouring will contrast well with most of them. My specimen was planted in a clearing in one of the wilder parts of the garden and was somewhat overtaken by nettles when young. Not wishing to spray herbicide in case it damaged the bamboo, I pulled and dug the invading weeds as much as I could but they continued to appear. Over the years *Yushania maculata* has truly dominated the nettle colony, which has given up to the superiority of the bamboo.

Yushania niitakayamensis

Hardiness: min. -18°C (0°F), zone 6
Aspect: light shade.
Height: 75 cm–1.5 m (2.5–5 ft.), average 1.2 m (4 ft.)

Spread: 50 cm.–1 m (1.6–5 ft.) in 10 years, usually clumping.
Habit: thin and elegant.
Culms: maximum diameter 0.5 cm. (0.2 in.), green ageing rich brown.
Leaves: very small, 6 x 1 cm. (2.4 x 0.4 in.), blue-grey.

This rare species has been attributed to *Yushania anceps* in previous publications but is in fact completely different, being very small and unusually congested in habit. It has a varied distribution in the wild, from Taiwan and the mountainous areas of Sichuan and Yunnan in China, at elevations up to 3,000 m (9,850 ft.) predominantly on open grassland.

A very difficult species to establish in gardens and as a result it is little known in its true form. I now own a single plant, which I had known previously in another garden for many years in a most unhealthy state and not long for this world. I was allowed to rescue it eventually and it has now recovered successfully over a period of eighteen months, producing many new culms and fresh rhizome.

Old culms turn a rich tawny brown, occasionally seared with oval black stains, and the congested base of the sheathed branches turns a reflective grey-silver. The narrow, glaucous leaves roll inwards during hot or cold windy weather, and this is more evident on the older culms. The foliage is held loosely by tight branching, which arches slightly from the culms and results in a slim fountain like habit.

Uses

A collector's item, which is rare and difficult, but very beautiful; it should be pampered accordingly.

Dark sheathing and pale emerging internodes on new culms of *Yushania maculata*.

Chapter 9
Close to the Edge

I make no excuses for separating these bamboos from the main alphabetical list. They are all fine bamboos and much in demand but, in terms of their suitability for the cool temperate garden, they are on the borderline or "close to the edge" of hardiness zone 8, with a minimum temperature range of -12.2 to 6.7°C (10 to 20°F). In fact many are less than happy in zone 9, which denotes an average annual minimum temperature only a few degrees above freezing.

It is not just the temperature range that is important in qualifying a bamboo's suitability for a particular climatic region; other factors include sunlight levels, wind exposure and seasonal fluctuations, heat as well as cold. There will always be reports of plants performing well in areas where they should not, surprising even the most sceptical bamboo enthusiast. It is certainly worth trying some of the plants described below, planting them in sheltered locations or town gardens, where they are less susceptible to the harsher climatic extremes of the open countryside. Failing that, a cool glasshouse with good ventilation is the next best thing.

Some of the following bamboos are arguably hardier than I have given them credit for and will indeed tolerate colder temperatures; however, they will not perform to the best of their ability or show their true worth, which in gardening terms is very important. It is fine to be a collector and possess a rare or difficult bamboo; there is value in this, even if only for the purposes of

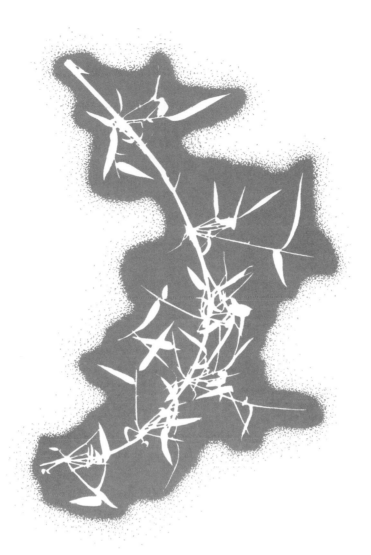

science, trialling or conservation, but for the average gardener success, reliability and value for money are more important. It is for these reasons the plants have been separated. Try them and reap the rewards if you can, but beware of cold winds.

Arundinaria gigantea

The only species native to North America, which at its best has the stature and habit of *Pseudosasa japonica*, but in poor conditions more resembles a short and unkempt *Pleioblastus*. Ecologically this was once a very important native plant in the United States before large areas of it were cleared for farmland. It formed huge cane meadows, which provided

food for migrating buffalo as well as livestock and a particular habitat for wildlife, including nesting birds.

There is variation within the species and undoubtedly some clones will be hardier than others. It is usually ragged in appearance and does not make a particularly good garden plant. The naturally occurring *Arundinaria gigantea* subsp. *tecta* is more suited to damper soil conditions than the true species.

Bambusa multiplex 'Alphonse Karr'

One of the most requested bamboos at the nursery and it is a pity that even here in the east of England it rarely survives, even under the protection of cold glass or polythene. Bright yellow culms are randomly striped green, sometimes pink tinted, and occasionally leaves show variegation. I have seen it grown successfully in a cool conservatory with its height much shortened. Other forms would also be suited to cool indoor culture; *Bambusa multiplex* var. *rivieriorum* and the cultivar B. *multiplex* 'Fernleaf' are both much shorter and plain green with lacy, fern-like foliage.

Bambusa ventricosa

This is the famous "Buddha's belly"; except, in my opinion, it is more a case of infamy because of the many people who request it after seeing a photograph or reading about it fleetingly in a magazine. In Western gardens it rarely produces the distorted internodes that are so appealing. I suggest a trip to China to see it in all its glory.

Swollen internodes of *Bambusa ventricosa*.

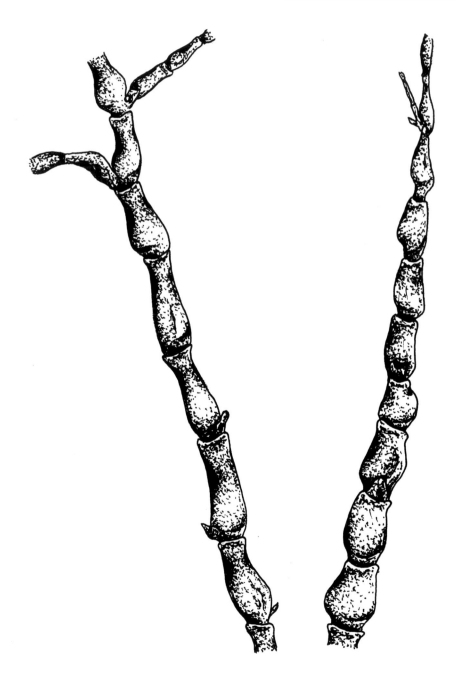

Brachystachyum densiflorum

Brachystachyum is quite similar to the genus *Semiarundinaria*. This species originates in the low foothills of the southeastern Chinese provinces and I admit it has survived in pots in the nursery, quite unscathed. I have yet to see good examples planted in gardens in England, so the hardiness is currently unknown. It is a very leafy bamboo with good culm sheath colouring of rich emerald green with white striae, and would offer ornamental value should it prove hardy.

Chusquea quila

A species native to the provinces in Chile that benefit from a Mediterranean or Californian-type climate. It is a scrambling plant that initially grows across the ground before clambering up and over anything in its path. The rhizome system is compact and the extending culms produce small clusters of branches and short, dark green leaves. It is particularly beautiful, and I would happily move to a Mediterranean island villa just to be able to grow this.

Chusquea valdiviensis

In its native Chile this could be likened to a monstrous rampaging bramble, so it is very much a bonus that the average cool temperate winter keeps it in check. In the warm temperate forests of its native country it swamps other vegetation with its marauding habit. The short, rigid and recurved branches of the culms act as hooks, enabling them to climb upwards. As soon as a

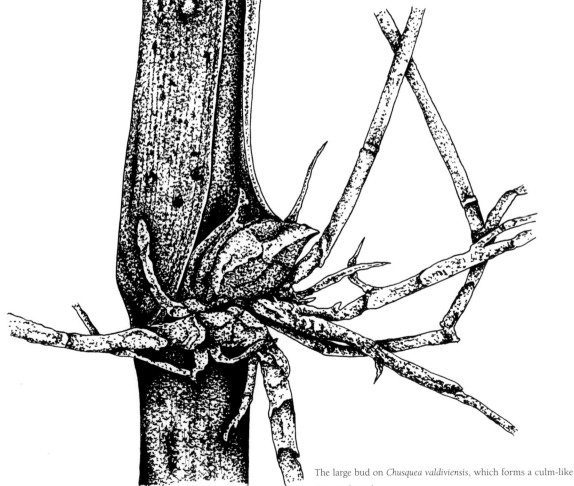

The large bud on *Chusquea valdiviensis*, which forms a culm-like primary branch.

The long trail of a *Chusquea valdiviensis* culm arching back to the ground.

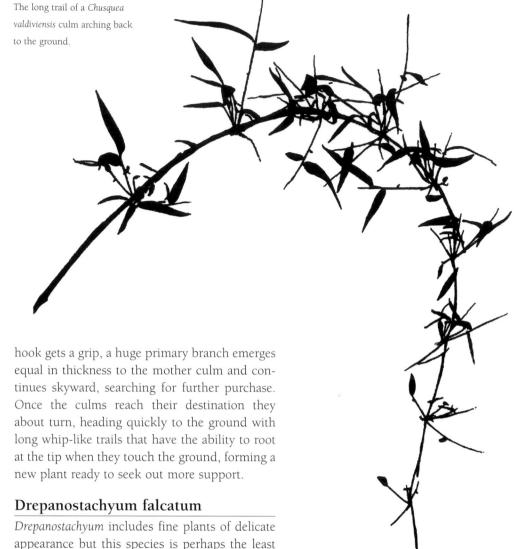

hook gets a grip, a huge primary branch emerges equal in thickness to the mother culm and continues skyward, searching for further purchase. Once the culms reach their destination they about turn, heading quickly to the ground with long whip-like trails that have the ability to root at the tip when they touch the ground, forming a new plant ready to seek out more support.

Drepanostachyum falcatum

Drepanostachyum includes fine plants of delicate appearance but this species is perhaps the least hardy. Very slender, arching culms with multiple branching that carry a huge mass of fresh foliage almost down to ground level. If it is severely damaged in the winter, it will often shoot again from the base, providing the rhizomes have been protected. If grown in this way, like an herbaceous perennial, it will rarely exceed 2 m (7 ft.), but a warm humid summer is preferred.

Drepanostachyum khasianum

A vertical growing species that can prove elegant in very mild, sheltered gardens. The tiny leaves rarely obscure the glossy culms with their crimson staining above the nodes. Regular thinning is required as the individual culms do not last long and can suffer dieback. This species has

Colourful oral setae on a fresh branch of *Drepanostachyum scandens*.

recently flowered and is currently unavailable until the resultant seedlings are deemed worthy for distribution.

Drepanostachyum microphyllum

Similar to *Drepanostachyum khasianum* and possibly hardier, but with leaves that are even smaller measuring only 1-5 cm. (0.4-2 in.). The culms mature to a dark, shiny purple-brown and give the plant a desirable appearance. Well worth trying.

Drepanostachyum scandens

A recent introduction to the United Kingdom from Guizhou, China; its specific name describes the scandent, or drooping, branch system. Very fresh, pale greenery is displayed on the manifold branching, the main branches develop strongly, but droop under the weight of foliage and further developing lateral branches. The effect is elegant but needs of plenty of space to be appreciated. My plant performs well under cold polythene but I have not been brave enough to try it outdoors.

Himalayacalamus falconeri

The genus *Himalayacalamus* is native to the cool and relatively moist forests of the Himalayas and although most species are able to withstand the cold they will not tolerate dry air, which can make them difficult to keep during long dry

summers in gardens. This species is an elegant leafy bamboo with a good culm structure and compact rhizome system. It is often razed to the ground in a cold winter but usually appears again the following spring. This is a popular choice for a cool but light position indoors, but try to provide some surrounding humidity or spray regularly with water.

Himalayacalamus falconeri 'Damarapa'

Of all the less hardy bamboos listed here, this is the one that performs the most satisfactorily outdoors in my cold, arid garden. It is, however, adequately protected by the large canopy of a *Sasa kurilensis* 'Shimofuri' which somehow manages to grow around instead of through this stunning cultivar. The culms are deliciously striped in shades of cream, yellow, pink and green, and hold dense branches of bunched and layered leaves. It is often hit hard in cold weather and has died back completely but reliably sprouts forth the following season. My plant rarely exceeds 1.5m (5ft) and I have to stoop low to see the culms under the leaf canopy, but it is worth the potential backache.

Himalayacalamus hookerianus

This, the once fashionable blue bamboo, now has a much hardier rival in *Thamnocalamus crassinodus* and its forms, with similar blue culms. However, *Himalayacalamus hookerianus* is very beautiful with pale blue waxy culms that mature to a pale yellow or pink-purple in good light. The species has recently flowered but seedlings with similar qualities are now available.

Oligostachyum oedogonatum

I first saw this bamboo labelled as *Clavinodum oedogonatum* at Peter Addington's Stream Cottage and was fortunate to be given a piece. I can find little reference to the genus *Clavinodum* and assume it is derived from the Latin *clava*, meaning club, and *nodes*, meaning knot, because the culms of this bamboo have obvious swollen nodes. It is not outstanding in cool gardens and

often short in stature with spindly culms, usually dull brown in colour. The leaves are quite long and narrow, bleaching irregularly during the winter. It did look beautiful in Peter's garden and I can understand his reluctance to divide it. If you can obtain a plant, it is well worth a try.

Schizostachyum funghomii

An attractive tropical-looking bamboo that in the warmest of conditions will produce thick, dark green culms with distinct buff-orange sheaths. The culms arch at the tips under the weight of the large leaves, unusual for a bamboo of this structure. In a cooler climate it will be more juvenile, quite arching, with smaller leaves but useful for the darker colouring.

Below: The unusual node and branch formation of *Schizostachyum funghomii*.

Left: Culm of *Himalayacalamus falconeri* 'Damarapa' showing yellow striping.

Sinobambusa intermedia

From a genus of subtropical bamboos this is one of a few species that will take some degree of cold and perform reasonably well. It grows strong and upright with almost white, powdery new culms. These are distinct with lengthy internodes and pronounced nodes, often hairy below the joint.

Sinobambusa tootsik

Known as the Chinese temple bamboo because it is traditionally planted adjacent to temples and monasteries, this is perhaps the best-known *Sinobambusa* species and widely used in Japan for creating a pompon effect with its tufted foliage. It can grow well in cool conditions if protected from cold wind and freezing at the roots to prevent desiccation of the leaves. It does lend itself to pruning and thinning and a finely worked plant is a beautiful sight.

Sinobambusa tootsik var. albovariegata

The variegated variety of the species can be equally robust, but prefers light shade. The variegation is quite bold and the colour is rarely lost as a result. Plants prefer good drainage and do not like the confines of a pot, especially in stagnant over-watered compost. Very beautiful if you can locate a specimen.

Yushania maling

Similar to *Yushania anceps*, but with sandpaper-like grey-green culms. On a mature plant the leaves weep luxuriously, but it only performs well in warm gardens, often dying back in cold regions.

Above: The tufted foliage of *Sinobambusa tootsik* resembles a pompon.

Right: The leaves of *Sinobambusa tootsik* var. *albovariegata*.

Chapter 10
Specific Qualities

These lists summarize the information given in the plant descriptions and will help you to select the right plant for a particular purpose or garden situation.

Very cold-hardy bamboos, for zones 4–6

Bashania fargesii
Chusquea culeou
Fargesia dracocephala
Fargesia murielae
Fargesia nitida (and forms)
Fargesia robusta
Fargesia rufa
Indocalamus tessellatus
Phyllostachys atrovaginata
Phyllostachys aureosulcata (and forms)
Phyllostachys bissetii
Phyllostachys humilis

1. *Phyllostachys iridescens*
2. *Chusquea culeou*
3. *Phyllostachys bambusoides* 'Castillonis'
4. *Phyllostachys aureosulcata* (dried culms)
5. *Himalayacalmus falconeri* 'Damarapa'
6. *Phyllostachys nigra* 'Megurochiku'
7. *Phyllostachys sulphurea*
8. *Phyllostachys aurea*
9. *Phyllostachys nigra*
10. *Phyllostachys glauca* f. *yunzhu*
11. *Phyllostachys vivax* f. *aureocaulis*
12. *Phyllostachys bambusoides* 'Allgold'
13. *Phyllostachys bambusoides* 'Castillonis Inversa'
14. *Phyllostachys aureosulcata* f. *pekinensis*
15. *Phyllostachys bambusoides*
16. *Borinda albocera*
17. *Phyllostachys violascens*

Phyllostachys mannii 'Decora'
Phyllostachys nuda
Phyllostachys parvifolia
Phyllostachys propinqua
Phyllostachys rubromarginata
Phyllostachys viridiglaucescens
Phyllostachys vivax (and forms)
Pleioblastus fortunei
Pleioblastus pygmaeus
Pleioblastus shibuyanus 'Tsuboi'
Sasa kurilensis (and forms)
Sasa palmata f. *nebulosa*
Semiarundinaria fastuosa (and var. *viridis*)
Shibataea kumasasa
Yushania brevipaniculata
Yushania maculata

Bamboos very tolerant of summer drought

Bashania fargesii
Chusquea culeou
Drepanostachyum (all species)
Fargesia robusta
Phyllostachys glauca
Pseudosasa japonica
Sasa palmata f. *nebulosa*
Sasa veitchii
Thamnocalamus tessellatus
Yushania maculata

Bamboos for wet soils, but not constantly waterlogged

Arundinaria gigantea subsp. *tecta*
Chimonobambusa quadrangularis
Chimonobambusa tumidissinoda
Phyllostachys atrovaginata
Phyllostachys heteroclada
Phyllostachys nidularia
Pseudosasa japonica
Shibataea kumasasa

Bamboos tolerant of deep shade

Chimonobambusa marmorea
Chimonobambusa quadrangularis
Fargesia murielae
Fargesia nitida
Indocalamus latifolius
Indocalamus tessellatus
Pleioblastus argenteostriatus 'Akebono'
Pleioblastus gramineus

Pleioblastus hindsii
Pleioblastus linearis
Pleioblastus simonii
Pseudosasa japonica
Sasa (most species)

Bamboos tolerant of seaside conditions and salt-laden winds

Chusquea culeou
Phyllostachys aureosulcata (and forms)
Phyllostachys bissetii
Phyllostachys nuda
Pleioblastus (all tall forms)
Pseudosasa japonica
Semiarundinaria fastuosa (and var. *viridis*, and most other species)

Grove-forming bamboos

Bashania fargesii
Chimonobambusa quadrangularis
Chusquea gigantea
Phyllostachys aureosulcata (and some forms)
Phyllostachys bambusoides (and some forms)
Phyllostachys dulcis
Phyllostachys glauca
Phyllostachys heteroclada
Phyllostachys nigra 'Boryana'
Phyllostachys nigra f. *henonis*
Phyllostachys violascens
Phyllostachys vivax (and forms)
Semiarundinaria fastuosa (and var. *viridis*)

Dwarf or ground cover bamboos

Indocalamus solidus
Indocalamus tessellatus
Pleioblastus argenteostriatus 'Akebono'
Pleioblastus argenteostriatus 'Okinadake'
Pleioblastus fortunei
Pleioblastus 'Gauntlettii'
Pleioblastus pygmaeus (and 'Distichus')
Pleioblastus viridistriatus (and forms)
Pseudosasa owatarii
Sasa kurilensis short
Sasa nipponica
Sasa veitchii
Sasaella masamuneana
Sasaella masamuneana 'Albostriata'
Sasaella ramosa
Shibataea (all species)

Phyllostachys aurea.

Bamboos for stabilizing banks and steep slopes

Arundinaria gigantea (and subsp. *tecta*)
Bashania fargesii
Chimonobambusa marmorea
Chimonobambusa tumidissinoda
Phyllostachys aurea (in warm areas)
Phyllostachys bissetii
Phyllostachys glauca
Phyllostachys humilis
Pleioblastus (many species)
Sasa oshidensis
Sasa palmata f. *nebulosa*
Sasa veitchii
Sasaella masamuneana (and forms)
Sasaella ramosa
Semiarundinaria kagamiana
Semiarundinaria okuboi
Semiarundinaria yashadake

Bamboos for hedging and screening

Many bamboos are suitable for hedges and screens, so rather than providing a long, unqualified list, here are a few pointers that you can follow up in the information given under "Uses" in the plant descriptions in chapter 8, "The Chosen Few".

Most of the small to medium bamboos, including the tiny leaved fargesias, are suitable for short hedges. Fargesias are tight and will need planting closely to form an impenetrable screen, and *Pleioblastus* are good for clipping, but will need more room to grow widthways as well as lengthways. *Indocalamus* will provide large-leaved screens of various heights according to species and will also require room to grow.

For taller hedges there are many species to choose from, particularly from the genera *Phyllostachys*, *Pseudosasa* and *Semiarundinaria*. Bamboos such as *Phyllostachys aurea* are especially good for clipping and shaping and others such as *Semiarundinaria fastuosa* and *Phyllostachys aureosulcata* will often grow naturally in straight lines, and can even be prompted to do so.

Bamboos for pots and containers outdoors

As well as the species listed here, many of the less hardy bamboos may well have to be grown in pots to control their environment, particularly in the winter months. By saying this it does not mean they are suitable and as general rule nearly all bamboos perform better in the ground than above it.

Chimonobambusa marmorea (and forms)
Fargesia (most species)
×*Hibanobambusa tranquillans* 'Shiroshima'
Indocalamus tessellatus
Phyllostachys aureosulcata f. *aureocaulis*
Phyllostachys aureosulcata f. *spectabilis*
Phyllostachys humilis
Phyllostachys nigra
Pleioblastus (most short species)
Sasa (most species)
Semiarundinaria kagamiana
Semiarundinaria makinoi
Semiarundinaria yashadake (and f. *kimmei*)
Shibataea kumasasa
Sinobambusa intermedia

Bamboos for growing indoors

Much against my will, here is a list of bamboos more suited to indoor culture. I am not an advocate of taking a hardy plant that requires a dormancy period indoors, and take no responsibility if you have little success; I get quite distressed when the telephone goes and the question is about a *Phyllostachys nigra* and its poor appearance, only to be told ten minutes into the conversation that it is situated in the kitchen next to the wood burner.

Bambusa multiplex (all forms)
Bambusa ventricosa
Chusquea (less hardy forms)
Drepanostachyum falcatum
Himalayacalamus falconeri (and 'Damarapa')
Indocalamus tessellatus
Pleioblastus fortunei
Pleioblastus pygmaeus
Pleioblastus shibuyanus 'Tsuboi'
Pseudosasa japonica
Shibataea kumasasa

Phyllostachys bambusoides 'Allgold'.

Bamboos with brightly variegated leaves

×*Hibanobambusa tranquillans* 'Shiroshima'
Pleioblastus argenteostriatus 'Akebono'
Pleioblastus argenteostriatus 'Okinadake'
Pleioblastus chino f. *elegantissimus*
Pleioblastus fortunei
Pleioblastus shibuyanus 'Tsuboi'
Pleioblastus viridistriatus (and forms)
Pseudosasa japonica 'Akebono' and 'Akebonosuji'
Sasa kurilensis 'Shimofuri'
Sasaella masamuneana 'Albostriata'
Sinobambusa tootsik var. *albovariegata*

Bamboos with medium or large leaves for a tropical effect

Bashania faberi
×*Hibanobambusa tranquillans* (and 'Shiroshima')
Indocalamus (most species)
Pseudosasa japonica (and forms)
Sasa (most species)
Sinobambusa (most species)

Timber bamboos capable of generating thick culms

Phyllostachys bambusoides (and some forms)
Phyllostachys edulis
Phyllostachys dulcis
Phyllostachys nigra var. *henonis*
Phyllostachys sulphurea (and forms)
Phyllostachys vivax (and forms)

Bamboos with unusual culm shapes

Bambusa ventricosa
Chimonobambusa tumidissinoda
Chusquea montana
Phyllostachys aurea (and forms)
Phyllostachys aureosulcata and forms
Phyllostachys bambusoides 'Marliacea'
Phyllostachys edulis 'Heterocycla'
Phyllostachys nidularia
Phyllostachys nuda
Pleioblastus gramineus f. *monstrispiralis*
Pseudosasa japonica 'Tsutsumiana'

Right: Swollen culm of *Pseudosasa japonica* 'Tsutsumiana'.

Right: Phyllostachys nigra.

Bamboos with yellow or yellow-striped culms (not including the sulci)

Bambusa multiplex 'Alphonse Karr'
Chimonobambusa quadrangularis 'Nagaminea'
Chimonobambusa quadrangularis 'Suow'
Phyllostachys aurea 'Holochrysa'
Phyllostachys aurea 'Koi'
Phyllostachys aureosulcata f. *aureocaulis*
Phyllostachys aureosulcata 'Lama Tempel'
Phyllostachys aureosulcata f. *spectabilis*
Phyllostachys bambusoides 'Allgold'
Phyllostachys bambusoides 'Castillonis'
Phyllostachys edulis 'Bicolor'
Phyllostachys praecox f. *viridisulcata*
Phyllostachys propinqua 'Bicolor'
Phyllostachys sulphurea ('Robert Young')
Phyllostachys vivax f. *aureocaulis*
Semiarundinaria yashadake f. *kimmei*

Bamboos with striped culms other than yellow (but including those with yellow sulci)

Chimonobambusa quadrangularis 'Yellow Groove'
Himalayacalamus falconeri 'Damarapa'
Phyllostachys arcana 'Luteosulcata'
Phyllostachys aurea 'Flavescens Inversa'
Phyllostachys aureosulcata
Phyllostachys aureosulcata 'Argus'
Phyllostachys aureosulcata 'Harbin'
Phyllostachys aureosulcata 'Harbin Inversa'
Phyllostachys bambusoides 'Castillonis Inversa'
Phyllostachys bambusoides 'Kawadana'
Phyllostachys edulis 'Goldstripe'
Phyllostachys iridescens
Phyllostachys nigra 'Megurochiku'

Left: A selection of distorted and oddly shaped culms, all useful for drying and ornamental decoration.

1. *Phyllostachys vivax*
2. *Phyllostachys aureosulcata* f. *spectabilis*
3. *Phyllostachys aureosulcata*
4. *Phyllostachys aurea*
5. *Chimonobambusa tumidissinoda*
6. *Pseudosasa japonica* 'Tsutsumiana'
7. *Phyllostachys aureosulcata* 'Argus'
8. *Phyllostachys aureosulcata* f. *pekinensis*
9. *Phyllostachys aurea* 'Koi'
10. *Phyllostachys nuda*

Phyllostachys sulphurea 'Houzeau'
Phyllostachys violascens
Phyllostachys vivax f. *huanvenzhu*

Bamboos with spotted or blotched culms

Phyllostachys bambusoides f. *lacrima-deae*
Phyllostachys bambusoides f. *mixta*
Phyllostachys glauca f. *yunzhu*
Phyllostachys nigra 'Boryana'
Phyllostachys nigra f. *punctata*
Phyllostachys nigra 'Tosaensis'
Sasa palmata f. *nebulosa*

Bamboos with black, grey, tawny, purple-tinted and blue culms

Bashania fargesii
Borinda albocera
Chusquea culeou (some clones)
Drepanostachyum (some species)
Fargesia nitida
Himalayacalamus hookerianus
Phyllostachys glauca
Phyllostachys heteroclada
Phyllostachys nigra (and 'Hale', 'Othello' and 'Wisley')
Phyllostachys nigra 'Fulva'
Thamnocalamus crassinodus (all forms)

Bamboos with colourful or attractive sheaths

Chimonobambusa marmorea
Fargesia robusta (and forms)
Fargesia rufa
Phyllostachys (many species and forms)
Pseudosasa usuwai
Sasa kurilensis 'Shimofuri'
Schizostachyum funghomii
Semiarundinaria fastuosa (and var. *viridis*)
Thamnocalamus (all species)
Yushania brevipaniculata
Yushania maculata

Left: Semiarundinaria fastuosa culm sheaths.

Above: A bright yellow sulcus on a culm of *Phyllostachys bambusoides* 'Castillonis Inversa'.

My top bamboos

"Which are the most suitable bamboos to start with for my garden?" is a frequent question, usually from people with little or no experience of growing bamboos. I hope this book has gone some way in convincing you that most bamboos really are quite easy to grow. This was going to be my top ten but choosing ten was an impossible task, so there are twelve listed here and not necessarily my favourites. They have been selected for their quick results and adaptability to many aspects in different gardens.

Chusquea gigantea
Fargesia nitida 'Nymphenburg'
Fargesia robusta
×*Hibanobambusa tranquillans* 'Shiroshima'
Phyllostachys aureosulcata f. *spectabilis*
Phyllostachys vivax
Phyllostachys vivax f. *aureocaulis*
Pleioblastus shibuyanus 'Tsuboi'
Pseudosasa japonica var. *pleioblastoides*
Semiarundinaria fastuosa var. *viridis*
Thamnocalamus crassinodus 'Kew Beauty'
Yushania maculata

Above: New shoots of *Fargesia robusta* are early and plentiful. This bamboo is very quick to establish in gardens.

Right: The strong vertical culms of *Chusquea gigantea* appear early in life and maturity comes quickly to this bamboo, which is still difficult to obtain.

From left to right, starting top left
Sasa veitchii
Semiarundinaria fastuosa
Sinobambusa tootsik var. *albovariegata*
Thamnocalamus crassinodus 'Merlyn'
Sasa palmata f.*nebulosa*
Yushania maculata
Pseudosasa japonica 'Akebonosuji'
Chimonobambusa marmorea 'Variegata'
Pleioblastus argenteostriatus 'Okinadake'
Pleioblastus viridistriatus
Sasaella masamuneana 'Albostriata'
Fargesia nitida

Feeling at Home

Chapter 11
Creative Culture

Purchasing a Bamboo

When you buy a bamboo you are paying for what is inside the pot, rather than what is on show above it. The root and rhizome are by far the most important parts of the young plant. Before you buy a plant look at it closely and take note of the following points.

I would always try to persuade you to buy a young bamboo. Young plants develop at their own pace and in balance, often overtaking larger specimens in the speed of their maturity. If you do insist on buying a large specimen, check with the supplier whether the plant is container grown or containerized. A container-grown plant is one that has been potted on from a young plant throughout its life and has matured equally in rhizome structure and culm formation. A containerized bamboo may have been lifted from the ground or split from a large stock plant. It may look impressive but the roots and rhizome will have been severed, resulting in thin weak growth. Always choose a container-grown plant, and if your supplier cannot confirm this method of culture, do not make the purchase.

Ensure the plant is not pale or yellowing in colour; if it is, it may be starved. A fresh green plant is likely to be recently potted and is unlikely to be starved or suffering from a check to its growth. Check for a high percentage of dead or dying culms, which signify the bamboo may be congested, old or woody and unable to produce new juvenile growth. If possible check the roots and rhizomes in the pot. Look for fresh white roots and rhizome, or buds near the edge of the pot or emerging from the surface. If there is an absence of all three, the bamboo may have been very recently potted and therefore not suitable for transplanting. Look closely for visible pests and disease (see chapter 13, "Beware of the Enemy"). Ask whether your supplier uses chemical control; sometimes plants overdosed on chemicals will be weaker in the garden and have no immune system. If the grower uses organic methods, the plants may stronger and the occasional aphid, although off-putting, will usually disappear once the bamboo is planted in your garden.

Buy according to your budget. Three young plants may be a better option than one large specimen, offering greater value in the long term. Bamboos grow quickly and large "instant plants", although impressive, are sometimes slow to establish and unbalanced, often having great top growth emerging from a small pot. It is always better to buy a balanced plant, which has sufficient root and rhizome to support the top growth.

Make sure you get "free" information when you buy a bamboo (or any plant for that matter). If the person you are buying the plant from cannot tell you a little about it, find someone who can, or go elsewhere. However, do not expect a guarantee. You are purchasing a living thing and as soon as you take it home it is your responsibility, so get some advice on how to look after it. After all, if you bought a hamster from a pet shop and it died two years later, would you take it back and demand another one?

In summary, I recommend that you buy a young plant after checking the root system and getting good advice. Start by choosing a bamboo with a reliable reputation and that is not too rare, so that you can get used to its needs without incurring too much expense.

Planting, Feeding, Mulches and Aftercare

One of the questions I am most often asked is how to plant bamboos. This is easy to answer but the follow up query about how a plant develops

A winter combination of Phyllostachys aureosulcata f. spectabilis, birch and mahonia – the vertical habits of the plants contrast well with the sharp horizontal line of the slate wall.

vigour and strength after planting is perhaps more difficult to explain. Many plants always look their best in nature – the gorgeous maples and groves of fresh dark green *Sasa* in the mountains of Japan, the North American woodlands with rich autumn colouring, the bright and textured evergreens of the South American low countries – all look their best without help from gardeners. Although management of some forested areas and, in particular, national parks is commonplace, this is usually limited to regeneration through thinning, cropping and replanting. You never see someone traipsing up a wild hillside with a long yellow hosepipe or bag of granular fertilizer to water and feed plants in the wild. Wild plants are survivors, they grow in the right place and at their own pace, developing the best habit and colouring.

When we bring plants into our gardens we introduce them to a habitat that they possibly have to adapt to or is unnatural to them. There is, however, a fault inbred in us to pamper things that are either close to our hearts, or we have spent money on, particularly if we have gone out of our way to obtain something we desire. I usually equate the life of a young plant to that of a child growing into the teenage years. If you mother and over cosset a child from birth into adulthood, not allowing some independence and space, the child will probably grow up less capable of standing on his or her own two feet, relying on your support for a greater length of time. Likewise a plant that has been overfed, given structural support and watered too frequently will look healthy to start with but may not have the strength to support itself later, when you devote your time a new acquisition.

Treat a new bamboo like a baby for the first two years and by all means give it your undivided attention. As the plant develops, just like a child going to school, give it some freedom, allow it to find its own way in life; occasional times of stress will help to make the plant grow

stronger. Allow the roots to search for water, let the culms blow in the wind and, when you feel the need to intervene, it will react positively to your care and attention. As a plant reaches maturity it should be more capable of looking after itself with minimal attention from you. This stage in life could possibly be equated to the late teenage years; you sometimes have to step in to keep your offspring in check but normally you have other things to devote to your time to.

The bamboos in my garden have always been given the bare minimum of care. Although the soil is reasonably fertile, it is quite gluey with an underlying pan of chalky clay. It can flood in winter and bake hard in summer, forming the occasional crevasse in the process. Planting has always been quick, with the minimum of ground disturbance, as I do not like to over cultivate the soil; it loosens the structure providing less stability for young plants and releases valuable water through evaporation. I prefer to plant in the autumn as I find watering young plants after spring planting a chore. Anything planted during the springtime will, however, get an initial watering. If I am feeling generous the young plant will be lightly mulched and, although this is something I recommend, I must admit that I do not often do it myself.

Supplementary watering and feeding have never been provided in my garden. Over the years, the natural organic content of the soil has improved with the decaying leaves of the surrounding broadleaved trees and shrubs, and also from the dropping leaves and sheaths of the bamboos. The organic matter from living plants is the only food my bamboos rely on. I admit that a new garden created from a building site will often be lacking in both organic and nutrient content, and in this situation it would be wise to enrich the soil with rotted manure, garden compost or similar bulky organic material before and after planting for a few years. The only way to persuade you that bamboos really do cope under stress, with low annual rainfall, no additional feeding and very little mothering is to trust my words, or come and see for yourself.

I know of some enthusiasts who annually mulch their beloved specimens with rich manure, and use drip watering throughout the summer months. The plants in their gardens look spectacular but, with respect, no better than the ones here. It is possible to speed up the maturity of a bamboo with feeding and watering but do not do this too soon on a juvenile plant. A plant that is just about to reach maturity has a greater demand for sustenance than one newly planted.

Summary of planting and early care

To give your bamboos a good start in life, please take heed of the following advice. You will notice that the planting and aftercare recommended for bamboos is not dissimilar to that of many other plants.

1. Prepare a hole in the soil a little bigger than the size of the pot or rootball of the plant. Fork the base and sides of the hole in case the soil is hard and panned; this will help the roots and rhizome grow into the surrounding area.
2. Moisten the hole before planting and allow it to drain.
3. Lightly tease or loosen some of the fibrous roots from the edge of the rootball, particularly if it has been confined in a pot. This can be done easily with your fingernails or a small stick, but take care not to damage rhizome or new buds and shoots. If the rhizome has circled the pot do not worry; a bamboo rhizome rarely strangles itself or the growing plant, and branches quickly outwards from any curving growth. This is an advantage over a tree, which sometimes relies on a few long woody roots that must grow outwards into the surrounding soil for stability; root circling on a tree can lead to its eventual death.
4. Plant the bamboo so the soil is level with the top of the rootball, or a little deeper if roots and rhizomes are visibly protruding from the top of the pot. Tread the soil firmly to give stability to the bamboo, but carefully so as not to damage any unseen shoots within the rootball.
5. Water immediately after planting.
6. Mulch with well-rotted leafmould or composted bark to a depth of no more than 5 cm.

(2 in.) around the base of the bamboo and lightly moisten the mulch if it is dry. If your soil is infertile, mix the mulch with some well-rotted manure or a smattering of balanced granular fertilizer. Never use pure peat for it has little nutrient value and dries out very quickly, often blowing away in the wind.

7. In the weeks following planting, give water when you think the plant requires it, not every day. Soak the soil occasionally with a slow running stream from a hosepipe so that the water penetrates the soil down to the roots. Do not use a sprinkler to top up soil moisture on a daily basis; this usually results in moistening the top few centimetres of soil and encouraging the roots to grow to the surface, making them more vulnerable in times of drought. Allow the soil and the roots to drain freely between irrigations; the root system must be allowed to breath and young plants do not like waterlogged soils.
8. Further mulching – in late winter to conserve moisture and prevent weeds germinating – and watering may be necessary in the first two years after planting, but should be gradually decreased in frequency. After this, try leaving the plant alone, only attending to its needs when under severe stress.
9. Thin out old and weak culms as the bamboo matures and prune some of the lower branches of the species with good culm colour to enhance their appearance.

Using Bamboos in Gardens and Landscapes

Whether you want to play at Capability Brown, envelop your house closely with a jungle-like screen to hide your neighbour's new building extension, reduce the wind or escape from the noise and urban pollution of the twenty-first century, there is a place for bamboos. Regardless of how small your garden, there is a suitable bamboo. If you do not have soil you can grow them in pots. Do you live in a second-storey apartment?

A strong Chusquea provides height and focus in this colourful planting.

Above: A large *Phyllostachys,* with phormium and grasses, seen in winter.

You have no excuse for not growing bamboos in pots on a balcony. Bamboos on roof gardens are popular and possible; short bamboos in window boxes and raised beds can be appreciated at close quarters, while on a larger scale bamboo mazes and secret areas in bamboo groves are enchanting examples of many other possibilities.

For plant associations you also have unlimited choice. Gardening should be personal, not dictated by fashion or other people's preferences. Plant as you like. Evergreens with larger leaves, including *Mahonia, Viburnum* and *Rhododendron* will complement your bamboos with their flowers. Boldly variegated plants look dramatic against the dark foliage or structural culms of many bamboos. You are spoiled for choice among the many deciduous shrubs, perennials and grasses that offer interest for the various seasons of the year as foils to the continuity that your bamboos provide.

Left: Phyllostachys nigra with *Cornus alternifolia* 'Argentea' (left) and *Euphorbia mellifera* (right).

We all have preferences and I prefer to use bamboos with other plants. The vertical structure of some bamboos is enhanced by association with ornamental grasses. The delicate greenery and branching systems can be made more obvious against a background of larger broadleaved plants. Low prostrate shrubs, conifers or perennials around the base of bamboos make strong contrast between the vertical and horizontal.

I do not intend to tell you what you should use for plant association and, although suggestions have been made in the individual plant descriptions, I would rather you make your choices after you have learned how versatile and complementary bamboos can be. If you still find you want help and tips, there are no shortages of gardening programmes, magazines, gardens to visit and general advice on the Internet or from specialists.

Bamboos successfully used to edge a path.

Use with materials and features

The simple use of hard landscape materials, such as stone, timber, small garden structures and ponds to create a different landscape setting within your garden can be very rewarding. The use of local materials or natural features is usually cheaper and more in keeping with the environment than introducing anything foreign, and failing that there are many concrete products that are very effective if used thoughtfully.

Small areas can be created within a garden in the style of a Japanese courtyard. Giant culms emerging alongside a gravel path, some discretely placed rocks and oriental ornaments, a plum tree, pine, some peonies and ferns will provide the imagery of a place thousands of miles away.

A bold *Phyllostachys* with bright golden culms or the large reflective leaves of *Indocalamus* and *Sasa* placed at the end of long path will create focus. Edging a narrow path with tall overhanging bamboos will create perspective. The willowy habits of *Fargesia* and *Yushania* by the side of a pond will be reflected and give depth to the landscape. Add to this simple horizontal fencing occasionally softened by broad mounds of the shorter *Pleioblastus* for an intermediate level for the eyes to view. A large tumble of sea-washed pebbles in the shade of a large bamboo creates brightness lower down, offering balance and a surface where the shadows and flickering light created by the foliage overhead can play. Sharp brick edging is a stark contrast to the smoothness of the huge rounded culms on some bamboos. If you prefer, the edging can be softened with small-leaved creeping ivy or blocks of ferns. Accentuate or punctuate the verticals and horizontals of a wooden pergola with bamboos erupting through the overhead struts, or grow them either side of an entrance to a large gazebo or summerhouse as an expression of formality. The possibilities are limited only by your imagination and bamboos will be more than accommodating to your special garden style.

A word of warning: bamboos should not be planted too close to a pond as the culms can penetrate the liner, whether it is flexible butyl rubber, a rigid preformed unit or other material.

Hedges and screens

Many bamboos are suitable for screening purposes and you only have to make a suitable choice of height, width, shape, colour and leaf size. In general, the more cold hardy a bamboo, the more tolerant it will be of the wind and therefore able to keep a fresh appearance all year round.

Some species are suitable for trimming. This should be done early in the growing season so that new branches and leaves can hide any cuts and bruises. In warm temperate gardens trimming can be carried out all year round, in which case do this little and often

A winding path lined with bamboos, including the golden-culmed *Phyllostachys bambusoides* 'Castillonis', and shining in the distance the large leaves of *Indocalamus tessellatus*.

Is it a culm or is it is a rhizome? A young plant of Phyllostachys aureosulcata f. aureocaulis produces a rhizome that snakes out from the surface of the pot. Instead of trying to escape over the rim, it has second thoughts and forms a weak culm instead.

rather than a single vicious flailing with a brush-cutter or motorized hedgetrimmer.

There are a few simple guidelines for planting hedges and screens. Firstly do not plant any closer than 1 m (3.3 ft.) apart. This allows each plant to develop individually without competing with the next one in line, so when they do grow together after a few years they will be strong enough to cope with the competition.

For a thick hedge, either choose a vigorous species with a broad culm formation or plant in two staggered rows. If possible plant a mixture of bamboos unless you insist on the formality and uniformity of a single species. If you only plant the one species and it happens to flower (and possibly die) that will be the end of your hedge.

If you plant bamboos by a wall, do so as far away from it as possible. This is because the soil

at the base of a wall is usually dry and growth will be restricted. Consider the aspects, too, as light is necessary to help the young plants mature.

A row of bamboos next to a fence will produce rhizomes in your neighbour's garden. To prevent this happening, sink a single line of overlapping concrete slabs vertically in the ground, or choose a more suitable clump-forming species.

Root and rhizome barriers

It is common to see rhizome barriers sunk into the soil to a depth of about 60 cm. (2 ft.) and protrude slightly above the ground; they are now used in some botanical gardens. The barriers are usually made from plastic or rubber compounds with a long life. Unfortunately, I disagree with their use with few exceptions. I can understand the need to control a bamboo, particularly if it is of great age or was already in situ when you moved to your house. I can also accept the use of a rhizome barrier should you desire the most rampant of bamboos but only have a small garden.

However, I have seen many bamboos with rhizomes that quickly grow over the top of a barrier, like snakes escaping from a basket. Unless the rhizomes are severed regularly the barrier will prove useless, because resistance is futile to a bamboo with great vigour and invasive qualities. Barriers may also affect the long-term quality of the bamboo; the translocation of water and nutrients across a large area of soil will be impeded and fresh, healthy growth will be reduced over time.

If you have a choice, always select a bamboo you know you have room for. If the plant does exceed your limits, control it by physical means, by removing some rhizome and culms from different sides of the plant each year using a sharp spade.

If a bamboo really gets out of control you may have to take the drastic measures I had to some years ago with a *Bashania fargesii* that had come to dominate one side of our house. After pruning the plant to about 1 m (3 ft.) high in the autumn, I sprayed it heavily the following spring with a systemic weedkiller and cut back to the ground any further growth that appeared. This treatment worked remarkably well and all I was left to deal with after a year was a matted rhizome. It could be that you will not be so lucky and may need to resort to a further spraying. (For the full story see the entry for *Bashania fargesii* in "Nothing but the Plants".)

Pots and containers

Most plants can be grown on in pots and the same can apply to many bamboos, but being able to, and being suitable for, are two completely different things. As a nurseryman I have to grow many bamboos in pots, particularly large ones for exhibition and, as it is my job, I know how best to look after them. There are many reasons for growing plants in pots, but the few advantages are far outweighed by the problems. I am not trying to put you off, merely warning you that you will have to give a bamboo in a container your undivided attention throughout its life.

The scenario: you are hiking across the Himalayan hillsides and forests and you climb over the next ridge, then stumble upon a *Fargesia* growing in a large, bright blue ceramic pot. I don't think so. Pots are unnatural, they do not exist in nature and as a result you will have to provide the plants with many of the things that nature gives freely, most importantly food and water. However, bamboos do look superb in pots when properly cared for; the contrast of colours, shapes and textures to go with your bamboo is infinite. Growing in pots gives you manoeuvrability in the garden and particularly where space is limited. The bamboo can be raised close to eye level for impact and invasive types can be grown with little fear of them taking over the garden. I have suggested some species suited to pots in the previous chapter, "Specific Qualities".

Rather than suggesting whether you do or you do not grow bamboos in pots, here are a few tips to help you decide or, if you have already decided, to help you succeed.

Situation

Choose a sheltered spot in the garden for a potted bamboo to reduce water loss and avoid exposure to strong wind. The wind not only takes moisture away from the plant, but also when it is dry, blows it over, sometimes cracking your pot in the process.

A bamboo in a pot can also suffer from drought in the winter because it does not have the natural supply from a wet winter soil. Also the bamboo is raised above the soil surface, so the roots can freeze solid. When the leaves transpire, the water supply is locked in the frozen rootball and your plant will desiccate. Be prepared either to water it, and/or give it some shelter in freezing weather, by moving the container into a cool glasshouse or even to a garage

temporarily. If this is not possible, insulate the pot with several layers of bubble wrapping or similar, or plunge it in the soil and protect the foliage from further moisture loss in the wind with heavy-duty fleece .

Containers and drainage

Use flexible plastic containers or rigid, good quality glazed ceramic pots with sides that are straight, or flare out towards the top. If you use a pot that narrows at the rim, you will either have to dissect and excavate your bamboo to remove it, or smash the pot with a sledgehammer. A wide shallow container avoids this problem and also has a low centre of gravity, which helps to prevent taller plants from blowing over. Terracotta pots are more brittle, and if used should be waterproofed on the inside to prevent moisture from evaporating through the side of the pot. A pot-bound bamboo with swelling rhizomes can eventually crack a terracotta pot – there you are, a late evening barbecue with your friends, glass of wine, soft music and chitchat, then your favourite terracotta pot complete with a giant *Phyllostachys* explodes under the pressure of the swelling rhizome.

Make sure there are numerous, well-spaced drainage holes in the pot and there is no need to place crocks or lumpy drainage material in the bottom. (When did you last buy a plant from a nursery with pieces of broken terracotta in the bottom of the pot?) The growing medium in the pot should be as close to the ground as possible to aid capillary action of water; although a bamboo is more likely to dry out in a pot it can occasionally get too wet. The only justifiable reason for using crocks is for weight, to lower the centre of gravity and give extra stability.

Compost

Choose your compost carefully. A heavy, soil-based compost gives weight and stability to the pot but over the years it will set like concrete, becoming devoid of air and making it difficult for water to permeate to the roots. A pure peat-based medium is too light, dries out rapidly and, if this happens, will prove difficult to remoisten. The

Bamboos in pots out of doors.

addition of water retention granules may help, but if the plant dries out too much these may have an adverse effect by taking moisture from the compost. If you grow tall bamboos in pots the growing medium will need to be heavier for extra stability than for shorter bamboos, which require less weight at the base.

I suggest a mixture of soil and peat-based compost at whatever percentage is necessary to add weight to the pot, approximately half and half if you are not sure. Add to this about 10 percent grit by volume for ballast (note the grit provides no additional drainage but merely adds weight to the compost) and between 5 and 10 percent of medium-grade composted bark; the large surface area of the pieces of bark will prevent the compost from clogging and provide the additional drainage, much better than grit. Finally mix in a slow-release, balanced fertilizer at the rate for the volume of the pot. Opt for a granular formulation and avoid using the small thimble-like pellets that are plugged into the compost; these plugs do not give an even balance of nutrients throughout the compost.

Often the best choice of compost is the one you are used too. As long as food and water is available and the plant looks healthy, the type of growing medium is irrelevant as long you know how to manage it.

Watering, feeding and pruning

Be prepared to water your bamboo as necessary. On the hottest and most arid of summer days this could be two or three times a day. If you go away for the weekend, you will need to employ a bamboo-sitter, or install automatic watering.

After the first year your potted bamboo will need supplementary nutrients. Liquid feeding is the best method, although a further top dressing with granular fertilizer is acceptable for second year. After a time the pH of the compost changes due of the build up of residual salts in the pot. The only way to overcome this is to pot on the bamboo to a larger container, or remove and divide it. There is no exact timescale for a bamboo to survive happily in a pot, but it is certainly not long term. The more vigorous the plant, the more often it will require food, water and therefore re-potting.

Fibrous roots and sometimes rhizomes will grow towards the surface of the compost. If you notice them exposed, cover them with grit, coarse bark or pebbles. Once this is done, the surface of the compost will no longer be visible, so you will not be able to see the change in colour or texture of the compost, which lets you know the plant is dry or wet. You will either have to estimate when the plant needs water or be prepared to lift the pot to judge its weight and water content: sore back means the compost is very wet; able to lift the pot with one arm means the plant is desperately in need of water.

If you notice your bamboo has closed its leaves through drought, you have only a matter of hours to water it. Once the leaf cells are damaged they will not be able to take in water and swell again. Should this happen, your bamboo is certainly not dead, but you will have to wait for it to grow new leaves.

Thinning out the old growth regularly reduces the leaf area and, in consequence, the amount of water required. On some species pruning and shortening the culms is also possible. Thinning and pruning are best done at a time when new culms are not emerging so as not to damage them; early spring is probably best.

Repotting

Remember any restriction to the roots and rhizomes, whether above or below ground, are one and the same, whether it is caused by a pot, large trough, small raised bed, or sunken concrete enclosure for lines of hedging. The larger the pot or enclosure, the longer the bamboo will last in situ. Having said that, potting on a plant from a 5-litre pot into a 50-litre container is not always a good idea. It is better to move a plant on in stages; from the 5-litre pot to a 15 or 20-litre pot, and then two years later into one of 50-litre capacity. A young plant wallowing in a large volume of wet compost is almost as bad as providing it with no water, and it usually sulks and takes time before growing strongly. Like thinning and pruning, repotting is best undertaken in early spring, so as not to damage the newly emerging young culms.

If I have put you off growing bamboos in containers I apologize, but the truth must be known. However, your skill, perseverance and best attention will provide an image of beauty, almost an art form. Bamboos in pots can add a touch of exotica and style to a patio or decked area, giving you total control over the plant and the ability to create new themes in your garden area.

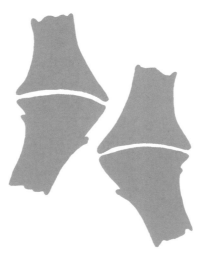

Chapter 12

Increasing the Fold

There are few techniques for propagating bamboos. Young temperate bamboos can only be raised from seed or by some form of division at the roots. Some tropical species can be reproduced from culm sections or by layering, but success with either of these techniques is very rare with temperate forms and you will be wasting your time if you try. To appreciate how to propagate temperate bamboos you should read this section in association with chapter 5 "Going Underground", which deals with rhizomes, and the section "Culm production and growing up", in chapter 6.

Propagating by Division

This process is best described as splitting a root system to make two or more plants. It may sound simple but there is much to learn to be successful. I am often asked when is the best time for bamboo division. As a commercial grower I divide bamboos all year round, but for the amateur gardener I suggest very early spring or during autumn, when the air is not too dry and temperatures not too extreme. At all costs avoid the time when the bamboo is shooting and producing new culms as this is when the most damage can be done.

Division from container stock

One of the reasons why bamboos are among the more expensive plants to buy is this most basic propagation method of division. As a novice with bamboos, many years ago, I soon learned not to be too greedy when dividing plants. If you have a pot filled with a mass of culms and rhizome, it would seem likely that many smaller plants can result. However, I was soon to realize that splitting a plant into many pieces is both wasteful and unrewarding, as most small divisions grow weakly

or do not survive. There is a simple rule: it is better to divide in half and produce two strong plants, than to divide into four and get one strong and three weak ones. A bamboo that does not grow strongly is a liability in a nursery; it has to be nursed, not kept too wet and takes up valuable growing space. A strong division can root fully in a pot in a matter of weeks and be sold well before a weak or small division has even started to recover. So learn the lesson and never be greedy.

The usual method for separating tough clumps of herbaceous plants, using two forks with a prising action, is not recommended for bamboos as it will disturb the root and rhizome and loosen the culms; it is better to employ a sharp, straight chopping action. To divide a bamboo growing in a relatively small pot, first take it out of its pot and then make a clean cut down the centre of the rootball with sharp secateurs or a handsaw. Expect these tools to blunt quickly, as the rhizomes are quite woody and grit in the compost makes matters worse. For larger plants in pots, use a stronger saw or sharp axe.

After potting up each division, remove any loose or damaged culms and be prepared to reduce the culm height, thereby reducing leaf area and moisture loss. If you have ever wondered why the tops have been pruned from the culms of a bamboo on a nursery, this is the reason; it is to create a balance between the amount of rhizome and the amount of top growth the roots are able to support. Keep the newly propagated plants in a sheltered and preferably humid environment until new roots are initiated and can be seen growing around the inside of the container.

A nurseryman wishing to produce a hundred plants of a particular bamboo species will require at least a hundred to start with. He will divide them in half to double the quantity, keeping a hundred for stock and selling an equal number. In reality, not every plant can be divided every year, and some of the very rare and slow-growing species may only be propagated once in every five years. The average bamboo nursery that is self-sufficient will have over 80 percent of the nursery devoted to stock plants. It is usual to keep three or four times the number of plants that are required for sale. The cost of this stock holding and the price of saws (you only get twenty to thirty divisions per saw), puts bamboos in the same price league as the rarer woody plants such as magnolias and Japanese maples, which are usually produced by the time-consuming and expensive method of grafting.

Division from mature stock plants or garden specimens

This method is most unproductive and rarely employed by commercial growers. Basically it involves removing a segment from an existing mature plant by brute force. As with the division of juvenile plants it is better to sever a generous-sized segment, as it will stand more chance of survival. Instead of a saw, you need a sharp spade or a specialist cutting tool with a sharp blade, such as a long-handled bolster chisel, and lump hammer. Chop downwards and do not prise, or the mother plant will be damaged. Where large pieces are required from a very old grove, I have seen a small mechanical digger used, but with much damage to the plant.

Sometimes this method is the only way to obtain a plant, particularly one from a friend's garden, so prepare yourself for hard work. The woody and matted structure of an established rhizome system is unbelievably resistant to physical damage or slicing. If you are allowed to pillage a plant for your own gain, take your time. Be aware you may not be successful and have respect for the bamboo you are trying to divide so as not to damage it more than necessary. Note too that dividing a clumping bamboo is more difficult than tackling one with runners. However, a runner often produces culms that have little root at the base, so a long section of rhizome must necessarily be removed while you are digging. With pachymorph bamboos it is wise to select a small colony of culms rather than a single culm, to ensure

sufficient quantity of roots and viable buds.

The aftercare of a mature division is much the same as for a juvenile plant. Reduce the leaf area by shortening the culms and keep the divided piece in a humid environment or regularly sprayed with water. Also because rhizome and buds are likely to have been damaged, do not expect strong growth in the first year or two; your new acquisition will probably revert to juvenile growth.

Rhizome sections and cuttings

Some leptomorph species can be propagated successfully by segmenting healthy sections of long rhizome with individual roots and buds present. These sections are usually known as rhizome sections, or rhizome cuttings, and do not necessarily need a culm or any greenery attached. The best time for taking sections is in spring, which gives a whole growing season for the buds on the rhizomes to break their dormancy. The sections are placed in pots or trays of free-draining compost so they are just below the compost surface, and then kept in a sheltered spot where they are not baked by the sun. Again, do not be greedy; large sections of rhizome with many buds stand more chance of producing culms than a tiny piece with a single bud. In the nursery we lay long pieces in trays, wait two years until the tray is bursting at the seams, and then section the mat of rhizomes and attached culms with a sharp saw. The sections are grown on in pots, and it takes another year for them to develop into saleable plants. Although this may seem like a free and easy method of production, it is in fact a lengthy and time-consuming process.

Culm offsets

This is the most difficult method of division and used for pachymorph bamboos. It requires patience and the protection of polythene or glass, and preferably some basal heat to help promote new root growth. Normally a single young culm with a piece of swollen rhizome and new bud is taken, and usually with very little root attached (the culm will have been supplied with nutrients via the short neck attached to another, older rhizome). After severing the young piece from the parent plant, cut back the culm to the node bearing the first branch above ground level and, if necessary, shorten the branch – very little root must be compensated by very little leaf. Place the offsets in shallow trays or small pots and do not allow them to become too wet. Keep the rhizome free from frost, and the air surrounding the culm cool, but humid. I have seen culm offsets propagated successfully in a mist unit with gentle heat at the base of 15° to 19°C (59° to 66°F). Although artificial heating is not essential it does provide warmth at night, preventing fluctuations in temperature. Young growth will be thin, and a saleable plant is often only achieved at the end of the second year after propagation.

Propagation from Seed

When seed is available it is one of the most productive and also a very cheap method of producing new plants. The guarantee that goes with seed-raised plants is that they are unlikely to flower for many years, possibly generations. Sow the seeds immediately after collection on the surface of free-draining compost and lightly cover them with fine grit or sharp sand. Place the sowings in a cool position, out of direct sunlight, either in a greenhouse or outdoors under netting for shade and protection against birds and vermin. Keep seedlings weed free and water only when the pot or tray feels light.

Some species germinate immediately and others can take more than a year, so be patient. Prick out young seedlings and look after them in the same way as for any other plant. Do not over pot them or keep them too wet, and make sure you protect the young plants from summer sun and low temperatures as they develop, probably for two or three years. They can then be hardened off and planted in the garden. The development of a bamboo from seed is quite quick, and at least matches the speed and type of culm production of a juvenile plant growing to maturity, as described under "Culm production and growing up", in chapter 6.

Chapter 13
Beware of the Enemy

When you buy a bamboo you can be safe in the knowledge that few pathogens can weaken it or predators cause it damage, for bamboos in the garden are usually pest and disease free. They are resistant to honey fungus (*Armillaria*) and only occasionally affected by aphids. Attacks from pests usually only occur in the optimum and sometimes forced growing conditions of a commercial nursery. Red spider mite, mealybug, whitefly and aphids are the main problems in this context, but they rarely occur in gardens.

However, in recent years the nuisance of the bamboo mite (*Schizotetranychus celarius*) has spread rapidly from Japan to North America and then Europe and is now seen occasionally in the United Kingdom. The lax import controls within the European Union are largely to blame for the spread of these, which inhabit the undersides of the leaves and protect themselves with webbing. They suck the sap from between the veins of a leaf, which results in small pale rectangular patches lacking chlorophyll. The tessellation on many bamboo leaves helps to show up the dam-

age and, as such, makes this pest easy to identify. There are very few bamboo species resistant to this mite and, once you have an infestation, it is difficult to control. Personally, I am not happy about using chemicals on plants but should you choose to use one, a standard miticide may control the pest in its early stages of spread. However, the safest way is to cut the bamboo to the ground and burn all the greenery, rake the surface free of debris and keep a close eye on new emerging growth for further signs of the pest. This may seem drastic but your bamboo will recover eventually. Prevention is better than cure, so inspect all plants and their surroundings before you purchase a plant. I would stress that the effect on the bamboo is mostly visual and there should be little evidence of poor growth unless the plant is already weak or very young.

Rabbits, deer and horses cause physical damage by grazing. In general they favour only the new culms, and there is usually an abundance of

Witches broom on *Phyllostachys nigra*.

other greenery in the summer months for them not to bother with your bamboo; although in the United Kingdom, near rural locations in particular, watch out for Muntjac deer. Squirrels like the occasional nibble and giant pandas can be a problem, but fortunately not in our gardens.

Very occasionally, physical abnormalities can be seen on bamboos. These are usually quirky in nature rather than having any lasting effect on the plant. Physical damage to a growing point may cause a culm to zigzag (mostly this zigzag formation is natural). Squirrels may gnaw holes in the sides of culms, which sometimes weaken them, but it is not usual. One of the more unusual deformities is "witches broom", which can occur on the branches of *Phyllostachys*. The distinctive dense twiggy growth is usually formed because of damage to cells by an insect, virus or fungus, and can sometimes be mistaken for flow-

ering. The deformity is very localised on the plant and has no ill effect on the overall growth. It is more common in China and usually evident on some imported stock.

The best way to summarize pests and diseases on bamboos is to tell you that in the seventeen or so years I have been growing bamboos in my garden I have never had need to use an insecticide or fungicide, or similar preparation. In addition, there has been no need to control animals of any description, even though the garden is surrounded by open fields, with only a few areas of woodland punctuating the skyline. On the contrary, the bamboos provide a safe haven for many birds roosting at night and, because of their few problems with pests and disease, and their ease of cultivation with little need for artificial fertilizer, they are some of the most environmentally friendly plants you could wish for.

Chapter 14
Myths, Legends and the Four Seasons

Dispelling Myths and Legends

After reading about the botany, structure and detail of the plants you will, I hope, have noted the underlying messages contained in this book. The simplest summary of these is that although bamboos are different in structure and appearance from other plant groups, they present little difficulty in their culture and, therefore, in their use in our gardens.

Ironically, as I write the last chapter in this book I have just put down the 'phone after talking at length to a potential customer. During the course of the conversation he said that many of his friends had tried to put him off growing bamboos. I was not at all surprised; I have heard the same tale, rather frustratingly, on many previous occasions. I asked him why and he listed invasive, not hardy, short lived, death from flowering, difficult to grow, lose all their leaves and something about needing a second mortgage to pay for them as his key points. This is precisely where I started in the Preface, explaining the taming of the dragon that people think bamboos are.

In discussion, the gentleman did not believe all these myths but he needed confirmation. Like him, I hope that by now you will have learned that bamboos should not be a worry; they are easily tamed and require little management. In answer to his questions I explained that many bamboos are clump forming and tidy; they are some of the hardiest plants we can grow; they have great life expectancy; they do not always die after flowering; they are very easy to cultivate; they are evergreen; and, unless you buy giant specimens, not that expensive. In fact, bamboos are one of the best investments you can make for your garden.

A culm of *Phyllostachys* in the rain.

The Four Seasons

As a conclusion to this book I thank you for coming this far. I hope that you can gain the same pleasure from bamboos that I already have. There have been mistakes along the way, during the years I have known bamboos, and I have learned from these. I hope you have picked up on this information, and will be more successful. Any mistakes in this book are purely mine. I have tried to translate much that is technical into easily digestible parts and simple terms, but it is so easy to falter along the way, human error being what it is.

A strong new shoot of *Phyllostachys bambusoides* 'Marliacea'.

I have tried to make my own views known throughout this book and summarize them in a way that will provide the reader with some insight for the best culture, use and careful selection of temperate bamboos. It is the adaptability of these plants to the cooler environment that is most questioned by others, and the main reason for this book is to allay those fears. Working from my experiences with bamboos in gardens, particularly those in cool regions, I have been selective with the plants and honest with my opinions.

It is almost impossible to give you a feel for bamboos without seeing them, touching them or hearing their almost constant movement, but I have tried. As I walk among the groves in the cold, low light of the winter sun, I see the sparkle of greenery and the shadows cast by the branches displayed crisply on the culms.

In spring I see the birds flitting through the culms and rustling the foliage with their evening manoeuvres, settling in the branches ready for the darkness of night. The first of the new, colourful shoots punctuate the soil in anticipation of warm summer days. Summer arrives and there is so much to enjoy – new sun-kissed culms aplenty with their sheathing in all the colours of the rainbow, the spotless unfolding leaves of the *Sasa* and the welcome shade cast by the tall foliage canopies is most refreshing on the hottest of days. Autumn brings rest and the colours can be admired. The foliage is at its freshest after the rains have washed away the late summer dust. As the wind starts to blow, the creaks and chattering from the culms and the rustling leaves provide a soothing background for the chores of tidying, before the approach of winter, while below ground, in the warm and moistening soil, the bamboos start to work unseen.

Enjoy your bamboos – do not be bound by the rules. Have no fear – just learn and succeed.

Vital Statistics

Appendix 1

Bamboos with an Award of Garden Merit

The Award of Garden Merit (AGM) is for plants judged to be of outstanding ornamental value. It is given to plants after long periods of assessment by the Royal Horticultural Society's Standing and Joint Committees in the United Kingdom and is intended to be of practical value to gardeners.

To qualify for an AGM a plant must meet the following criteria:

It must be available.

It must be of outstanding excellence for the garden or decoration use.

It must be of good constitution.

It must not require highly specialist growing conditions or care.

It must not be particularly susceptible to any pest or disease.

It must not be subject to an unreasonable degree of reversion.

The following bamboos currently hold the Award of Garden Merit:

Chusquea culeou
Fargesia murielae
Fargesia murielae 'Simba'
Fargesia nitida 'Nymphenburg'
x Hibanobambusa tranquillans 'Shiroshima'
Indocalamus tessellatus
Phyllostachys aurea
Phyllostachys aureosulcata f. *aureocaulis*
Phyllostachys aureosulcata f. *spectabilis*
Phyllostachys nigra
Phyllostachys nigra f. *henonis*
Phyllostachys vivax f. *aureocaulis*
Pleioblastus fortunei (syn. *P. variegatus*)
Pleioblastus viridistriatus (syn. *P. auricomus*)
Pseudosasa japonica
Semiarundinaria fastuosa

Appendix 2
Synonyms and Common Names

As an example of the need for a lengthy list of possible synonyms, there have been over twenty changes in bamboo nomenclature in the last two years, some of them minor and a few changed completely from their previous listing. The names used by A. H. Lawson in his work *Bamboos: A Gardener's Guide to their Cultivation in Temperate Climates*, are now almost unrecognizable, bearing in mind his work was published less than forty years ago in 1968. Although this list could be much longer, it is confined to the species and cultivars described in this book.

Common name (in bold), Chinese or Japanese synonym, or botanical synonym.	**Current botanical name used** throughout this book.
Allgold bamboo	*Phyllostachys sulphurea*
Alphonse Karr bamboo	*Bambusa multiplex* 'Alphonse Karr'
Arrow bamboo	*Pseudosasa japonica*
Arundinaria albomarginata	*Sasa veitchii*
Arundinaria amabilis	*Pseudosasa amabilis*
Arundinaria anceps	*Yushania anceps*
Arundinaria anceps 'Pitt White'	*Yushania anceps* 'Pitt White'
Arundinaria argentiostriata	*Pleioblastus argenteostriatus* 'Okinadake'
Arundinaria argenteostriata var. *disticha*	*Pleioblastus pygmaeus* 'Distichus'
Arundinaria auricoma	*Pleioblastus viridistriatus*
Arundinaria chino	*Pleioblastus chino*
Arundinaria chino var. *argenteostriata*	*Pleioblastus argenteostriatus* 'Okinadake'
Arundinaria disticha	*Pleioblastus pygmaeus* 'Distichus'
Arundinaria falconeri	*Himalayacalamus falconeri*
Arundinaria fargesii	*Bashania fargesii*
Arundinaria fastuosa	*Semiarundinaria fastuosa*
Arundinaria fastuosa var. *kagamiana*	*Semiarundinaria kagamiana*
Arundinaria fastuosa var. *yashadake*	*Semiarundinaria yashadake*
Arundinaria fortunei	*Pleioblastus fortunei*
Arundinaria fortunei var. *viridis*	*Pleioblastus humilis*
Arundinaria funghomii	*Schizostachyum funghomii*
Arundinaria gauntletti	*Pleioblastus* 'Gauntlettii'
Arundinaria glabra	*Sasaella masamuneana*
Arundinaria graminea	*Pleioblastus gramineus*
Arundinaria hindsii	*Pleioblastus hindsii*
Arundinaria hindsii var. *graminea*	*Pleioblastus gramineus*
Arundinaria hookeriana	*Himalayacalamus hookerianus,* or *H. falconeri* 'Damarapa'
Arundinaria humilis	*Pleioblastus humilis*
Arundinaria japonica	*Pseudosasa japonica*
Arundinaria jaunsarensis	*Yushania anceps*
Arundinaria khasiana	*Drepanostachyum khasianum*
Arundinaria kokantsik	*Chimonobambusa marmorea*
Arundinaria kurilensis	*Sasa kurilensis*
Arundinaria kurilensis var. *paniculata*	*Sasa senanensis*
Arundinaria linearis	*Pleioblastus linearis*
Arundinaria macrosperma	*Arundinaria gigantea*
Arundinaria maling	*Yushania maling*
Arundinaria marmorea	*Chimonobambusa marmorea*
Arundinaria matsumarae	*Chimonobambusa marmorea*

Arundinaria maximowiczii	Pleioblastus chino
Arundinaria metake	Pseudosasa japonica
Arundinaria murielae	Fargesia murielae
Arundinaria nagashima	Pleioblastus humilis
Arundinaria narahira	Semiarundinaria fastuosa
Arundinaria nitida	Fargesia nitida
Arundinaria nobilis	Himalayacalamus falconeri
Arundinaria oedogonata	Clavinodum oedogonatum
Arundinaria owatarii	Pseudosasa owatarii
Arundinaria palmata	Sasa palmata
Arundinaria pumila	Pleioblastus argenteostriatus f. pumilus
Arundinaria purpurea	Sasaella masamuneana
Arundinaria pygmaea	Pleioblastus pygmaeus
Arundinaria pygmaea var. disticha	Pleioblastus pygmaeus 'Distichus'
Arundinaria qingchengshanensis	Bashania qingchengshanensis
Arundinaria quadrangularis	Chimonobambusa quadrangularis
Arundinaria racemosa	Yushania maling
Arundinaria ragamowskii	Indocalamus tessellatus
Arundinaria ramosa	Sasaella ramosa
Arundinaria simonii	Pleioblastus simonii
Arundinaria simonii var. chino	Pleioblastus chino
Arundinaria spathacea	Fargesia murielae
Arundinaria spathiflora	Thamnocalamus spathiflorus
Arundinaria tessellata	Thamnocalamus tessellatus
Arundinaria tootsik	Sinobambusa tootsik
Arundinaria vagans	Sasaella ramosa
Arundinaria variabilis f. glabra	Pleioblastus pygmaeus 'Distichus'
Arundinaria variabilis var. pumila	Pleioblastus argenteostriatus f. pumilus
Arundinaria variabilis var. variegata	Pleioblastus fortunei
Arundinaria variabilis var. viridi-striata	Pleioblastus viridistriatus
Arundinaria variegata	Pleioblastus fortunei
Arundinaria variegata var. viridi-striata	Pleioblastus viridistriatus
Arundinaria veitchii	Sasa veitchii
Arundinaria viridistriata	Pleioblastus viridistriatus
Azuma-nezasa	Pleioblastus chino
Azumazasa	Sasaella ramosa
Bai-bu-ji zhu	Phyllostachys dulcis
Bai-jia zhu	Phyllostachys bissetii
Bai-ke-bu-ji zhu	Phyllostachys dulcis
Bambusa albo-marginata	Sasa veitchii
Bambusa alphonse karrii	Bambusa multiplex 'Alphonse Karr'
Bambusa angulata	Chimonobambusa quadrangularis
Bambusa aurea	Phyllostachys aurea
Bambusa boryana	Phyllostachys nigra 'Boryana'
Bambusa chino	Pleioblastus chino
Bambusa disticha	Pleioblastus pygmaeus 'Distichus'
Bambusa edulis	Phyllostachys edulis
Bambusa erecta	Pleioblastus hindsii
Bambusa fastuosa	Semiarundinaria fastuosa
Bambusa flexuosa	Phyllostachys flexuosa
Bambusa floribunda	Himalayacalamus falconeri
Bambusa fortunei	Pleioblastus fortunei
Bambusa fortunei var. aurea	Pleioblastus viridistriatus
Bambusa fortunei variegata	Pleioblastus fortunei
Bambusa glaucescens f. alphonse karrii	Bambusa multiplex 'Alphonse Karr'

Common name (in bold), Chinese or Japanese synonym, or botanical synonym.	Current botanical name used throughout this book.
Bambusa graminea	*Pleioblastus gramineus*
Bambusa henonis	*Phyllostachys nigra* f. *henonis*
Bambusa japonica	*Pseudosasa japonica*
Bambusa kumasaca	*Shibataea kumasasa*
Bambusa kurilensis	*Sasa kurilensis*
Bambusa marmorea	*Chimonobambusa marmorea*
Bambusa metake	*Pseudosasa japonica*
Bambusa metallica	*Sasa palmata*
Bambusa mitis	*Phyllostachys edulis*
Bambusa multiplex 'Fern Leaf'	*Bambusa multiplex* 'Floribunda'
Bambusa nagashima	*Pleioblastus humilis*
Bambusa nana var. *alphonse karrii*	*Bambusa multiplex* 'Alphonse Karr'
Bambusa newmanii	*Arundinaria gigantea*
Bambusa nigra	*Phyllostachys nigra*
Bambusa nipponica	*Sasa nipponica*
Bambusa palmata	*Sasa palmata*
Bambusa puberula	*Phyllostachys nigra* f. *henonis*
Bambusa pumila	*Pleioblastus argenteostriatus* f. *pumilus*
Bambusa pygmaea	*Pleioblastus pygmaeus*
Bambusa quadrangularis	*Chimonobambusa quadrangularis*
Bambusa quiloi	*Phyllostachys bambusoides*
Bambusa ragamowski	*Indocalamus tessellatus*
Bambusa ramosa	*Sasaella ramosa*
Bambusa senanensis	*Sasa senanensis*
Bambusa senanensis f. *albo-marginatus*	*Sasa veitchii*
Bambusa simonii	*Pleioblastus simonii*
Bambusa sulphurea	*Phyllostachys sulphurea* f. *viridis*
Bambusa tessellata	*Indocalamus tessellatus*
Bambusa tootsik	*Sinobambusa tootsik*
Bambusa variegata	*Pleioblastus fortunei*
Bambusa veitchii	*Sasa veitchii*
Bambusa viminalis	*Shibataea kumasasa*
Bambusa viridi-glaucescens	*Phyllostachys viridiglaucescens*
Bambusa viridistriata	*Pleioblastus viridistriatus*
Bambusa viridistriata var. *simonii*	*Pleioblastus simonii*
Beautiful bamboo	*Phyllostachys decora*
Bergbamboes	*Thamnocalamus tessellatus*
Bioji-chiku	*Phyllostachys edulis*
Biotan-chiku	*Phyllostachys edulis*
Birodona	*Semiarundinaria okuboi*
Black bamboo	*Phyllostachys nigra*
Block bamboo	*Chimonobambusa quadrangularis*
Blue bamboo	*Himalayacalamus hookerianus*
Borinda angustissima	*Fargesia angustissima*
Borinda frigida	*Fargesia frigida*
Borinda frigidorum	*Fargesia frigida*
Borinda fungosa	*Fargesia fungosa*
Bory bamboo	*Phyllostachys nigra* 'Boryana'
Buddha bamboo	*Bambusa ventricosa*
Buddha's belly bamboo	*Bambusa ventricosa*
Bundodake	*Shibataea kumasasa*

Bungozasa	*Shibataea kumasasa*
Butsumen-chiku	*Phyllostachys edulis* 'Heterocycla'
Candy cane	*Himalayacalamus falconeri* 'Damarapa'
Candy-stripe bamboo	*Himalayacalamus falconeri* 'Damarapa'
Cane reed	*Arundinaria gigantea*
Canebreak bamboo	*Arundinaria gigantea*
Chigo-zasa	*Pleioblastus fortunei*
Chimakizasa	*Sasa palmata*
Chimonobambusa hookeriana hort.	*Himalayacalamus falconeri* 'Damarapa'
Chimonobambusa intermedia	*Sinobambusa intermedia*
Chimonobambusa tumidinoda	*Chimonobambusa tumidissinoda*
Chinese temple bamboo	*Sinobambusa tootsik*
Chinese weeping bamboo	*Phyllostachys flexuosa*
Chishimazasa	*Sasa kurilensis*
Chusquea aff. *culeou*	*Chusquea gigantea*
Chusquea breviglumis	*Chusquea culeou*, or *C. gigantea*
Chusquea tenuis	*Chusquea culeou* 'Tenuis'
Clavinodum oedogonatum	*Oligostachyum oedogonatum*
Colihue	*Chusquea culeou*
Cui zhu	*Pleioblastus pygmaeus* 'Distichus'
Culeu	*Chusquea culeou*
Daba-shan 2	*Fargesia dracocephala*
Dai-ming zhu	*Pleioblastus gramineus*
Dan zhu	*Phyllostachys meyeri*
David Bisset bamboo	*Phyllostachys bissetii*
Deo-bih	*Phyllostachys bambusoides*
Dragon's head bamboo	*Fargesia dracocephala*
Drepanostachyum falconeri	*Himalayacalamus falconeri*
Drepanostachyum hookerianum	*Himalayacalamus falconeri* 'Damarapa', or *H. hookerianus*
Dwarf fern-leaf bamboo	*Pleioblastus pygmaeus* 'Distichus'
Dwarf white-stripe bamboo	*Pleioblastus fortunei*
Fang zhu	*Chimonobambusa quadrangularis*
Fargesia albocera	*Borinda albocera*
Fargesia crassinoda	*Thamnocalamus crassinodus* forms
Fargesia frigidorum	*Fargesia frigida*
Fargesia spathacea	*Fargesia murielae*
Fei-bai zhu	*Pleioblastus fortunei*
Fish-pole bamboo	*Phyllostachys aurea*
Fishscale bamboo	*Phyllostachys heteroclada*
Forage bamboo	*Phyllostachys aureosulcata*
Fountain bamboo	*Fargesia nitida*
Fuiri-shiiyazasa	*Sasaella masamuneana* 'Albostriata'
Gamaizasa	*Shibataea kumasasa*
Gang zhu	*Phyllostachys sulphurea* f. *viridis*
Gansu 95-1	*Fargesia rufa*
Gansu 95-2	*Fargesia nitida* 'Gansu'
Genkei-chiku	*Sasaella masamuneana*
Giant cane	*Arundinaria gigantea*
Giant hairy-sheath bamboo	*Phyllostachys edulis*
Giant timber bamboo	*Phyllostachys bambusoides*
Ginmei-chiku	*Phyllostachys bambusoides* 'Castillonis'
Girl's bamboo	*Phyllostachys rubromarginata*
Golden bamboo	*Phyllostachys aurea*
Golden crookstem bamboo	*Phyllostachys aureosulcata* f. *aureocaulis*

Common name (in bold), Chinese or Japanese synonym, or botanical synonym.	Current botanical name used throughout this book.
Golden golden bamboo	*Phyllostachys aurea* 'Holochrysa'
Golden-striped hedge bamboo	*Bambusa multiplex* 'Alphonse Karr'
Gomadake	*Phyllostachys nigra*
Gosan-chiku	*Phyllostachys aurea*
Green bamboo	*Phyllostachys nuda*
Green onion bamboo	*Pseudosasa japonica* 'Tsutsumiana'
Green sulcus bamboo	*Phyllostachys aureosulcata* f. *spectabilis*
Green sulphur bamboo	*Phyllostachys sulphurea* f. *viridis*
Gui zhu	*Phyllostachys bambusoides*
Gyoya-chiku	*Pleioblastus linearis*
Ha-chiku	*Phyllostachys nigra* f. *henonis*
Han zhu	*Chimonobambusa marmorea*
Hardy bamboo	*Pseudosasa japonica*
Hardy timber bamboo	*Phyllostachys bambusoides*
Heavenly bamboo	*Nandina domestica* (this is a woody shrub of the *Berberis* family, and not a bamboo)
Hei zhu	*Phyllostachys nigra*
Henon bamboo	*Phyllostachys nigra* f. *henonis*
Himalayan blue bamboo	*Himalayacalamus hookerianus*
Hime-hachiku	*Phyllostachys humilis*
Hirouzasa	*Pleioblastus humilis*
Ho-o-cjiku	*Bambusa multiplex* 'Alphonse Karr'
Hong-bian zhu	*Phyllostachys rubromarginata*
Hotei-chiku	*Phyllostachys aurea*
Houchiku	*Chimonobambusa quadrangularis*
Hua xian-shun zhu	*Bambusa multiplex* 'Alphonse Karr'
Huang pi gong zhu	*Phyllostachys sulphurea* f. *viridis*
Huang-cao zhu	*Phyllostachys aureosulcata*
Huang-gu zhu	*Phyllostachys angusta*
Huang-ku zhu	*Phyllostachys mannii* 'Mannii'
Hyondake	*Phyllostachys bambusoides* 'Castillonis'
Ibuki-zasa	*Sasa tsuboiana*
Incense bamboo	*Phyllostachys atrovaginata*
Indocalamus tessellatus f. *hamadae*	*Indocalamus hamadae*
Japanese timber bamboo	*Phyllostachys bambusoides*
Jian zhu	*Fargesia nitida*
Jiao-ku dan zhu	*Phyllostachys propinqua*
Jin zhu	*Phyllostachys sulphurea* f. *viridis*
Kamura-zasa, or kamuro-zasa	*Pleioblastus viridistriatus*
Kan-chiku	*Chimonobambusa marmorea*
Kanzanchiku	*Pleioblastus hindsii*
Karadake	*Phyllostachys bambusoides*
Kasan-chiku	*Phyllostachys aurea*
Kasurazasa	*Shibataea kumasasa*
Kawa-take	*Pleioblastus simonii*
Ke-oroshuma-chiku, or ke-oroshima-chiku	*Pleioblastus pygmaeus*
Keelee	*Chusquea quila*
Khasia bamboo	*Drepanostachyum khasianum*
Kikku-chiku	*Phyllostachys edulis* 'Heterocycla'
Kili	*Chusquea quila*
Kimmei-chiku	*Phyllostachys bambusoides* 'Castillonis'

Kin-chiku	*Phyllostachys sulphurea* f. *viridis*
Kokuradake	*Phyllostachys bambusoides*
Kou-chiku	*Phyllostachys sulphurea* f. *viridis*
Kovan-chiku	*Phyllostachys edulis*
Ku-chiku	*Phyllostachys bambusoides*
Kuma bamboo grass	*Sasa veitchii*
Kumaizasa	*Sasa palmata*
Kumazasa	*Sasa veitchii*
Kurio-zasa	*Sasaella masmuneana*
Kuro-chiku	*Phyllostachys nigra*
Kurodake	*Phyllostachys nigra*
Leopard-skin bamboo	*Phyllostachys nigra* 'Boryana'
Leleba multiplex f. *alphonse karrii*	*Bambusa multiplex* 'Alphonse Karr'
Lohan-chu	*Phyllostachys edulis* 'Heterocycla'
Lucky bamboo	*Dracaena* (this is an indoor novelty plant, and not a bamboo)
Luo-han zhu	*Phyllostachys aurea*
Lyozasa	*Shibataea kumasasa*
Madake	*Phyllostachys bambusoides*
Mai-pang puk	*Phyllostachys mannii* 'Mannii'
Makino bamboo	*Phyllostachys makinoi*
Makinoi	*Semiarundinaria makinoi*
Makko-chiku	*Phyllostachys nigra* f. *henonis*
Mao zhu	*Phyllostachys edulis*
Mao-jin zhu	*Phyllostachys nigra* f. *henonis*
Maradake	*Phyllostachys nigra* 'Boryana'
Marbled bamboo	*Chimonobambusa marmorea*
Marliac's bamboo	*Phyllostachys bambusoides* 'Marliacea'
Maso-chiku	*Phyllostachys edulis*
Mato-chiku	*Phyllostachys edulis*
Mazel's bamboo	*Phyllostachys bambusoides*
Me-dake	*Pleioblastus simonii*
Medake	*Pseudosasa japonica*
Mei-chu	*Phyllostachys mannii* 'Decora'
Meizhu	*Phyllostachys mannii* 'Decora'
Meyer bamboo	*Phyllostachys meyeri*
Mikayo sasa	*Sasa nipponica*
Mizakozasa	*Sasa nipponica*
Moso bamboo	*Phyllostachys edulis*
Mosodake	*Phyllostachys edulis*
Narihira bamboo	*Semiarundinaria fastuosa*
Narihiradake	*Semiarundinaria fastuosa*
Nastus tessellatus	*Thamnocalamus tessellatus*
Ne-zasa	*Pleioblastus pygmaeus*
Nemagaridake	*Sasa senanensis*
Neosasamorpha kurilensis	*Sasa kurilensis*
Neosasamorpha masamuneana	*Sasaella masamuneana*
Neosasamorpha nipponica	*Sasa nipponica*
Neosasamorpha owatarii	*Pseudosasa owatarii*
Neosasamorpha palmata	*Sasa palmata*
Neosasamorpha ramosa	*Sasaella ramosa*
Neosasamorpha senanensis	*Sasa senanensis*
Neosasamorpha tessellata	*Indocalamus tessellatus*
Neosasamorpha tsuboiana	*Sasa tsuboiana*
Neosasamorpha veitchii	*Sasa veitchii*

Common name (in bold), Chinese or Japanese synonym, or botanical synonym.	Current botanical name used throughout this book.
Nigadake	*Phyllostachys bambusoides*
Nigala Nepal	*Chimonobambusa macrophylla* f. *intermedia*
Nipponobambusa kurilensis	*Sasa kurilensis*
Nipponobambusa masamuneana	*Sasaella masamuneana*
Nipponobambusa nipponica	*Sasa nipponica*
Nipponobambusa owatarii	*Pseudosasa owatarii*
Nipponobambusa palmata	*Sasa palmata*
Nipponobambusa ramosa	*Sasaella ramosa*
Nipponobambusa senanensis	*Sasa senanensis*
Nipponobambusa tessellata	*Indocalamus tessellatus*
Nipponobambusa tsuboiana	*Sasa tsuboiana*
Nipponobambusa veitchii	*Sasa veitchii*
Nipponocalamus argenteostriata var. *disticha*	*Pleioblastus pygmaeus* 'Distichus'
Nipponocalamus argenteostriatus	*Pleioblastus argenteostriatus* 'Okinadake'
Nipponocalamus chino	*Pleioblastus chino*
Nipponocalamus fortunei	*Pleioblastus fortunei*
Nipponocalamus nagashima	*Pleioblastus humilis*
Nipponocalamus pumilus	*Pleioblastus argenteostriatus* f. *pumilus*
Nipponocalamus simonii	*Pleioblastus simonii*
Noble bamboo	*Semiarundinaria fastuosa*
Nu-er zhu	*Phyllostachys rubromarginata*
Ogon-chiku	*Phyllostachys sulphurea* f. *viridis*
Okamazasa	*Shibataea kumasasa*
Okame-zasa	*Shibataea kumasasa*
Okinadake	*Pleioblastus argenteostriatus* 'Okinadake'
Oligostachyum lubricum	*Semiarundinaria lubrica*
Oroshima-chiku	*Pleioblastus pygmaeus* 'Distichus'
Ougon-kou-chiku	*Phyllostachys sulphurea* ('Robert Young')
Owodake	*Phyllostachys nigra* f. *henonis*
Pah koh poo chi	*Phyllostachys dulcis*
Pao mung	*Himalayacalamus falconeri*
Phoenix bamboo	*Phyllostachys aurea*
×*Phyllosasa*	×*Hibanobambusa*
Phyllostachys assamica	*Phyllostachys mannii* 'Mannii'
Phyllostachys aurea f. *formosana*	*Phyllostachys aurea* f. *takemurai*
Phyllostachys aureosulcata f. *alata*	*Phyllostachys aureosulcata* f. *pekinensis*
Phyllostachys aureus	*Phyllostachys aurea*
Phyllostachys bambusoides 'Castillon'	*Phyllostachys bambusoides* 'Castillonis'
Phyllostachys bambusoides 'Holochrysa'	*Phyllostachys bambusoides* 'Allgold'
Phyllostachys bambusoides f. *tanakae*	*Phyllostachys bambusoides* f. *lacrima-deae*
Phyllostachys bambusoides 'Violascens'	*Phyllostachys violascens*
Phyllostachys bambusoides var. *albomarginata*	*Sasa veitchii*
Phyllostachys bambusoides var. *aurea*	*Phyllostachys aurea*
Phyllostachys bambusoides var. *sulphurea*	*Phyllostachys sulphurea* f. *viridis*
Phyllostachys bawa	*Phyllostachys mannii* 'Mannii'
Phyllostachys boryana	*Phyllostachys nigra* 'Boryana'
Phyllostachys boryanus	*Phyllostachys nigra* 'Boryana'
Phyllostachys castillonii var. *holochrysa*	*Phyllostachys bambusoides* 'Allgold'
Phyllostachys cerata	*Phyllostachys purpurata* 'Straight Stem'
Phyllostachys congesta	*Phyllostachys atrovaginata*
Phyllostachys decora	*Phyllostachys mannii* 'Decora'

Phyllostachys edulis f. pubescens	Phyllostachys edulis
Phyllostachys edulis subconvexa	Phyllostachys viridiglaucescens
Phyllostachys elegans	Phyllostachys viridiglaucescens
Phyllostachys faberi	Phyllostachys sulphurea f. viridis
Phyllostachys fastuosa	Semiarundinaria fastuosa
Phyllostachys faurei	Phyllostachys nigra f. henonis
Phyllostachys filifera	Phyllostachys nigra
Phyllostachys flexuosus	Phyllostachys flexuosa
Phyllostachys formosana	Phyllostachys aurea
Phyllostachys fulva, or P. fulvus	Phyllostachys nigra 'Fulva'
Phyllostachys henonis	Phyllostachys nigra f. henonis
Phyllostachys henryi	Phyllostachys nigra f. henonis
Phyllostachys heteroclada 'Solid Stem'	Phyllostachys heteroclada f. solida
Phyllostachys heteroclada 'Straight Stem'	Phyllostachys heteroclada
Phyllostachys heterocycla 'Hikku-Chiku'	Phyllostachys edulis 'Heterocycla'
Phyllostachys heterocycla	Phyllostachys edulis 'Heterocycla'
Phyllostachys heterocycla var. pubescens	Phyllostachys edulis
Phyllostachys kuma-saca	Shibataea kumasasa
Phyllostachys kumasasa	Shibataea kumasasa
Phyllostachys mannii	Phyllostachys mannii 'Mannii'
Phyllostachys marliaci	Phyllostachys bambusoides 'Marliacea'
Phyllostachys mazelii, or P. mazeli	Phyllostachys bambusoides
Phyllostachys mitis	Phyllostachys edulis, or P. sulphurea f. viridis
Phyllostachys montana	Phyllostachys nigra f. henonis
Phyllostachys nevinii, or P. nevinni	Phyllostachys aureosulcata, or P. nigra f. henonis
Phyllostachys nevinii var. hupehensis	Phyllostachys nigra f. henonis
Phyllostachys niger	Phyllostachys nigra
Phyllostachys niger boryanus	Phyllostachys nigra 'Boryana'
Phyllostachys nigra 'Bory'	Phyllostachys nigra 'Boryana'
Phyllostachys nigra 'Henon'	Phyllostachys nigra f. henonis
Phyllostachys nigripes	Phyllostachys nigra
Phyllostachys nitida	Fargesia nitida
Phyllostachys puberula	Phyllostachys nigra f. henonis
Phyllostachys puberula var. boryana	Phyllostachys nigra 'Boryana'
Phyllostachys puberula var. henonis	Phyllostachys nigra f. henonis
Phyllostachys puberula var. nigra	Phyllostachys nigra
Phyllostachys puberula var. punctata	Phyllostachys nigra f. punctata
Phyllostachys pubescens	Phyllostachys edulis
Phyllostachys pubescens var. heterocycla	Phyllostachys edulis 'Heterocycla'
Phyllostachys punctata	Phyllostachys nigra f. punctata
Phyllostachys punctatus	Phyllostachys nigra f. punctata
Phyllostachys purpurata	Phyllostachys heteroclada f. purpurata
Phyllostachys purpurata 'Straight Stem'	Phyllostachys heteroclada
Phyllostachys purpurata 'Solid Stem'	Phyllostachys heteroclada f. solida
Phyllostachys quadrangularis	Chimonobambusa quadrangularis
Phyllostachys quiloi, or P. quilioi	Phyllostachys bambusoides
Phyllostachys reticulata	Phyllostachys bambusoides
Phyllostachys reticulata var. aurea	Phyllostachys aurea
Phyllostachys reticulata var. holochrysa	Phyllostachys bambusoides 'Allgold'
Phyllostachys reticulata var. sulphurea	Phyllostachys bambusoides 'Allgold'
Phyllostachys rubicunda	Phyllostachys concava
Phyllostachys ruscifolia	Shibataea kumasasa
Phyllostachys stauntonii	Phyllostachys nigra f. henonis
Phyllostachys sulphurea var. holochrysa	Phyllostachys bambusoides 'Allgold'
Phyllostachys tranquillans	×Hibanobambusa tranquillans

Common name (in bold), Chinese or Japanese synonym, or botanical synonym.	Current botanical name used throughout this book.
Phyllostachys veitchiana	Phyllostachys nigra f. henonis
Phyllostachys viridis	Phyllostachys sulphurea f. viridis
Phyllostachys viridis f. youngii	Phyllostachys sulphurea ('Robert Young')
Phyllostachys viridis 'Houzeau'	Phyllostachys sulphurea 'Houzeau'
Phyllostachys viridis 'Robert Young'	Phyllostachys sulphurea ('Robert Young')
Phyllostachys viridis 'Sulphurea'	Phyllostachys sulphurea ('Robert Young'), or P. bambusoides 'Allgold'
Pleioblastus akebono	Pleioblastus argenteostriatus 'Akebono'
Pleioblastus auricomus	Pleioblastus viridistriatus
Pleioblastus chino f. pumilus	Pleioblastus argenteostriatus f. pumilus
Pleioblastus chino 'Vaginatus Variegatus'	Pleioblastus chino f. argenteostriatus
Pleioblastus distichus	Pleioblastus pygmaeus 'Distichus'
Pleioblastus glaber	Sasaella masamuneana
Pleioblastus masamuneanus	Sasaella masamuneana
Pleioblastus maximowiczii	Pleioblastus chino
Pleioblastus nagashima	Pleioblastus humilis
Pleioblastus pubescens	Pleioblastus pygmaeus
Pleioblastus pumilus	Pleioblastus argenteostriatus f. pumilus
Pleioblastus simonii heterophyllus	Pleioblastus simonii 'Variegatus'
Pleioblastus variegatus	Pleioblastus fortunei
Pleioblastus variegatus 'Fortunei'	Pleioblastus fortunei
Pleioblastus variegatus 'Tsuboi'	Pleioblastus shibuyanus 'Tsuboi'
Pleioblastus viridistriata	Pleioblastus viridistriatus
Praong	Himalayacalamus falconeri 'Damarapa'
Pseudosasa japonica 'Variegata'	Pseudosasa japonica 'Akebonosuji'
Pseudosasa kurilensis	Sasa kurilensis
Pseudosasa pleioblastoides	Pseudosasa japonica var. pleioblastoides
Pummon	Himalayacalamus falconeri
Qiong zhu	Chimonobambusa tumidissinoda
Qiongzhuea tumidinoda	Chimonobambusa tumidissinoda
Quila	Chusquea quila
Ren-mian zhu	Phyllostachys aurea
Riben emao zhu	Shibataea kumasasa
Riben shi zhu	Pseudosasa japonica
Rikuchudake or Rikuchu-dake	Semiarundinaria kagamiana
Rito-chiku	Phyllostachys edulis
River cane	Arundinaria gigantea
Robert Ougon-chiku	Phyllostachys sulphurea ('Robert Young')
Robert Young bamboo	Phyllostachys sulphurea ('Robert Young')
Ruo-zhu	Indocalamus tessellatus
Ruscus-leaved bamboo	Shibataea kumasasa
Ryuku-chiku	Pleioblastus linearis
Sacred bamboo	Nandina domestica (this is a woody shrub of the Berberis family, and not a bamboo)
Sasa albomarginata	Sasa veitchii
Sasa argenteostriata	Pleioblastus argenteostriatus 'Okinadake'
Sasa auricoma	Pleioblastus viridistriatus
Sasa cernua 'Nebulosa'	Sasa palmata f. nebulosa
Sasa disticha	Pleioblastus pygmaeus 'Distichus'
Sasa fastuosa	Semiarundinaria fastuosa
Sasa fortunei	Pleioblastus fortunei

Sasa glabra	*Sasaella masamuneana*
Sasa humilis	*Pleioblastus humilis*
Sasa japonica	*Pseudosasa japonica*
Sasa kurilensis 'Shima-shimofuri'	*Sasa kurilensis* 'Shimofuri'
Sasa masamuneana	*Sasaella masamuneana*
Sasa nana	*Sasa veitchii* f. *minor*
Sasa owatarii	*Pseudosasa owatarii*
Sasa palmata	Ususally refers to *Sasa palmata* f. *nebulosa*, as the green form is rare in cultivation.
Sasa palmata var. *senanensis*	*Sasa senanensis*
Sasa paniculata	*Sasa senanensis*
Sasa pumila	*Pleioblastus argenteostriatus* f. *pumilus*
Sasa pygmaea	*Pleioblastus pygmaeus*
Sasa ramosa	*Sasaella ramosa*
Sasa ruscifolia	*Shibataea kumasasa*
Sasa tessellata	*Indocalamus tessellatus*
Sasa vagans	*Sasaella ramosa*
Sasa variegata	*Pleioblastus fortunei*
Sasa variegata var. *pygmaea*	*Pleioblastus pygmaeus*
Sasa veitchii f. *nana*	*Sasa veitchii* f. *minor*
Sasaella glabra	*Sasaella masamuneana*
Sasaella kurilensis	*Sasa kurilensis*
Sasaella nipponica	*Sasa nipponica*
Sasaella owatarii	*Pseudosasa owatarii*
Sasaella palmata	*Sasa palmata*
Sasaella senanensis	*Sasa senanensis*
Sasaella tessellata	*Indocalamus tessellatus*
Sasaella tsuboiana	*Sasa tsuboiana*
Sasaella veitchii	*Sasa veitchii*
Sasamorpha kurilensis	*Sasa kurilensis*
Sasamorpha masamuneana	*Sasaella masamuneana*
Sasamorpha nipponica	*Sasa nipponica*
Sasamorpha owatarii	*Pseudosasa owatarii*
Sasamorpha palmata	*Sasa palmata*
Sasamorpha ramosa	*Sasaella ramosa*
Sasamorpha senanensis	*Sasa senanensis*
Sasamorpha tessellata	*Indocalamus tessellatus*
Sasamorpha tsuboiana	*Sasa tsuboiana*
Sasamorpha veitchii	*Sasa veitchii*
Semiarundinaria fastuosa var. *yashadake*	*Semiarundinaria yashadake*
Semiarundinaria nitida	*Fargesia nitida*
Semiarundinaria tranquillans	×*Hibanobambusa tranquillans*
Semiarundinaria villosa	*Semiarundinaria okuboi*
Shakotan-chiku	*Sasa palmata*
Shi-zhu	*Phyllostachys nuda*
Shibataea ruscifolia	*Shibataea kumasasa*
Shibo-chiku	*Phyllostachys bambusoides* 'Marliacea'
Shiho-chiku	*Chimonobambusa quadrangularis*
Shikakudake	*Chimonobambusa quadrangularis*
Shimadake	*Phyllostachys bambusoides* 'Castillonis'
Shima-dake	*Pleioblastus fortunei*
Shimofuri	*Sasa kurilensis* 'Shimofuri'
Shinegawadake	*Pleioblastus chino*
Shiro-chiku	*Phyllostachys nigra*
Shiro-shima-inyou	×*Hibanobambusa tranquillans* 'Shiroshima'

Common name (in bold), Chinese or Japanese synonym, or botanical synonym.	Current botanical name used throughout this book.
Shiwa-chiku	*Phyllostachys bambusoides* 'Marliacea'
Shui-zhu	*Phyllostachys heteroclada*
Simon bamboo	*Pleioblastus simonii*
Sinarundinaria anceps	*Yushania anceps*
Sinarundinaria anceps 'Pitt White'	*Yushania anceps* 'Pitt White' (and forms)
Sinarundinaria aurea	*Phyllostachys aurea*
Sinarundinaria hookeriana	*Himalayacalamus hookerianus*
Sinarundinaria maling	*Yushania maling*
Sinarundinaria murielae	*Fargesia murielae*
Sinarundinaria nigra	*Phyllostachys nigra*
Sinarundinaria nigra f. *boryana*	*Phyllostachys nigra* 'Boryana'
Sinarundinaria nigra f. *punctata*	*Phyllostachys nigra* f. *punctata*
Sinarundinaria nigra var. *henonis*	*Phyllostachys nigra* f. *henonis*
Sinarundinaria nitida	*Fargesia nitida*
Sinarundinaria pubescens	*Phyllostachys edulis*
Sinobambusa tootsik 'Variegata'	*Sinobambusa tootsik* var. *albovariegata*
Slender crookstem	*Phyllostachys bambusoides* 'Slender Crookstem'
Smooth sheathed bamboo	*Phyllostachys vivax*
Snake-skin bamboo	*Phyllostachys nigra* 'Boryana'
Solid stem bamboo	*Indocalamus solidus*
Sou-chiku	*Bambusa multiplex* 'Alphonse Karr'
Southern cane	*Arundinaria gigantea*
Square bamboo	*Chimonobambusa quadrangularis*
Square-stemmed bamboo	*Chimonobambusa quadrangularis*
Stake bamboo	*Phyllostachys aureosulcata*
Stoke and forage bamboo	*Phyllostachys aureosulcata*
Straight stem	*Phyllostachys heteroclada*
Stone bamboo	*Phyllostachys nuda*
Sudore-yoshi	*Pleioblastus argenteostriatus* f. *pumilus*
Sui-chiku	*Phyllostachys nigra* f. *henonis*
Suisho-chiku	*Phyllostachys nigra* f. *henonis*
Sulphur bamboo	*Phyllostachys sulphurea* f. *viridis*
Sweetshoot bamboo	*Phyllostachys dulcis*
Switch cane	*Arundinaria gigantea*
Tai-min-chiku	*Pleioblastus gramineus*
Taibo-chiku	*Phyllostachys aurea*
Taiwan gui zhu	*Phyllostachys makinoi*
Tan-chiku	*Phyllostachys nigra* f. *henonis*
Tang zhu	*Sinobambusa tootsik*
Tao-chiku	*Phyllostachys nigra* f. *henonis*
Tea stick bamboo	*Pseudosasa amabilis*
Tetragonacalamus angulatus	*Chimonobambusa quadrangularis*
Tetragonacalamus quadrangularis	*Chimonobambusa quadrangularis*
Thamnocalamus aristatus	*Thamnocalamus spathiflorus*
Thamnocalamus aristatus (hort. U.S.)	*Thamnocalamus crassinodus* cultivars
Thamnocalamus crassinodus	*Thamnocalamus crassinodus* 'Gosainkund'
Thamnocalamus crassinodus 'Glauca'	*Thamnocalamus crassinodus* 'Gosainkund'
Thamnocalamus falconeri	*Himalayacalamus falconeri*
Thamnocalamus funghomii	*Schizostachyum funghomii*
Thamnocalamus hindsii	*Pleioblastus hindsii*
Thamnocalamus hindsii var. *graminea*	*Pleioblastus gramineus*

Thamnocalamus khasianus	*Drepanostachyum khasianum*
Thamnocalamus maling	*Yushania maling*
Thamnocalamus quadrangularis	*Chimonobambusa quadrangularis*
Thamnocalamus spathaceus	*Fargesia murielae*
Thamnocalamus spathiflorus var. *crassinodus*	*Thamnocalamus crassinodus* forms
Tian zhu	*Phyllostachys flexuosa*
Tian-sun zhu	*Phyllostachys viridiglaucescens*
To-chiku	*Sinobambusa tootsik*
Tonkin bamboo	*Pseudosasa amabilis*
Tonkin cane	*Pseudosasa amabilis*
Toocu-chu	*Chimonobambusa quadrangularis*
Tortoise shell bamboo	*Phyllostachys edulis* 'Heterocycla'
Tovooka-zasa	*Pleioblastus humilis*
Tsuboi	*Pleioblastus shibuyanus* 'Tsuboi'
Tsuboi-zasa	*Sasa tsuboiana*
Tsushi-chiku	*Pleioblastus gramineus*
Tung Chuan 3	*Fargesia utilis*
Tung Chuan 4	*Yushania maculata*
Ueda-zasa	*Pleioblastus shibuyanus* 'Tsuboi'
Umbrella bamboo	*Fargesia murielae*
Unmou-chiku	*Phyllostachys nigra* 'Boryana'
Vivax	*Phyllostachys vivax*
Water bamboo	*Phyllostachys heteroclada*
White crookstem	*Phyllostachys bambusoides* 'White Crookstem'
Withered sheath bamboo	*Phyllostachys propinqua*
Wrinkled bamboo	*Phyllostachys bambusoides* 'Marliacea'
Wu-bu-ji zhu	*Phyllostachys vivax*
Wu-ke-bu-ji zhu	*Phyllostachys vivax*
Xian zhu	*Fargesia murielae*
Yadake	*Pseudosasa japonica*
Yadakeya japonica	*Pseudosasa japonica*
Yadakeya owatarii	*Pseudosasa owatarii*
Yajuno	*Phyllostachys bambusoides*
Yakibazasa	*Sasa veitchii* f. *nana*
Yakushimadake	*Pseudosasa owatarii*
Yashadake	*Semiarundinaria yashadake*
Ye-ping zhu	*Semiarundinaria fastuosa*
Yellow bitter bamboo	*Phyllostachys mannii* 'Mannii'
Yellow groove bamboo	*Phyllostachys aureosulcata*
Yellow stem bamboo	*Phyllostachys aureosulcata* f. *aureocaulis*
Yunnan 1, 2 3A and 3B	*Borinda albocera* (clones)
Yunnan 4	*Borinda edulis* or *B. lushuiensis*
Yunnan 5	possibly a *Yushania* species
Yunnan 6	*Borinda perlonga*, but possibly a *Fargesia*
Yu-ziang-jin zhu	*Phyllostachys aureosulcata*
Yushania chungii	*Yushania brevipaniculata*
Yushania jaunsarensis	*Yushania anceps*
Zhejiang dan zhu	*Phyllostachys meyeri*
Zi zhu	*Phyllostachys nigra*

Glossary

Adventitious Usually refers to aerial roots. See below.

Aerial root Any root above ground level produced from the culms. These are usually for support or have no apparent purpose.

Amphimorph Refers to a rhizome system that has both leptomorph and pachymorph rhizomes.

Amphipodial Refers to a bamboo that has both a sympodial and monopodial branching habit, with reference to the formation of the culms.

Arborescent Tree like, with reference to the taller, woody bamboos.

Auricle Ear-like extensions that may or may not be present at the top of the culm and branch sheaths on either side of the blade, depending on the species.

Axis A main growing point on a rhizome, culm or branch.

Blade Refers to the true leaf and also the extension at the top of a culm sheath. The true leaf blade is very obvious and an extension of the branch sheath, to which it is linked by a petiole. The true leaf blade is the main site for photosynthesis. The culm sheath blade is less prominent than the true leaf blade, variable in size and occasionally absent. When present it is capable of photosynthetic activity.

Bloom Refers to the pale, delicate, powdery surface deposit found particularly on young culms.

Bract The scale-like leaf structures that protect the buds on rhizomes, culms and leaf branches. Sometimes used instead of the term sheath.

Branch complement The number of branches at a culm node.

Branch sheath More correctly known as a leaf sheath, it is the scale-like structure on the branches that protects the nodes, buds and emerging tissue of the true leaf. The sheath remains as part of the branch structure with a true leaf attached via a petiole. However, on some species there can be a supplementary sheath at the base of a branch, which is shed and does not produce a true leaf.

Bud A dormant growth point on a rhizome, culm or branch that produces culms, branches and leaves respectively. It appears as a small swelling.

Caespitose Tightly clumping formation of culms that arise from rhizome systems with short necks.

Chlorosis A nutrient deficiency, usually of iron, which can reduce the green coloration of leaves so they appear yellowish.

Cilia Fine hairs or bristles on the edge or surface of a growing part. An example is the hairiness of the outer surface on some culm sheaths.

Clone Plants that originate from a single parent by vegetative propagation and are genetically identical.

Clumping Tight formation of culms.

Cotyledon A seed leaf. Monocotyledons, which include bamboos and grasses, have one seed leaf, and dicotyledons, which include broad-leaved trees and shrubs, have two.

Culm The above-ground stem of a bamboo and other grassy plants.

Culm leaf The term mostly used in the United States for the culm sheath. This protects and gives support to the emerging culm and, in cases where it is persistent, protects the buds.

Culm sheath The term used for culm leaf throughout this book. See above.

Deciduous Refers to the shedding of leaves or sheaths during certain seasons.

Diffuse Refers to the habit of culms that emerge widely spaced, rather than in clumps.

Fimbriae The bristles or hairs that usually extend from the auricles on a sheath, depending on species, and more usually referred to as oral setae. They are not always present.

Foliage leaf The true leaf responsible for photosynthetic activity on the ends of the branches.

Fringe A fine row of hairs at the top of a sheath that may be present with or without oral setae and auricles.

Geniculation Refers to the lower parts of culms that appear crooked or zigzag in formation on some species. There is no clearly defined reason for this occurrence.

Glabrous Not hairy, but not necessarily smooth.

Glaucous A plant surface covered in a fine bluish bloom.

Gregarious flowering Simultaneous flowering of a species or generation, irrespective of location or age.

Internode The section of a bamboo culm or rhizome between two nodes.

Lanceolate Usually a reference to a leaf, shaped longer than wide and tapering at both ends.

Leaf blade The correct term for the sheath blade attached to the leaf sheath. In other words the true leaf and main organ for photosynthesis.

Leaf sheath The sheath that encircles a branch and produces a true leaf attached by a petiole.

Leptomorph Refers to a rhizome type usually associated with running bamboos, although there are variations.

Ligule A small extension of the sheath at the base of a blade that clings tightly to the culm or branch. This feature prevents moisture from entering the inside of the sheath and damaging the newly forming buds and nodes. It varies in size according to species and is not always obvious.

Linear Usually refers to long and narrow leaves with parallel sides.

Meristem A point where growth is initiated and cell division takes place. It is used in micropropagation techniques.

Microclimate A niche within a broad climatic area that offers different growing conditions. A microclimate can sometimes be created artificially by introducing protection, for example by planting a shelterbelt.

Micropropagation Test tube grown cultures of the growing points, or meristems, of a plant.

Monocarpic Refers to a single flowering followed by the death of the plant. Pachymorph bamboos that flower gregariously are mostly monocarpic but flowering is rare and not predictable. Leptomorph bamboos are not classed as monocarpic usually surviving gregarious flowering.

Monocotyledon Often abbreviated to monocot A plant that produces only a single seed leaf at germination.

Monopodial Usually refers to the culm habit in relation to a leptomorph rhizome system but was formerly used to describe the rhizome formation of long lateral growth and secondary growth points producing either new rhizomes or culms.

Neck Usually refers to the portion joining two growing points on a bamboo and is generally associated with rhizome structure.

Nodal diaphragm The solid section of node that separates two hollow sections of internode.

Node The solid, usually pronounced point on a rhizome, culm or branch where roots, buds, branches, leaves and flowers occur.

Oral setae The bristles or hairs that usually extend from the auricles on a sheath, but depending on species may not be present. The term used throughout this book for fimbriae.

Pachymorph Usually associated with clumping bamboos although there are exceptions. This rhizome type turns upwards, always forming a culm that is thinner than the rhizome from which it has been produced.

Palmate With reference to a leaf formation where three or more leaves emerge from a central point.

Persistent sheath Refers to a culm sheath that, in general, is not immediately shed and adheres to the culm for a season or more.

Petiole The section of leaf sheath that attaches the true leaf to the leaf sheath on a branch.

pH A measure of the acidity or alkalinity of soil.

Pluricaespitose Refers to culms that arise in spaced clumps and that have long and short rhizome necks on pachymorph bamboos. Leptomorph bamboos that display this habit usually have tillering culms.

Progagule A section of rhizome used for propagation purposes.

Pruinose Usually a pale, powdery coating on the culms. See bloom.

Pubescent Covered with tiny, fine hairs.

Rhizome The underground stem of the bamboo with a similar structure to the above-ground culm.

Scandent Refers to a climbing habit.

Sheath The protective scale-like formation that encircles parts of the culms and branches. This acts as protection to soft emerging growth and buds. Very obvious on the culms, but not always noticeable on the branches. This structure also occurs on the rhizome as it develops, but rarely seen because it is underground.

Sheath scar The ring left at the lower part of the node where a sheath was attached.

Sinuous Parts of the plant that are wavy or undulating.

Sport A mutation on a plant that is different in appearance to the form.

Stoma (plural **Stomata**) Minute pores present in the epidermis of a leaf.

Sulcus (plural **Sulci**) A groove that runs the length of an internode. This is formed by the development of a prominent bud at the base of the internode that causes the grooving of the internode as it develops. Very noticeable in the genus *Phyllostachys*.

Supranodal ridge The usually swollen upper part of a node, which varies in its prominence according to species.

Sympodial Used loosely in reference to a pachymorph rhizome system. It describes the rhizome branching habit by which each new rhizome turns upwards to develop a culm.

Tessellation The fine grid-like cross veining of leaves on some species of bamboo. Leaves that are tessellated generally denote cold hardiness, and this structure is only evident on temperate bamboos.

Tillering On bamboos this refers to the production of new culms from the base of existing culms.

Transpiration The evaporation of water from the surface of a plant, mostly through the stomata.

Type Often used in the phrase "type form" and refers to the true species of a genus.

Vascular bundle Strands of tissue that transport water and nutrients throughout the plant.

Bibliography

Addington, P. 1992. *Chusquea* in Europe. *Journal of the European Bamboo Society* 1: 33–34.

Ardle, J. 1997. Horticultural Techniques: Cultivating Bamboos in Containers (Taming the Dragon). *Journal of the Royal Horticultural Society, The Garden.* 122: 632–635.

——. 2002. Design: Using Temperate Bamboos in British Gardens (Culmination of the Grasses). *Journal of the Royal Horticultural Society, The Garden.* 127: 524–529.

Bamboo Society, (EBS Great Britain). 1998. *General Information Booklet: Bamboo: A Guide to the Plant and its Cultivation in the British Isles.* Oxford: The Bamboo Society.

Bareis, K. 1998. The Curious History of Qiongzhu. *Journal of the Bamboo Society* (EBS Great Britain) 29: 16–18.

Bell, M. 2000. *The Gardener's Guide to Growing Temperate Bamboos.* Newton Abbot, Devon: David & Charles.

——. 1998. *Phyllostachys bambusoides. Journal of the Bamboo Society* (EBS Great Britain) 29: 23–27.

——. 2002. New Bamboo Introductions. *Journal of the Bamboo* Society (EBS Great Britain) Autumn: 7–10.

——. 2003. New Bamboo Introductions. *Journal of the Bamboo Society* (EBS Great Britain) Spring: 13–15.

——. 2003. My Favourite Bamboo (*Phyllostachys* bambusoides 'Kawadana'). *Journal of the Bamboo Society* (EBS Great Britain) Summer: 13, 16–17.

——. 2004. Bamboo information sheet and price list: Treraven Plants, Wadebridge, Cornwall, England.

Brisbane, M. General catalogue and information cards: Jungle Giants, Ludlow, England.

Chao, C. S. 1989. *A Guide to Bamboos Grown in Britain.* Royal Botanic Garden, Kew.

Crawford, M. 1997. *Bamboos.* Totnes, Devon: Agroforestry Research Trust.

Crouzet, Y. General catalogue: *Nurseries of the Bambouseraie.* Anduze, France.

Darke, R. ed. 1994. *The New Royal Horticultural Society Dictionary, Manual of Grasses.* Series editor M. Griffiths. London: Macmillan.

Eberts, W. General catalogue: *Bambus.* Baden Baden, Germany.

Farrelly, D. 1996. *The Book of Bamboo.* London: Thames and Hudson.

Gauntlett, V. N. circa 1908. General catalogue: *Hardy Plants Worth Growing.* Chiddingfold, Surrey.

Grounds, R. 1989. *Ornamental Grasses.* London: Christopher Helm.

Jaquith. N. General catalogue: *The Bamboo Garden.* Oregon.

Kingsbury, N. 2000. *Grasses and Bamboos.* London: Ryland, Peters and Small.

Lawson, A. H. 1968. *Bamboos: A Gardener's Guide to their Cultivation in Temperate Climates.* London: Faber and Faber.

McClure, F. A. 1993. *The Bamboos.* Washington and London: Smithsonian Institution Press.

Meredith, T. Jordan. 2001. *Bamboos for Gardens.* Portland. Oregon: Timber Press.

Ohrnberger, D. and J. Goerring. 1983–1987. *The Bamboos of the World.* Germany. Reprint. Dehra Dunn, India: International Book Distributors, 1990.

Olpin, S. 1998. Bamboos in the North. *Journal of the Bamboo Society* (EBS Great Britain) 29: 7–10.

Pike, A. 1992. Supersonic Bamboo: *Phyllostachys aureosulcata* 'Harbin'. *Journal of the European Bamboo Society* 1: 8–9.

PW Plants. General catalogue. *Hardy Bamboos.* Norfolk, England.

Recht. C. and Max F. Wetterwald. 1992. *Bamboos.* Trans, M. Walters. London. Batsford.

van der Palen, Jos. 2003. *Fargesia* sp. rufa. Trans. T. Willems. *Journal of the Bamboo Society* (EBS Great Britain) Autumn: 19–21.

Wang, D. and S. Shen. 1987. *Bamboos of China.* London: Christopher Helm.

Zhu, S., N. Ma, and M. Fu, principals eds. 1994. *A Compendium of Chinese Bamboo.* Peking: China Forestry Publishing House.

Electronic sources

Agricultural Systems. Bamboo.
http://agsyst.wsu.edu/bamboo.htm. Online! Accessed November 2003.

American Bamboo Society. *Introduction to Hardy Bamboos.* Online!
http://www.americanbamboo.org/GeneralInfoPages/BarnhartIntro.html. Accessed November 2003.

Australian Bamboo Network. Plant Listings.
http://www.ctl.com.au/abn/abnp.htm. Accessed November 2003.

Bamboo Select. Bamboos in Europe. Online!
http://www.bambooselect.com/UK/bamboo_in_europe.htm. Accessed December 2003.

Bamboos in Scandinavia. Online!
http://hem.passagen.se/snowpalm/swe/bamboo.html. Accessed October 2003.

Canada BambooWorld. *Cold Hardy Bamboo Plants.* Online! http://www.bambooworld.com/. Accessed November 2003.

European Bamboo Society. *Index.* Online!
http://www.rsl.ox.ac.uk/users/djh/ebs/ebsindex.htm. Accesed October 2003.

Jmbamboo, Bamboo Nursery. *Cold Hardy Bamboo and Bamboo Products.* Online!
http://www.jmbamboo.com/. Accessed January 2004.

Lewis Bamboo Groves. *Cold Hardy Bamboos.* Online!
http://www.lewisbamboo.com/. Accessed December 2003.

PW Plants. *Hardy Bamboos.* Online!
http://www.hardybamboo.com. Accessed November 2003.

University of Melbourne. *Multilingual Multiscript Plant Name Data Base, Sorting the Names of Bamboos. Online*!
http://gmr.landfood.unimelb.edu.au/Plantnames/Sorting/Bamboo_names.html. Accesed January 2004.

van der Palen, Jos. *New Garden Bamboos.* Trans. E. Soldaat. Online!
http://home.iae.nl/users/pms/jpl_art/lezing/bam_eng.html. Accessed October 2003.

Where to see bamboos

The best way of finding up to date information about events, nurseries and gardens is to access the internet. Many organizations now have websites and, failing that, the many bamboo societies will offer good advice. Some gardens and catalogues have been listed in the Bibliography and also in the Index.

Bamboo societies

European Bamboo Society (EBS):
http://www.bodley.ox.ac.uk/users/djh/ebs

American Bamboo Society:
http://www.bamboo.org/abs/

Australian Bamboo Network:
http://www.ctl.com.au/abn/abn.htm

General Index

Picture Acknowledgements

All drawings and line images by the author, except for the painting of the giant panda on p272, which is by copyright © Kate Blackmore.

The author would like to thank Richard Childs and Tim Sandall for their help with the photos used in this book:

Photos © Richard Childs: front cover, pp4, 13, 21, 28, 30, 34, 37, 41, 53, 57, 63, 70, 71, 74, 75, 82, 85, 87, 89, 92, 94, 97 (top), 99, 103, 109, 111, 113, 114, 115 (left), 116, 117, 118, 119, 121 (top left and bottom right), 124, 125, 128, 130, 131, 132, 134, 136, 137, 139, 141, 143, 145, 151, 152, 153, 155, 158, 159, 160, 163, 165, 171, 173, 180, 189, 194, 196 (right), 198, 199, 206, 209, 211, 214 (top), 215, 216 (left), 219, 221, 223, 225, 226, 235, 237, 241, 249, 250, 273, 276

Photos by Tim Sandall, © Paul Whittaker: pp11, 14, 36, 56, 69, 88, 246, 259, 266

Photos © Tim Sandall/Royal Horticultural Society: pp25, 104, 142, 147, 157, 191, 196 (left)

Photos © Paul Whittaker: pp13, 16, 18, 22, 33, 39, 41, 47, 51, 72, 73, 80, 87, 91, 96, 97 (right), 101, 112, 115 (right), 121 (bottom left), 123, 127, 133, 135, 138, 148, 149, 154, 156, 162, 164, 166, 169, 170, 171 (right), 175, 176, 181, 185, 187, 192, 193, 197, 201, 202, 203, 205, 213, 214 (bottom), 216 (right), 217, 218, 222, 233, 234, 239, 243, 245, 248, 251, 253, 255, 256, 260, 261, 262, 263, 264, 275

Richard Childs is responsible for contributing many of the images and deserves my special thanks for being in the right place, at the right time. He is a prize-winning photographer specializing in landscape and botanical work. His images are regularly published in magazines and his work is sold through art galleries nationwide as well as from his own website. A self-confessed "bamboo nut", Richard has also built up a collection of over seventy bamboos.

Locations

Many thanks to the proprietors and directors of the following gardens for giving permission for photographs to be taken either by the author or the photographers listed here:

All photos (with the exception of the ones listed below) were taken at the author's garden, "Sunnyside", or at the author's nursery, P W Plants, both in Norfolk, England.

Mike Bell's garden: pp138, 162, 218

Richard Childs' garden: pp67, 223

Tony Churly's garden: pp101 (left), 121 (bottom left), 170, 176, 216 (right), 251, 275

The gardens of the late Mr. Maurice Mason: pp51, 109, 118, 133, 152, 173, 180, 196 (right), 202, 206 (left)

The Royal Horticultural Society Gardens at Rosemoor: pp72, 104, 164, 175, 209, 213, 214 (bottom), 255, 261, 262, 263

The Royal Horticultural Society Gardens at Wisley: p259

(Thanks to the RHS Director of Horticulture and the Director of Rosemoor.)

Sylvia Whittaker's (the author's mother) garden: pp22, 33, 135 (right), 245